# Conversations with Neil Gaiman

Literary Conversations Series
*Monika Gehlawat*
*General Editor*

# Conversations with Neil Gaiman

Edited by Joseph Michael Sommers

University Press of Mississippi / Jackson

www.upress.state.ms.us

The University Press of Mississippi is a member of
the Association of University Presses.

First printing 2018
∞

Library of Congress Cataloging-in-Publication Data

Names: Sommers, Joseph Michael, 1976– editor. | Gaiman, Neil, interviewee. ive
Title: Conversations with Neil Gaiman.
Description: Jackson: University Press of Mississippi, [2018] | Series:
  Literary conversations series | Includes bibliographical references and
  index. |
Identifiers: LCCN 2018021270 (print) | LCCN 2018028977 (ebook) | ISBN
  9781496818713 (epub single) | ISBN 9781496818720 (epub institutional) |
  ISBN 9781496818737 (pdf single) | ISBN 9781496818744 (pdf institutional)
  | ISBN 9781496818690 (cloth) | ISBN 9781496818706 (pbk.)
Subjects: LCSH: Gaiman, Neil—Interviews. | Authors, English—20th
  century—Interviews.
Classification: LCC PR6057.A319 (ebook) | LCC PR6057.A319 Z46 2018 (print) |
  DDC 823/.914 [B]—dc23
LC record available at https://lccn.loc.gov/2018021270

British Library Cataloging-in-Publication Data available

# Works by Neil Gaiman (Edited Volumes Not Listed)*

## Comics and Graphic Novels

*2000 AD*:

> "You're Never Alone with a Phone," 1986 (with John Hicklenton in No. 488)
>
> "Conversation Piece," 1986 (with Dave Wyatt, in No. 489)
>
> "I'm a Believer," 1987 (with Massimo Belardinelli, in No. 536)
>
> "What's in a Name?," 1987 (with Steve Yeowell)

*Judge Dredd Annual '88*: "Judge Hershey: Sweet Justice," 1987 (with Lee Baulch)

*Revolver Horror Special*: "Feeders and Eaters," 1990 (with Mark Buckingham)

*Violent Cases*, 1987 (with Dave McKean)

*Outrageous Tales from the Old Testament,* 1987:

> "The Book of Judges" (with Mike Matthews)
>
> "Jael and Sisera" (with Julie Hollings)
>
> "Jephthah and His Daughter" (with Peter Rigg)
>
> "Journey to Bethlehem" (with Steve Gibson)
>
> "The Prophet Who Came to Dinner" (with Dave McKean)
>
> "The Tribe of Benjamin" (with Mike Matthews)

*Blaam!* #1: "The Great Cool Challenge," *1988* (with Shane Oakley)

*Seven Deadly Sins*: "Sloth," 1989 (with Bryan Talbot)

*AARGH!* #1: "From Homogenous to Honey," 1998 (with Bryan Talbot)

*Black Orchid*, 1988–89 (with Dave McKean)

*Redfox* #20: "Fragments," 1989 (with SMS)

*Signal to Noise*, 1989 (with Dave McKean)

*Trident* #1: "The Light Brigade," 1989 (with Nigel Kitching)

*The Sandman*, 1989–1996 (With Sam Keith, Mike Dringenberg, Chris Bachalo, Dave McKean et al)

*The Sandman*'s 75 issues have been collected in 10 volumes:

> Vol. 1 *Preludes and Nocturnes*, 1991
>
> Vol. 2 *The Doll's House*, 1990
>
> Vol. 3 *Dream Country*, 1991
>
> Vol. 4 *Season of Mists*, 1992

*Cherry Deluxe* #1: "The Innkeeper's Soul," 1998 (with Larry Welz)

*Frank Frazetta Fantasy Illustrated* #3: "The Facts in the Case of the Departure of Miss Finch," 1998 (with Tony Daniel)

*Oni Double Feature* #6–8: "Only the End of the World Again," 1998 (with P. Craig Russell)

*Shoggoth's Old Peculiar* (with Jouni Koponen, one-shot, Dream Haven, 1998)

*The Spirit: The New Adventures* #2: "The Return of the Mink Stole," 1998 (with Eddie Campbell)

*Vertigo: Winter's Edge* #1, "The Flowers of Romance," 1998 (with John Bolton)

*Neil Gaiman's Midnight Days*, 1999 (various artists)

*Sandman: The Dream Hunters*, 1999 (with Yoshitaka Amano)

*Vertigo: Winter's Edge* #2, "A Winter's Tale," 1999 (with Jeffrey Catherine Jones)

*Green Lantern/Superman: Legend of the Green Flame*, 2000 (various artists)

*Vertigo: Winter's Edge* #3, "How They Met Themselves," 2000 (with Michael Zulli)

*Harlequin Valentine*, 2001 (with John Bolton)

*Heroes*: "The Song of the Lost," 2001 (with Jae Lee)

*Murder Mysteries*, 2002 (with P. Craig Russell)

*The Extraordinary Works of Alan Moore*: "True Things," 2003 (with Mark Buckingham)

*Marvel 1602*, 2003 (with Andy Kubert)

*Creatures of the Night*, 2004 (with Michael Zulli)

*Melinda*, 2005 (with Dagmara Matuszak)

*Eternals*, 2007 (with John Romita Jr)

*John Romita Jr. 30th Anniversary Special*: "Romita—Space Knight," 2007 (with Hilary Barta)

*Sandman: The Dream Hunters*, 2008–09 (with P. Craig Russell)

*Batman: Whatever Happened to the Caped Crusader?*, 2009 (with Andy Kubert, et al)

*CBLDF Presents: Liberty Comics* #2: "100 Words," 2009 (with Jim Lee)

*The Collected Death*, 2009 (with Dave McKean, Chris Bachalo et al)

*Wednesday Comics*, 2009 (With Mike Allred)

*The Sandman: Overture*, 2013–2015 (with JH Williams III)

*The Graveyard Book Vol. 1 and 2* (*Graphic Novel*), 2014 (with P. Craig Russell)

## *Drama*

"The Wolves in the Walls," 2006

"Mr. Punch," 2008

## *Film (screenwriter)*

*Princess Mononoke*, 1997 (English translation & adaption)

*A Short Film About Jon Bolton*, 2003

*MirrorMask*, 2005

*Beowulf*, 2007

## Nonfiction

*Duran Duran: The First Four Years of the Fab Five*, 1984

*Don't Panic: The Official Hitchhiker's Guide to the Galaxy Companions*, 1988

*Don't Panic: Douglas Adams & The Hitchhiker's Guide to the Galaxy*, 1993

*Dustcovers: The Collected Sandman Covers 1989–1996*, 1997 (with Dave McKean)

*Gods & Tulips*, 1999

*Alchemy of MirrorMask*, 2005 (with Dave McKean)

*Beowulf: The Script Book*, 2007

*Make Good Art*, 2013

*Dream State: The Collected Dreaming Covers*, 2014 (with Dave McKean)

The View from the Cheap Seats: Selected Nonfiction, 2016

## Long Fiction

(Note: as Gaiman chooses not to distinguish between "Adult" and "Non-Adult" Fiction, this list does not either.)

*Good Omens*, 1990 (with Terry Pratchett)

*Neverwhere*, 1996

*The Day I Swapped My Dad for Two Goldfish*, 1997 (with Dave McKean)

*Stardust*, 1999

*American Gods*, 2001

*Coraline*, 2002

*The Wolves in the Walls*, 2003 (with Dave McKean)

*Anansi Boys*, 2005

*MirrorMask*, 2005

*MirrorMask* (Children's Edition), 2005

*InterWorld*, 2007 (with Michael Reaves)

*The Dangerous Alphabet*, 2008 (with Gris Grimly)

*The Graveyard Book*, 2008

*Odd and the Frost Giants*, 2008

*Blueberry Girl*, 2009 (with Charles Vess)

*Crazy Hair*, 2009 (with Dave McKean)

*Instructions*, 2010 (with Charles Vess)

*Chu's Day*, 2013 (with Adam Rex)

*Fortunately, the Milk*, 2013 (with Skottie Young)
*The Silver Dream*, 2013 (with Michael and Mallory Reaves)
*The Ocean at the End of the Lane*, 2013
*Chu's First Day of School*, 2014 (with Adam Rex)
*Hansel and Gretel*, 2014 (with Lorenzo Mattotti)
*The Sleeper and the Spindle*, 2014 (with Chris Riddell)
*The Truth Is a Cave in the Black Mountains*, 2014 (With Eddie Campbell)
*Eternity's Wheel*, 2015 (with Michael and Mallory Reaves)
*Norse Mythology*, 2017

## Short Fiction (Collected)

*Angels and Visitations*, 1993
*Smoke and Mirrors*, 1998
*Adventures in the Dream Trade*, 2002
*Fragile Things*, 2006
*M is For Magic*, 2007
*Who Killed Amanda Palmer*, 2009 (with Kyle Cassidy and Beth Hommel, 2009)
*Trigger Warnings*, 2015

## Short Fiction (Uncollected)

"I Cthulhu: or What's a Tentacle-Faced Thing Like Me Doing in a Sunken City Like This (Latitude 47°9′S, Longitude 126°43′W)?," 1987
"Culprits Or Where Are They Now?," 1990 (with Kim Newman and Eugene Byrne)
"Now we are Sick," 1991
"An Honest Answer," 1993 (with Bryan Talbot)
"Cinnamon," 1995
"The False Knight on the Road," 1996 (with Charles Vess)
"The Shadow," 2009
"House," 2013
"How the Marquis Got His Coat Back," 2014
"Kissing Song," 2014

## Television (screenwriter)

*Neverwhere*, 1996
*Babylon 5*, "Day of the Dead," 1998
*10 Minute Tales*, "Statuesque," 2009

*Doctor Who*
    "The Doctor's Wife," 2011
    "Nightmare in Silver," 2013
    "Rain Gods," 2013

## Video Game

*Wayward Manor*, 2013

\*Originally published in *Critical Concepts*: *Neil Gaiman* (Grey House/ Salem Press, 2016)
    with minor emendation

# Contents

# Introduction

Neil Richard MacKinnon Gaiman has been called many things as a writer and is known by many people in many, many different ways. According to Jelena Krstovic, he is "widely credited with elevating the literary status of the graphic novel and demonstrating its potential to embrace and develop theological, philosophical, and psychological themes."[1] Others might simplify that statement to indicate that he is the author and primary creator of DC Comics/ Vertigo's landmark comics series, *The Sandman.* In many circles, that comic alone would be enough to qualify him for consideration within the *Conversations* series, having won some two dozen-plus Harvey, Eisner, World Fantasy, Bram Stoker awards among others. Adding in the prizes for his other comics from 1991 forward would require an introduction all their own and more than justify Gaiman's position amongst the pantheon of the greatest modern comics writers with names such as Alan Moore, Frank Miller, Grant Morrison, and Bryan K. Vaughn—writers who have transcended the medium of comics and graphic novels and became better known, arguably, than their creations themselves. And, had he stopped at comics, Gaiman would have carved out a polite niche in the annals of prose writing that would have been a career for any dozen other writers. Fortunately for the reader, however, his highly-allusive writing career branched out into short stories, novellas, and novels as widely-known, if not more so, than his work in comics: From his partnership with the late Terry Pratchett on the mercilessly funny *Good Omens,* to his collaborations on the BBC television series cum novel cum comic cum radio play for *Neverwhere,* to his novelized fairy tale *Stardust,* to arguably his magnum opus, *American Gods*—itself, alone, the winner of the Hugo, Nebula, Locus, and Bram Stoker Awards, all for Best Novel . . . and that is just naming the early work traditionally labeled as "for adults." It would be ill-advised to forgo *The Graveyard Book,* the first novel to win both the Carnegie and Newbery Medals for children's literature among his many literary achievements. Gaiman has become one of the most celebrated authors of the late-twentieth and early-twenty-first centuries regardless of audience or medium having written in every conceivable type of narrative form from prose, to non-fiction, to comic, to drama, to poem and song, to picture book, to screenplay for adults, children, and every age in-between.

And, as important as prizing is to an author's cultural and literary renown, Gaiman would have likely been content with his lot in life simply had he been known and remembered as little more than a storyteller. He has said, "Stories are important. Stories are vital. Storytellers are in some sense very vital. I'm somebody who makes things up for a living. When I was a kid, people said, 'Neil, don't make things up—you're making that up.' And these days, what I do is make stuff up" (Campbell 8).[2] Those are the words of a thirty-four-year-old man reflecting upon his childhood, the better part of which was spent in a library as he was, in his mind, a reader, first and foremost. As critics have argued, this youthful bookworm, first reading at the tender age of four digging through the works and worlds of C. S. Lewis, J. R. R. Tolkien, Lewis Carroll, and Dennis Wheatley learned "empathy" for the common human being (McIlhagga 196) as well as "nostalgia, horror, melancholy, hope, laughter and almost everything in between" (Eveleth and Wigard 14)[3] in the local branch of his West Sussex library. He learned how one builds worlds and populates them with characters both kind and cruel and sometimes both, and he crafted those experiences, including ones from his own life, into the fictions he composed as an adult. Much of Gaiman's work, as the interviews forthcoming show, arise from his own life, history, and the experiences he gathered while traversing it. Interestingly enough, in a collection devoted to the interviews and conversations had with Neil Gaiman throughout the years, if we look back far enough, we will find the seeds of a young man who read G. K. Chesterton, William Shakespeare, H. P. Lovecraft, and Horace Walpole and wove them together into a comic book surrounding a gaunt and gothic dream lord who desperately needed to step out into the sun every once and a millennia.

Captivated by world-builders and cosmologists at a young age, myth and legend would come to populate Gaiman's own writing throughout his life. And, as he aged, his reading habits would evolve but continue to gravitate towards those fantastic thinkers who would build worlds with more replete and complex universes such as Roger Zelazny, Terry Pratchett, Ursula LeGuin, Douglas Adams, and Diana Wynne Jones. Fantasy and mytho-poeia (Gaiman would likely call it "imaginative"[5] writing) would become his passion and the most fertile ground in which he planted the seeds of his future fictions be they in comics, long or short fictions, movies, or whatever medium happened to hold his fancy at the moment.

In the terminology of theorist Julia Kristeva[6] and the further application of her theories by Roland Barthes,[7] Gaiman's writings are living, breathing literary intertextuality. Fictional or nonfictional, comic or strictly textual, his writings bring together a mélange of traditions, histories, mythopoeia, and the collectors of such things (The Inklings, immediately, spring to mind.), and filters them through as unique and refined a literary voice as one has read in recent centuries into a symphony instantly identifiable by the adjective frequently applied and always baffling to him, "The Gaiman-esque." It baffles few else. The laundry list of his work thus far illustrates (no pun intended) his erudition in the classics, in children's literature, and, of course, comics, due to a large parcel he received as a young man filed with copies of *Fantastic Four, Spider-Man, Silver Surfer,* among others (Campbell 26).[8] Neil Gaiman is as much a student of Jack Kirby and Will Eisner as he is C. S. Lewis and G. K. Chesterton. Looking through works such as *The Sandman, Death: The High Cost of Living, Stardust, The Day I Swapped My Dad for Two Goldfish, American Gods, Coraline,* the English adaptation and translation of *Princess Mononoke, Crazy Hair, The Graveyard Book, The Ocean at the End of the Lane,* and *Norse Mythology*—as he states in the interview he gave me (and my precocious seven-year-old daughter, Maggie)—shows that he has many voices, but they are all distinctly and immediately recognizable to a consumer as Neil Gaiman. It breeds familiarity with the reader who can sense the traces of the authors in Gaiman's library of the mind, however the voice in the reader's mind is unmistakably Gaiman's: a librarian as well-read as any other eager, nearly giddy, to tell a story. As such, the interviews contained here are still Gaiman's words, and they tell his story.

The interviews in this volume have been reprinted as they appeared or transcribed from the source when available. In compiling the interviews, I was faced with a unique set of challenges. The first, and most immediate one was the fact that Gaiman gives (and has taken) many interviews; many *thousands* of interviews, from the age of seven to nearly fifty-seven. Fortunately, anyone who has heard him speak knows that, by way of one's homework, reading and listening to his voice and mannerisms is not the worst way in the world to spend one's time. But, by way of selecting and presenting interviews and conversations for this collection, there were few things that demanded insertion any more than any other. His first interview, with Keith Graves of the BBC, who I must openly and gratefully thank for donating it to this collection at no cost, was brought about due to Gaiman's expulsion from school due to, of all things, his parents' association with the Church of Scientology, and needed to be shown to articulate the sort of innate brilliance, if not eloquence, that Gaiman had even as a small child. It was news of his expulsion that persuaded the British Broadcasting Company to come and visit with him to talk about the matter. "Precocious" doesn't seem appropriate enough to describe Gaiman here. Rather, as Graves states, I think one could easily conclude that Neil Gaiman, aged seven, would have been found to be as an extraordinary of a mind then as he has been found since undertaking his career in writing.

A piece of his own writing, as Gaiman began his writing career not as a fantasist or comics scribe, but as a freelance journalist, seemed appropriate. An argument might be made, as Gaiman has said that one finds his authorial voice after learning many others' voices, that through his early career as a journalist he met and spoke with a great many people, borrowing their voices. In this case, it's the interview he took with Alan Moore in 1987, the man who, by Gaiman's own admission, taught him how to write comics. Likewise, given their long history and friendship, an interview with Terry Pratchett, an interview with them *together* speaking on their collaborative work *Good Omens,* felt *very* appropriate. Pratchett once told Gaiman in an interview in *Time Out* that he composed "a vein of humor that you can really only explore through fantasy. . . . You look at something taken for granted logically. Often when you do that it becomes funny."[9] It's an object-lesson Gaiman took to heart and explored through *Good Omens* with Pratchett, and that work also stands as a testament to Gaiman's commitment to collaboration with others in his writing be they writers, illustrators such as Dave McKean or P. Craig Russell, musicians like Tori Amos or even his own wife, Amanda Palmer, and certainly with his readers—the people who he keeps up a nearly-daily correspondence with on a variety of social networking platforms and never-ending book tours, readings, and speaking engagements. After that, if this collection has a central argument found through the chronology, I would have to argue that it is one of watching Gaiman's voice grow in power as he became more confident in letting his work sound less like others and more like him ,regardless of which version of himself he chose to present.

Of course, breadth of topics matters, and I attended to those matters within the realms of time, space, and, of course, budget. Most all contributors gave freely, and all others made generous reductions to their normal licensing rate in order to allow me to place their work here. And, by way of what was selected, we all wanted a variety of types and kinds: smaller publications (such as the short-lived *Hero Illustrated,* a publication of a time and vein akin to the more widely-remembered *Wizard*) next to larger national outlets, such as interviews with National Public Radio; personal interviews from blogs and podcasts like Jessa Crispin's *Bookslut* interview set alongside newspapers interviews from *The Minnesota Daily*. Sometimes an interview was included simply because it was an amazing piece that told more of a story than the subject matter ostensibly under discussion; Neil being interviewed by his then ten-year-old daughter, Maddy, fit that bill. Most interviews were not repackaged pieces where the author wished to showcase their acumen with the written word, but rather, were the raw text of a conversation between two (or sometimes many, many more) people having a fascinating conversation. In several cases, some of these interviews have been out of print for many years and, contextualized against the other interviews, provide a more complete picture of Gaiman's growth over time. To my knowledge, this is the first work seeking to compile a longitudinal study of what Gaiman's recorded thinking has been over the course of his life and career, and as such, it struck me that the most important thing to show the reader was the evolution of a young boy with an already brilliant mind, oft full of piss and vinegar, along his journey to becoming a self-proclaimed "old dad"[10]: far more patient, far more reflective on his almost forty years in publishing. Even the way Neil and the interviewer got on merited consideration. This might be the first academic collection on Neil Gaiman openly discussing his lunch, perhaps the most posh fish and chips he'd ever seen; Pádraig ó Méalóid knows how to evoke that kind of intimate conversation. Other times there were children, and while Neil Gaiman is a storyteller, generally-speaking, he becomes something otherworldly and marvelous when faced with the straight-forward queries of a young child.

There are interviews missing from the anthology, of course. One can fit only so much between two covers and roughly 96,000 words. I wish there had been space and opportunity to fit in another piece from the BBC. However, that would have been *slightly* cost prohibitive. A piece devoted entirely to his work on movies and adaptation was something sought after and, ultimately, not obtainable. On voicemails, answering machines, and floating about the aether or beyond somewhere (perhaps extra-terrestrials shall one day return my phone calls) are countless requests for things that shall not go mentioned but shall still be long sought-after. No one I actually spoke with and asked for something said no, and for that I am eternally grateful.

I could not have produced this volume without help and patience from a great many friends, colleagues, and people who have become both those things. First and foremost, my wife, Sulynn, and my girls, Maggie and Gwendolyn—the latter who patiently read and reread endless books and interviews on Gaiman with glee and the former who, in addition to that, helped me conduct an interview with him as well. They got a playhouse out of the deal. If Gaiman is the subject of the work, the contributors are the instruments by which we are allowed to examine the course of his career—and I am grateful to have met, conversed, and compared notes with all of them. Katie Keene at the University Press of Mississippi approached me about working on this volume after meeting me at a conference. She is one of the kindest, most encouraging, and most tolerant people I have ever met. Likewise, her assistant, Mary Heath, answered more questions I didn't know I had, and the work benefited from it. My friend and colleague from the United Kingdom, James Underwood, kindly saved me considerable international phone charges by obtaining materials for me from The British Library, and I owe him a pint for that. Similarly, my colleagues and fellow contributors to the *Conversations* series, Brannon Costello and Pete Kunze were endlessly helpful just trying to help me understand how to make thousands of interviews turn into hundreds turn into dozens and eventually turn into slightly under twenty . . . for very little cost. To that end, Vicky Mitchell at the BBC worked with me across several time zones on a very quick turn around to inform me that the BBC would grant me permission to print their transcription of the Keith Graves interview with Neil for free (as opposed to their regular fee), and for that I can't express gratitude enough. Similarly, on this side of the pond, Jenna Molster from National Public Radio not only helped me secure the interview with Neal Conan that I wanted, but convinced me to reconsider another one that I eventually also used. Hal Phillips scanned a copy of *Hero Illustrated #4* from his own private collection so I could include it here, and he found it and scanned it amidst a move, making him a hero to me. Mike Hendrickson (and his Dad) provided similar service to me at the University of Minnesota, helping me find a newspaper interview with Gaiman that existed only in a bound clippings file before the paper began scanning entries into PDFs. Interviews and the lovely cover for this volume were purchased with funds provided by the Department of English here at Central Michigan University and its generous chairperson, Melinda Kreth—they have funded many of my projects, and my debt to my home department extends with every project I craft. A special note of thanks to my student assistant, Mikah Whipple, a truly inquisitive and brilliant young mind in our Honors Program at Central, who dug through and catalogued decades of interviews for me to read for nothing more than the joy of learning about Neil Gaiman. Similarly to Justin Wigard, a former student assistant and now PhD candidate and University Fellow at Michigan

State University, who granted me access to a great many pieces of Gaiman scholarship that I otherwise did not have locally. Micki Christiansen, the executive secretary of the Department of English here at Central, helped me pay the bills for various trips out of town looking for things and Gary Lane, assistant manager of technology here in Anspach Hall at Central, showed me how to save endless hours using technology to reduce the time in transcribing things as opposed to retyping them myself in their entirety. A special note of thanks goes to the folks I will hereby dub Team Gaiman: Cat Mihos, Stephanie Bryant, Rebecca Eskildsen, and Merrilee Heifetz, among others who got me to this core group of people (such as Lisa Von Drasek, curator of the Children's Literature Research Collections at the University of Minnesota, who quite literally shoved me through the door to meet these fine folks), were absolutely a joy and pleasure to work with over the last year. They are encouraging, generous, and strong women without whose aid this book would not have been possible. Thank you so much for everything, all of you. You are the best.

Finally, I would like to thank Neil Gaiman himself for his time and energy to work with me around an impossible schedule (his, not mine). More than that, though—I would like to thank him for his kindness, for the things he said that I will not share (as they are for me and my children), and for being the reason that I'm permitted to do things such as this. You will likely be associated with dreams for as long as you are read; and it's not just because you wrote *The Sandman*. It's because you really do make dreams come true.

**JMS**

## Notes

1. "Neil Gaiman," Ed by Lawrence Trudeau. *Children's Literature Review* Vol 207 (2016): 1. Print.

2. Campbell, Hayley. *The Art of Neil Gaiman*. New York: Harper Collins, 2014. Print.

3. Both essays, McIlhagga, Kristin. "Crafting Advocacy through Intimacy and Empathy: A Rhetorical Analysis of The Reading Agency Lecture" and Eveleth, Kyle and Justin Wigard. "'We have an obligation to imagine': A Critical Reception of the Work of Neil Gaiman," come from *Critical Insights: Neil Gaiman* Ed by Joseph Michael Sommers. Ipswich: Salem/ Grey House, 2016. Print.

4. "BBC Audio of 7 Year Old Scientologist Neil Gaiman." *YouTube*. YouTube, 09 Feb. 2017. Web. 29 July 2017.

5. Blaschke, Jayme. *Voices of Visions.* Lincoln: University of Nebraska Press, 2005. Print. 132.

6. See *Desire in Language: A Semiotic Approach to Literature and Art.* New York: Columbia UP, 1980.

7. Barthes' best essay addressing this subject is probably "Theory of the Text" (1981), however, Gaiman would be the first person to tell you that most of his characters embodied elements of himself—so, while Barthes may assert that nothing exists outside the text, Gaiman does. However, Gaiman would likely also tell you that you don't need to know any of that enjoy his work.

8. Campbell, Hayley. *The Art of Neil Gaiman.* New York: Harper Collins, 2014. Print.

9. Gaiman, Neil. "Deeply Weird: Terry Pratchett." *Time Out.* October 26-November 2 (1988) Print. 13.

10. From Joseph Michael Sommers and Maggie Grace Sommers' interview in this collection.

# Chronology*

1960    Neil Richard Gaiman is born on November 10, 1960 to Sheila and David Bernard Gaiman in Portchester, Hampshire, UK.

1965    The Gaiman Family moves to East Grinstead, West Sussex and Gaiman begins to supplement his reading at the local library with the works of J. R. R. Tolkien, C. S. Lewis, Lewis Carroll, and a bevy of American comic books which he received around 1967–68.

1968    Gaiman is interviewed by Keith Graves with the BBC Radio after being expelled from school, supposedly due to his family's relationship to Scientology.

1970    Begins Ardingly College.

1974    Begins Whitgift School.

1977    After graduating Whitgift, Gaiman becomes a freelance journalist writing for newspapers and outlets such as *The Sunday Times*, *The Observer, Knave,* and *Time Out.*

1983    With Mary McGrath, Gaiman has first child, a son, named Michael Richard.

1984    Gaiman's first professional short story, "Featherquest" is published. Proteus Publishing Company hires him to write a biography of Duran Duran entitled *Duran Duran: The First Four Years of the Fab Five*. He also produces a book of quotations with Kim Newman entitled *Ghastly Beyond Belief*. Rustling through a comics kiosk in Victoria station, Gaiman happens upon an issue of *The Saga of The Swamp Thing* by Alan Moore; this would begin his fascination with Moore and his work, and a friendship ensued. Moore would introduce him to the process of scripting comics in 1985.

1985    Marries Mary McGrath in March. Later that year, Holly Miranda, a daughter, is born to Mary McGrath. Gaiman begins writing further short stories such as "How to Be a Barbarian" and "How to Spot a Psycho." He also meets Terry Pratchett through an interview for the first time.

1986    Gaiman writes his first comic for *2000 AD* entitled "You're Never Alone with a Phone" and "Conversation Piece." He meets Karen Berger at DC Comics and pitches *Black Orchid* (which would be published between 1988–89); she offers him the opportunity to revive a DC property. This conversation leads to the genesis of *The Sandman*.

1987    Gaiman formally quits his job as a professional journalist. Gaiman meets illustrator Dave McKean in New York City where the two collaborate on *Violent Cases*. It will be the first of many collaborations between the two.

1988    As an avid fan of Douglas Adams, Gaiman writes *Don't Panic: The Official Hitchhiker's Guide to the Galaxy Companion*

1989    With Mark Buckingham, Gaiman publishes *Total Eclipse* featuring the character Miracleman; this becomes his first published work with the character.

1990    Publishes *Good Omens* with Terry Pratchett. Picks up and begins writing the comic book *Miracleman* (formerly *Marvelman*) at issue #17 from Alan Moore.

1991    Gaiman wins his first Eisner Awards for *The Sandman* in the categories of Best Continuing Series, Best Graphic Album, and Best Writer. He would win again (in multiple categories) in 1992, 1993, 1994, 2000, 2004, 2007, and 2009 (more than twenty six to this date). He would also win Harvey Awards and Hugo Awards, among others, in the same year. Perhaps most notably, *The Sandman* #19 "A Midsummer Night's Dream" wins the prestigious World Fantasy Award, becoming the first comic to ever do so.

1992    Gaiman and family move to America near Menomonie, Wisconsin, to be closer to McGrath's family.

1993    Publishes the collection of short stories *Angels and Visitations*. Publishes *Death: The High Cost of Living* with Chris Bachalo.

1994    Madeleine Rose Elvira, a daughter, is born to Mary McGrath in August. Publishes *The Tragical Comedy or Comical Tragedy of Mr. Punch: A Romance* with Dave McKean.

1995    Publishes *Sandman: Midnight Theatre*.

1996    Scripts the television series *Neverwhere* (with Lenny Henry) and, dissatisfied with the BBC treatment, subsequently publishes the work as a novel.

1997    Adapts the English version of the film *Princess Mononoke* from Studio Ghibli. Publishes *The Day I Swapped My Dad for Two Goldfish*.

1998    Publishes the collection of short stories *Smoke and Mirrors*. Writes the screenplay "Day of the Dead" for the television series *Babylon 5*.

1999    Publishes *Stardust*. Publishes *Sandman: The Dream Hunters*.

2001    Publishes *American Gods*. Opens *Neil Gaiman's Journal*, his ongoing blog.

2002    Publishes *Coraline*. Gaiman wins the Hugo, the Nebula, the Locus, and the Bram Stoker award for best novel for *American Gods*.

2003    Publishes *The Wolves in the Walls*. Publishes *The Sandman: Endless Nights*. Gaiman wins the Nebula and Hugo awards for *Coraline*.

2004    Publishes *Marvel: 1602*. In *Legends II*, a collection of short stories edited by Robert Silverberg. Gaiman publishes "The Monarch of the Glen," the first official sequel to *American Gods*. "Black Dog," the second sequel, will be later published in *Trigger Warning*.

2005    Writes screenplay for *MirrorMask*. Publishes *Anansi Boys*.

2006    Publishes short story collection *Fragile Things*.

2007    Divorces Mary McGrath. Publishes short story collection *M Is for Magic*. Writes the screenplay for *Beowulf*. Gaiman also visits the Republic of China and is inspired by the trip to start a series about a panda named Chu.

2008    Writes *The Graveyard* Book and *Odd and the Frost Giants*. Wins the Newbery and Carnegie Medals for *The Graveyard Book* becoming the first author to do so for the same work.

2009    Pens the poem "Blueberry Girl" for friend Tori Amos. The poem is later illustrated by Charles Vess and published as *Blueberry Girl*. Gaiman wins the Hugo Award for *The Graveyard Book*.

2010    Publishes the poem "Instructions" with illustrations by Charles Vess as *Instructions*.

2011    Marries Amanda Palmer. Writes his first episode of long-time BBC series *Doctor Who*, "The Doctor's Wife."

2012    Gaiman is awarded an honorary doctorate and is invited to give the commencement speech at The University of the Arts in Philadelphia. The speech becomes viral online becoming known as the "Make Good Art" speech published in 2013. Additionally, he forms the non-profit organization, The Gaiman Foundation, dedicated to supporting free speech.

2013    Publishes *The Ocean at the End of the Lane* which is voted Book of the Year in the British National Book awards. Also publishes *Chu's Day*, the first in an ongoing series aimed at younger readers.

Publishes *Fortunately, The Milk* with illustrator Skottie Young. Writes first video game, *Wayward Manor*. Writes the screenplay for "Nightmare in Silver" and "Rain Gods" for the television series *Doctor Who*. Gaiman returns to write the prequel to *The Sandman* with J. H. Williams III entitled *The Sandman: Overture* which will be published from 2013–15 after numerous delays.

2014    Gaiman is called upon by United Nations High Commission for Refugees to visit Jordan during the Syrian Civil War to account for the tragedies he sees. He makes a short film with the UNHCR and writes a piece for *The Guardian* to account for the trip.

2015    Publishes the collection *Trigger Warning*. With Amanda Palmer, has son, Anthony, in September.

2016    Publishes collection of nonfiction pieces entitled *The View from the Cheap Seats*.

2017    Publishes *Norse Mythology*. The adaptation of *American* Gods premieres on *STARZ* to terrific acclaim with Gaiman serving as executive producer. Begins writing, adapting, and executive producing *Good Omens* for Amazon to be released as a limited six-episode series in 2018. Begins sequel to *Neverwhere*, entitled *The Seven Sisters*, and accepts fundraiser challenge to read the entirety of the Cheesecake Factory menu if $500,000 can be raised for charity.

*Originally published in *Critical Concepts*: *Neil Gaiman* (Grey House/ Salem Press, 2016) with minor emendation.

# Conversations with Neil Gaiman

# World at Weekend

## Keith Graves / 1968

From BBC Radio 'World at Weekend,' August 1968. Reprinted by permission.

**Keith Graves:** What is Scientology?
**Neil Gaiman:** It is an applied philosophy dealing with the study of knowledge.

**KG:** Do you know what philosophy is?
**NG:** I used to, but I've forgotten.

**KG:** Who told you that meaning of Scientology?
**NG:** In clearer words, it's a way to make the able person more able.

**KG:** What does it do for you—Scientology—does it make you feel [like] a better boy?
**NG:** Not exactly that, but when you make a release you feel absolutely great.

**KG:** Do you get what you call a release very often, or do you have this all the time?
**NG:** Well, you only keep a release all the time when you get Clear. I'm six courses away from Clear.

**KG:** You're on a particular grade are you?
**NG:** Well, I've just passed Grade I; I'm not Grade II yet.

**KG:** What is Grade I?
**NG:** Problems Release.

**KG:** And what does this mean to you, Problems Release?
**NG:** It helps you to handle quite a lot of problems.

**KG:** What problems do you have as a little boy that this helps you with?
**NG:** Only one big problem.

**KG:** What's that?
**NG:** My friend Stephen.

**KG:** Oh, I see. Is he a Scientologist?
**NG:** Yes.

**KG:** He is? But I mean, how does this grade that you've got, Problems Release, help you to deal with Stephen?
**NG:** Well, you know, I've dealed [sic.] with every single problem except Stephen, one thing Problems Release can't help me to handle.

**KG:** So you still fight with Stephen?
**NG:** It's more of a question he fights with me.

**KG:** He's older than you, presumably.
**NG:** Yes.

**KG:** And he's three grades ahead of you?
**NG:** In a way, but you see, there are six main courses; but there are ever so many in-between courses. I've just finished three, and that's Engrams.

**KG:** What are Engrams?
**NG:** Engrams are a mental image picture containing pain and unconsciousness.

**KG:** And what does this mean to you?
**NG:** Well, shall I tell you?—I'll give you a demonstration. You're walking along the street, and a car hooted and somebody shouted, "shooo,"and a dog barked, and you tripped over a bit of metal and hurt your knee. Three years later, say, you were walking along that same place and someone shouted "shooo," and a car hooted, and a dog barked, and suddenly you feel pain in your knee. I've had one Engram that I can remember. I was jumping off the television set. We've got a gigantic television set, but it doesn't work. Onto my mom's bed and, you see, I jumped and I hit my head on the chandelier, and you know it really hurt; and I looked up and I saw it swinging, and a few minutes later I tried to test an Engram, so I set it swinging and I looked up there, and I suddenly had a headache.

**KG:** And how old were you when this happened?
**NG:** Around three months ago.


**KG:** Oh, I see. How long have you been studying Scientology?
**NG:** I started at five, now I'm seven.
**KG:** Seven years old. Extraordinary, isn't it?

# The British Invasion: Alan Moore

## Neil Gaiman / 1987

"The British Invasion: Alan Moore" Interview by Neil Gaiman, *American Fantasy* V.2 #2
© copyright 1987 by Neil Gaiman. Reprinted by permission.

Many horror readers may not know Alan. He writes comic books. But *what* comic books! His latest series for DC Comics, *Watchmen,* has been heralded by London's *Time Out* as "a . . . phenomenon . . . a legitimate novel . . . the first series in nearly thirty years to assume that comic reading doesn't stop with the advent of adolescence."

His forte is revitalizing old characters who are drowning in their own clichés. He approaches these comic book characters as if they were ordinary people with real thoughts and emotions. He brings contemporary horror and suspense writing techniques to a medium traditionally reserved for quick philosophizing between fist-fights.

This interview was conducted in Britain by Neil Gaiman over the last few months.

✦ ✦ ✦

What do the following have in common: A huge, green, animated heap of bog muck, used to explore issues of sexism, racism, and the dumping of nuclear wastes?

A world on the brink of nuclear war, in which a lone, crazed vigilante tries to find out who, if anyone, is killing his old business partners?

Two alien juvenile delinquents, who, in their passion for thermonuclear weaponry and mindless destruction, make the *Young Ones** look boringly stay-at-home?

A sensitive portrayal of a young woman caught up first in a future society with no hope, then recruited as a soldier in a war she can never win?

There is more than one answer. They are all products of the fertile mind of Alan Moore; they have all won awards and critical respect; and they are all comic-strips, respectively, *Swamp Thing, Watchmen, D.R. and Quinch,* and *The Ballad of Halo Jones.*

Alan Moore is a phenomenon; a six-foot-two inhabitant of Northhampton, long-haired and bearded, who would look somewhere between a remnant of the Sixties and a Yeti were it not for his penchant for expensive suits and leopard skin shoes, and for the look of humor and intelligence in his deep-set eyes.

He is a superstar in a field—comics—in which fame, fortune, and artistic credibility would have been unthinkable a few years ago.

He isn't even an artist. He's a writer.

Suddenly, comics are hip. They're in. Kathy Acker raves about Moore's *Swamp Thing* in print; Malcolm McLaren, trend Svengali, has just hired Alan Moore to write a film script for him (*Fashion Beast,* somewhere between the life of Christian Dior and the story of *Beauty and the Beast*).

Moore is a perceptive and voracious reader with an almost photographic memory who has become, after seven years of writing comics, an overnight success . . .

"I left school at the age of seventeen, and my first job was hacking up sheep carcasses for the Co-op Hide and Skin Division. It certainly gave me an insight into life, because we had to turn up at 7:30 A.M., and drag these blood-stained sheep carcasses out of these vats of freezing cold water, blood, and various animal by-products. Then we used to mutilate them in a variety of strange ways . . . but oddly, a form of concentration-camp humor arose, and many was the happy hour that we had, throwing whacked-off sheep's testicles at each other. It doesn't sound that funny, out of context. Y'had to be there, I suppose. . .

"Then I started as a toilet cleaner, which seemed to be more my line, and I've worked my way down since then, eventually ending up as a comics writer. Somewhere along the line, back when I was a teenage werewolf, the arts lab movement was spreading. Small cells of people who'd do poetry readings, concerts, magazines, and theatre; everybody who joined the group would learn a little bit of what everybody else was doing—it was great. It wasn't a formal artistic training, but it was influential.

"Northhampton, where I live, is a small, dark, grimy town. A friend of mine described it as the 'Murder Mecca of the Midlands'—we have a fantastic number of completely bizarre murders up there, and they're different from murders anywhere else, because they're more *warped.* You get head-lines in Northhampton papers like, 'Vampire Killer Gets Life' and it's *true!* A boring town with a lot of evil shit going on. And a very small Bohemian intelligentsia, only four of us, and we all know each other."

So how did he wind up writing comics?

"Getting into comics for me was a matter of going round the back, poison-ing the dogs, and climbing the fence. I didn't go into it the route that people normally do, in that I didn't go straight into writing comics. I had a period of two or three years when I had delusions of adequacy as an artist, and I started drawing a strip for *Sounds,* writing and drawing it every week. First a Private Eye parody, called *Rosco Mosco,* then a SF comedy, and then—having done it for a couple of years—I was forced to the terrifying conclusion that I couldn't actually *draw.* However, I had learned an awful lot about telling a story during that time—how to get the pictures to move in sequence, and all the other things you find out, and I realized that I could write faster, write better, and make a lot more money writing than I could drawing. So I started sending sample scripts in to things like *2000 AD* and after a couple of tries I got some accepted, and I've worked my way up from there."

After working on *2000 AD* and the short-lived *Warrior* (of which more anon) Alan turned his talents across the Atlantic to work on the horror comic, *Swamp Thing.* It was a comic sunk in the bog of mediocrity, but Alan soon began to take it places that no horror comic had gone before, and attracting an audience that usually did not read comics.

*Swamp Thing* at its best was an Eighties Horror Comic, cerebral, and scary horror in the Clive Barker, Ramsey Campbell tradition, in which a heap of bog muck is the most human character in a Louisiana populated by underwater vampires, zombies, menstrual werewolves, and serial killers. It was the first intelligently written comic to be seen in America for many years. The early Alan Moore-written issues now fetch as much as $25.00, the first time that the writer of a comic, as opposed to an artist, has ever made a difference to the collector's market.

What did he do that was so different?

"I think it's mainly in terms of the way I put things together. I did things to the character that, in terms of his history, were quite startling. But the main thing I did was to bring a different sensibility to it.

"The way I tend to approach comics is, there's no reason to think of them as just for kids. The fact they've got stuck in a children's ghetto is not entirely their own fault, it's just that from their inception they've been regarded as children's entertainment and nothing more.

"When I write comics I try to write them as if I were writing a book for adults, or a film, or TV and try to get the same kinds of concerns and sensibilities into it. So when I took over *Swamp Thing* I tried to make the stories more credible—which is a bit difficult when you're dealing with a huge animated mound of bog-muck. But you get round that by making the stories talk about real, relevant, social issues that will mean something to the reader, instead of having an endless succession of people in skin-tight costumes wrestling with each other (sure it's fun, but not anything to base an art-form upon).

"So I've tried to do stories dealing with nuclear waste, feminism, all sorts of things. Keeping it well away from the Batman syndrome of an endless number of bizarre and improbable villains wanting to take over the world, and equally as bizarre heroes trying to stop them. I wanted to do something more intense, that would put the wind up people a bit."

After just eight issues with Alan at the helm, *Swamp Thing* lost the "Approved by the Comics Code Authority" seal from the cover—the seal that guarantees purity from corruption for American Youth.

"Well, for anyone who doesn't know what the Comics Code is, back in the fifties, when America was in the throws of all kind of witchhunts, a man called Frederic Wertham produced a book called *Seduction of the Innocent*. He said that disturbed kids he had treated had all read comics at some time or the other, so therefore they were disturbed *because* they read comics—he could probably have drawn the same conclusions about *milk.*

"He reprinted panels from comics out of context: one, for example, showed a tight close-up of Batman's armpit, so it's just a triangle of darkness—Wertham managed to imply that this was a secret picture of a vulva the artist had put in to titillate his younger readers. Reading *Batman* must have been an endlessly enriching erotic experience for Wertham . . . I mean, if you can get that much out of an *armpit*!

"As a result of the book, the comics publishers imposed a code of practice on themselves, and the result was the little white sticker in the top corner of comics. It was like *The Dick Van Dyke Show*, where he and Mary Tyler Moore not only had to sleep in separate beds, they also had to have a table lamp and a table in between, y'know?

"In comics, female characters couldn't have breasts any more, (although admittedly, before the code certain women characters would literally not have been able to stand up) there was no sex, violence vanished completely. So the good comics and the bad were stamped out together.

"Now when I started doing *Swamp Thing*, I decided I'd just ignore the code and let them slap me into line, rather than try to second-guess them.

So when we got to issue 29, and the theme of the issue was incest and necrophilia, (apparently still frowned on in America, although they're part of the social fabric over here) we did the story in such a way that anyone not old enough to have understood the concepts would not have understood the comic, it was written very subtly.

"But we did have a double page spread of five rotting zombies attacking a girl.

"Now, apparently the Comics Code Authority are just a bunch of old people who sit in a room and thumb through comics all day, at an amazing speed. And if they don't see any mammeries or four-letter words, they assume it's all OK. So they thumb through *Swamp Thing*, get to this scene, and immediately have coronaries, and the breather team outside the door have to come in to give them a heart massage.

"They said, 'This is *horrible!*' so they went back and read it *very carefully*, discovered it was all about incest and necrophilia, and said, 'We cannot allow this comic to go out on the stands.' So DC, in a move for which I shall forever salute them, said 'Alright, put it out without the seal.'

"And they did.

"And nothing happened. The code is a toothless anachronism. *Swamp Thing* is still on the newsstands, it's extremely violent and horrible, nobody's said a word, and frankly, I wouldn't expect them to. We're just carrying on."

How about *Warrior?*

"The original idea for *Warrior* was that the creators would be getting less money up-front, but that we'd be getting complete control and creative freedom to do what we wanted to do. We'd have copyright control, a share of the merchandising (if there was any) . . . it was good, it made you feel more honorable and less like someone who was turning out writing and drawing by the yard.

"You see, comics in the UK are a long way behind other industries in the way that creators are treated—everything is bought outright, for very little money. If they made *Judge Dredd: The Movie*, for example, the writers and the creators would get no money. It's a criminal set-up, but it's something you've got to work within if you want to work at all.

"Unfortunately the things we were promised on *Warrior* didn't turn out to be the things that were delivered. The creative freedom was only gotten after a lot of arguments with the editor; the money we were promised never materialized; there were personal problems. Like a lot of good ideas before it, the creative people got alienated. But we did get a chance in the twenty or so issues it endured, to do stuff that *we* enjoyed doing.

"I did three strips for *Warrior,* one called *Marvelman,*" (renamed *Miracleman* in US reprints due to threats from Marvel Comics) "a revival of a 1950's character—a really endearingly *stupid* superhero. I decided to bring him back in a really harsh, urban environment. He's married, he's forty, he's paunchy, he can't remember his magic word.

"I felt it touched on aspects of the superhero that hadn't been touched on before.

"Then there was *V for Vendetta*—it's one of my favorite things I've done. It's set in the near-future, in around 1997, when Britain is under a very tight right-wing government and everyone hates the police (I know, you'll find that very hard to believe!). And set against this bleak world we have a character who dresses up as Guy Fawkes.

"In the first issue he blew up the Houses of Parliament, and we've been working up to a climax since then. That's gone down quite well—there's obviously a place for a deranged, urban terrorist in the hearts of today's comics readers.

"The other strip we did was a thing called *The Bojeffries Saga.* I really liked it—it's one of the few comedy strips I've done. It's basically about a family of mutants living in an unnamed urban mass—possibly Birmingham, possibly Northhampton—and me and the artist, Steve Parkhouse, have been trying to get the feel of the really *stupid* bits of England we can remember from when we were kids.

"Like you see the same motorbike propped up on four bricks without any wheels on your way to work each morning, and you don't know why it's there. And you pass factories and you don't know what they *do* in there, and you suspect the people who work there don't know either. So we boiled all this down into a fantasy on the British landscape in which we set these various werewolves and mutants. In a funny way it's a lot more personal than a lot of the strips I've done.

"Although *Warrior's* gone down the tubes, all the strips will eventually be appearing in different formats in American editions, since I've been snapped up as part of the brain drain."

Encouraged by the success of *Swamp Thing,* DC gave Moore and British artist Dave Gibbons complete artistic freedom to create *Watchmen,* a 12-issue graphic novel about a world much like our own, but in which 'superheroes' actually exist (they won the Vietnam war; Nixon is still president; nuclear armageddon is just around the corner). It's state of the art stuff.

As literary critic John Clute explained, "*Watchmen* is the first comic to take the icons, the material of the superheroes and fantasies that have built up around them and make them a legitimate part of fictional discourse about America. It's the first time a novel—and make no mistake, *Watchmen is* a legitimate novel—has been written that assimilates these grotesque childhood fantasies into an adult model of the state of the US and its future."

The world of *Watchmen* is much like our own. But in the thirties a few people, for their own reasons, began wearing masks and fighting crime. Then in 1960 the superman was created, and he was American. And the world has never recovered. By the 1985 we are presented with, nuclear armageddon is looking likely.

As Moore explains: "If you actually talk about the world in which we live at the moment, you are going to run into a lot of emotional feedback. You are going to run into people's emotional feelings about political issues. If I were to do a comic that slagged off Ronald Reagan for an American audience (much as I detest Ronald Reagan, and would like to do that) it wouldn't be a wise thing to do. The majority of Americans *like* Ronald Reagan, therefore only the ones that didn't like Ronald Reagan to start with would read my comic. The rest of the people would switch off.

"The beauty of *Watchmen*—and indeed much comics and fantasy, if used correctly, is they don't have to be escapist. You can use them to make a statement about the world without bumping up against people's prejudices.

"In *Watchmen,* the president is Richard Nixon. You can say what you like about Nixon and nobody cares! So by having a parallel universe, in which there were just two *Washington Post* reporters found dead in an underground garage somewhere, you can depict this world, in which there are lots of wonderful things—electric cars, airships, superheroes—but the feeling of the world, the approaching feeling of doom and apocalypse, the feeling of disconnection, all these things are things which I'm obviously drawing from the world in which I live in. And by making the statement in terms of a world in which superheroes exist, and instead of the atom bomb unbalancing the culture, it's the superhero, you can say the same things, get the same attitudes over while sidestepping people's prejudices.

"On one level that's what *Watchmen* is about. Given the fact that it is a very dense series that lasts twelve issues, it's also about a number of other things. Issue four is about the implications of the Theory of Relativity, which sounds a bit dry and boring. What Einstein said and what it means for humanity."

Dave Gibbons, illustrator of *Watchmen,* suggested one reason why British creators have been making such an impact on America. "There's something about a non-American drawing or writing about America. You've got a more detached view. You see the quirks. On the surface our stuff looks like American stuff. But when you look a bit deeper you find there's enough of a warped view, enough of a sideways twist to make it more interesting than the home-grown product.

"What happened in America was that you had a generation who had grown up on American comics—it got very incestuous. It became very ritualized. They needed a Beatles . . ."

Alan Moore interrupted, "That's me and Dave. We're the Lennon and McCartney of comics. Now we just have to decide who gets shot and who gets to marry Linda Eastman . . ."

While not all Alan's projects have won him the fame he feels he deserves, (his single, with a band called The Sinister Ducks, was described as "silly" by the *New Musical Express,* thus ruining its chances of making the top ten) he currently enjoys a cult status for his work in comics, especially in the US— something he finds slightly unnerving.

"It's very disorienting. I'm a complete nonentity for the other 364 days a year. Round the corner shop I'm not famous. Then suddenly I'm the idol of thousands of thirteen-year-old boys. I start to realize how Hayley Mills must have felt. All I have to do is sit in a room and write—it must be one of the most boring existences in the world. But it's especially odd in the US, where they love you for just being English, and they believe anyone with an English accent is Oscar Wilde—y'know, you say 'Hello' and they crease up. I get treated as a real novelty—at the last big convention I wound up having dreams of clawing hands all over me.

"I like the undeserved adulation, but in some way I'd almost rather write anonymously (although I couldn't sell much like that) as when I started nobody expected comics writing to be any good. So if I did a good one it was a bonus. If I did a bad one it didn't matter. These days I do as many duff stories as ever, but people expect them all to be brilliant, so it's a pressure I could do without. But it *is* nice to be feted and acclaimed for doing something so essentially trivial."

What made him decide to write comics with adult sensibilities? "I cannot write down to people. I cannot write stuff I'm not interested in. If I cannot find something to interest me then I won't do it, because it won't work.

"So, wanting to get into comics, my tastes in literature had already gone beyond most comics which presented me with a problem. Then I saw *2000 AD* and saw that what Wagner and Grant were doing on *Judge Dredd* was very intelligent, and there could be a place that I could do the stories I wanted to do. Too much stuff is aimed at a hypothetical reader who doesn't exist. You get comics that almost gear themselves towards a lowest common denominator, so the stuff isn't very interesting if you aren't either very young or perhaps not terribly bright.

"Comics seemed to me to be an area which, in comparison with other media, is still in its infancy, and there's a lot of innovation that's yet to be brought to bear. Obviously, if you're going to be an artist, the point of art is communication: you want to communicate what you have to say as truly and powerfully as possible and to the optimum audience. Effect is everything. By using new techniques you can surprise the reader enough to cut through the cultural callouses.

"Comics have greater opportunity for new directions, to actually reach the reader on that level."

What does he think of the accusations that comics are for illiterates, or for lazy readers?

"You have to be fairly literate to read my comics or the Hernandez', or Frank Miller's. I think in complexity something like *Watchmen,* for example, is as or more complex than a lot of mainstream novels on the shelves.

"One of the prejudices against comics is this rather snotty attitude that people who need pictures in their stories are in some way subliterate, which is to ignore and deny the main thrust of the twentieth century: we are a visually-oriented society, visually-oriented in almost every way you'd care to conceive of: films, television, video . . .

"With the new wave of comics there is something very sophisticated beginning to emerge. A comic has a potential for enormous density: you can read it at your own pace, you can absorb a huge amount of information; it also has an image track which means there's no need for obtrusive descriptive passages, but you can still get the same depth and complexity as a novel."

He points to *Watchmen* as an example. The average script he sends to Dave Gibbons is over 120-pages long.

"Comics are starting to form their own language which is not just words and pictures, but a strange interrelationship between the two. People are starting to work out how to use them in ironic counterpoint to each other. You can get effects which there is no real critical language to describe as yet, because very little attention has been paid to them, but it seems something that seems ideal for the sensibilities that are emerging in the latter-half of the twentieth century. People want smaller information packets, but they still demand stuff that's as forceful and has as much information as a novel. It's an ideal situation for comics to come into their own."

How about the money—has it changed him?

"When I was poor I had complete contempt for the stuff. Now, I've got money it means I can ignore it a bit more. And it means I can have a delayed adolescence—because age 14 to 20, not only didn't I have the money to do all the teenage pursuits I wanted to, like clothes and singles, but I was also part of a generation that was vehemently anti-fashion. Looking good was politically not on. But now I can buy more clothes and comics and records."

Does he believe his work in comics will have any long term effects?

"Eventually, everything has an effect. The effect I hope it *doesn't* have, is that people will take the worst aspects of my writing, like the floweriness of the prose, which is a fault, not a virtue, and copy them. Steal the wrong licks as it were. I'd like to think that if I did enough stuff it might have the effect of making people *expect* reasonably written comics. If it did that, I'd be pleased.

"I don't see any reason why comics should be a second-rate medium. To me, it's as if the first few films had been children's cartoons, and someone said 'It's a wonderful medium for kids,' and it stayed there. You wouldn't have *Citizen Kane*, or any good films. There's no *reason* why comics should be seen as a medium for children or illiterates. What I'd like to do is make it acceptable enough for adults to read on busses."

After a brief discussion of his hairstyle ("I'm not doing anything—it's everyone else that's doing things! Scraping hideously sharp pieces of metal across their faces, dousing themselves with aftershave that *stings* and smells terrible! I *hate* going to barbers—there were all these things I didn't understand there, like styptic pencils, and sprays and things. Long hair's a lot easier to maintain . . . but as a concession to normality I *do* bite my nails. The earthy, unkempt look will be popular in another twenty years, and I'll be laughing and you'll all be sorry . . .") I asked him about future projects.

"I'd like to perform on stage again. And do films. But I do plan to keep in comics, because a lot of the big creative leaps have yet to be made—there's a lot of ground left to be broken. But there's really a world full of possibilities. All of the things people need words for.

"I mean, I'd quite like to be one of the people who write those letters that say 'Dear——, you may not be aware of it, but you could already have won . . . ' 'cause somebody has to write them."

*The Young Ones* is a British television show featuring four punkers living together in one house. One is wealthy due to his bestseller, *How to Be a Bastard.*

# Pratchett & Gaiman: The Double Act

## *Locus* / 1991

From *Locus*. Reprinted by permission.

**Neil Gaiman:** "The first radio interview we did in New York, the interviewer was asking us 'Who is Agnes Nutter? What is her history? Is Armageddon happening?" and so on and so forth. After a while, we twigged he hadn't realized this was fiction. He thought he'd been given two kooks who'd come across these old prophecies and were predicting that the world was going to be ending."

**Terry Pratchett:** "Once we realized, it was great fun. We could take over the interview, since we knew he didn't know enough to stop us."

**NG:** "And at that point, we just did the double act."

**NG:** "We're working on seeing how many smart-alec answers we can come up with when people ask us how we collaborated."

**TP:** "I wrote all the words, and Neil assembled them into certain meaningful patterns . . . What it wasn't was a case of one guy getting 2/3 of the money and the other guy doing 3/4 of the work."

**NG:** "It wasn't, somebody writes a three-page synopsis, and then somebody else writes a whole novel and gets their name small on the bottom."

**TP:** "That isn't how we did it, mainly because our egos were fighting one another the whole time, and we were trying to grab the best bits from one another."

**NG:** "We both have egos the size of planetary cores."

**TP:** "Probably the most significant change which you must have noticed [between the British and American editions] is the names get the other way 'round. They're the wrong way 'round on the American edition [where Gaiman is listed first]—"

**NG:** "They're the wrong way 'round on the English edition."

**TP:** "Both of us are prepared to admit the other guy could tackle our subject. Neil could write a *Discworld* book, I could do a *Sandman* comic. He wouldn't do a good *Discworld* book and I wouldn't do a good *Sandman* comic, but—"

NG: "—we're the only people we know who could even attempt it."

TP: "I have to say there's a rider there. I don't think either of us has that particular bit of magic, if that's what it is, that the other guy puts into the work, but in terms of understanding the mechanisms of how you do it, I think we do."

NG: "There's a level on which we seem to share a communal undermind, in terms of what we've read, what we bring to it."

TP: "In fact, people that have read a lot of the *Discworld* books and a lot of the *Sandman* comics will actually find, for example, Neil put into one of the *Sandman* comics a phrase lifted out of a *Discworld* book. I spotted it in a shop and said, 'You bastard! You pinched my sentence. Everyone liked that line, and you pinched it.'"

*Locus*: So how did the collaboration on *Good Omens* begin?

TP: "Neil wrote several thousand words a couple of years ago, which was part of the main plot of *Good Omens*."

NG: "I didn't know what happened next, so I put it aside and I showed it to Terry. One day I got this phone call from Terry, saying 'Remember that plot? I know what happens next. Do you want to collaborate on it, or do you want to sell it to me?' And I said, 'I'll collaborate, please.'"

TP: "Best decision he ever made! I didn't want to see a good idea vanish. It turned out, more and more things kind of accreted 'round it as the book was written. Also, Neil went and lost them anyway, so it all had to be retyped."

NG: "I'd lost it on disk, so I gave him a hard copy, which meant he had to type it in. He kept changing it."

TP: "I changed it so I could make the next bit work. The thing kind of jerked forward quite quickly, as both of us raced one another to the next good bit, so we would have an excuse to do it. Both of us cornered certain plot themes which we stuck to like glue."

NG: "Like the reluctance with which I handed over the Four Horsepersons of the Apocalypse to Terry when they got to the airbase."

TP: "I seldom let Neil touch any of the bits involving Adam Young himself."

NG: "When we got to roughly the end, we could actually see which characters we hadn't written. So we made a point of going in and writing at least one or two scenes with any of the characters that up until then we hadn't written."

**TP:** "Insofar as there's any pattern at all, we worked out what the themes were and then we each took a theme and wove that particular strand."

**NG:** "The other pattern, of course, was that you'd do your writing in the morning and I'd do mine late at night."

**TP:** "Which means there was always someone, somewhere, physically writing *Good Omens*."

**NG:** "It took nine weeks."

**TP:** "We look upon *Good Omens* as a summer job. The first draft for nine weeks was sheer, unadulterated fun. Then there were nine months of rehashing, then there was the auction."

**NG:** "When you have situations when you've got three agents, five publishers, all that kind of stuff. . . ."

**TP:** "Our friendship survived only because we had other people to shout at. So I could say, 'Take that, you bastard!' and hit his agent."

**NG:** "One thing Terry taught me, when we were writing the book together, was how not to do it. Too many funny books fail because people throw every single joke they can think of in, and have an awful lot of fun, and eventually it just becomes a collection of gags."

**TP:** "The big problem you face if you're working collaboratively on a funny book is that you start with a gag and it's great, it's very amusing, but with the two of you discussing it, eventually it's not good anymore. It's an old gag from your point of view, so you avoid it and you take it further and further. What you're putting in is a kind of specialized humor for people who work with humor. There's an old phrase, 'Good enough for folk music.' As you work, you have to stand back and say, 'Never mind whether we are bored with this particular gag, is the reader going to be bored with it, coming to it fresh?'"

**NG:** "One of the great things about humor is, you can slip things past people with humor, you can use it as a sweetener. So you can actually tell them things, give them messages, get terribly, terribly serious and terribly, terribly dark, and because there are jokes in there, they'll go along with you, and they'll travel a lot further along with you than they would otherwise."

**TP:** "The book has got its gags, and we really enjoyed doing those, but the core of the book is where Adam Young has to decide whether to fulfill his destiny and become the Antichrist over the smoking remains of the Earth, or to decide not to. He's got a choice, and so have we. So to that extent I suppose he does symbolize humanity."

**TP:** "Bear in mind that we wrote *Good Omens* while the Salman Rushdie affair was really just coming to a boil in the UK. But no one's going to go around burning copies of *Good Omens*, no one would think about that."

**NG:** "Yet everything is blasphemous. Technically speaking, *Good Omens* is blasphemous against religious order, as blasphemous as you can get. And Gollancz have just bunged it in for the big religious award in the UK, which we find very strange. They actually asked the archbishop of Canterbury to send vicars 'round to have serious tea with us."

*Locus*: Future plans?

**TP:** "There's always another *Discworld* book. The way I look at it, if I don't have to force them—if I want to do them, if publishers want me to do them, and readers want me to do them, I can go on doing them. The current *Discworld* book, *Moving Pictures*, is about the *Discworld* film industry. There are so many cinema industry gags that you can do, the problem was cutting ones out. There's a natural attraction to the subject for fantasy writers, because movies are not real in any case.

"Then, in *Reaper Man* [the next *Discworld* novel], you find out how shopping malls breed, and what the purpose of a shopping mall actually is. You're familiar with the idea of 'metalife,' the idea that cities are living things. Shopping malls are city predators. They spring up around the outside like starfish on a reef, and they draw the life out, the people, so the city starts to die in the middle. This is actually a minor plot in *Reaper Man*.

"There is no shortage of ideas for *Discworld* books. It's probably going to slow down a wee bit, because I've got some other stuff planned. I'm going to do another children's book. There's my big science fiction novel I've been trying to do for three years, and I'm going to have to get that one finished now. I've finished the first draft for the script for the film of *Mort*, which may or may not happen. And finally, I'm toying with the idea of a comic, but it's got nothing to do with *Discworld*. It's called *Stalin* and it's what would happen if Superman landed in Russia in 1904. The direct translation of the word *Stalin* is 'man of steel.' I'm not intending it to be a particularly funny comic. It has to be tragic, not because that's the fashion for superheroes, but because when you consider Russian history, it is tragic."

**NG:** "What am I doing next? I'm still writing *Sandman*. The *Rolling Stone* plug for *Sandman* in their 'hot' issue last year, combined with the actual graphic novel collection, has done wonders for increasing the readership. The first eight will also be collected by DC, which will mean a problem with how we number that collection, having brought out the second collection first.

"*Sandman* is going to keep going for about another two years. *Miracleman* is great fun. I'm doing it roughly bi-monthly for *Eclipse*. It's utopian

SF, and it's getting stranger and stranger, because I don't even have the commercial constraints that I have in *Sandman*. The next one is done as if Andy Warhol were doing comics. Then I'm doing a horror comic series which will be appearing in *Taboo*, about Sweeney Todd. *Signal to Noise,* a graphic series I did with Dave McKean, which was serialized in English trendy-style magazine *The Face,* has just been bought in a two-book deal by Gollancz. We'll be expanding it slightly, and that will be coming out early in the launch of their new graphic novel line. And I've started work on a fantasy novel, which won't be funny and may not even be very scary. It's called *Wall.*"

**TP:** "We've both got lots of stuff to do. So if you allow time for eating and sleeping, *Good Omens* 2 doesn't seem to fit in there very well."

**NG:** "It will probably never happen. We actually know how it would go. We know the theme— '668, The Neighbor of the Beast.'"

**TP:** "We even know some of the main characters in it. But there's a huge difference between sittin' there chattin' away, saying, 'Hey, we could do this, we could do that,' and actually physically getting down and doing it all again. One problem is, we've been saying it fliply, but it's almost true these days, we're not on the same continent for nine weeks at a time anymore."

# Sleep of the Just: Neil Gaiman on the Act of Creating and the Perils of Fame

## Steven Darnall / 1993

From *Hero Illustrated* #4. Reprinted by permission.

*The scene is the 1993 Chicago Comiccon, and at the moment, Neil Gaiman is more than the guest of honor; he's also the prime player in what appears to be a smaller, sweatier version of Beatlemania. As Comiccon coordinator Bevin Brown leads us on a beeline through a throng of fans ("Always look straight ahead and never stop moving," seem to be the orders of the day), Neil—the renowned leather jacket and shades in place—gets that little Beatle-like hop in his step as he reaches the foot of the stairs, and I can't resist asking: "Did you ever think you'd be the next Paul McCartney?"*

*"No," he responds. "I just wanted to write and have my writing published. I hoped people would read it. I didn't expect anything more than that."*

*It's easy to forget it was only about five years ago when DC Comics unleashed* Sandman *on the world. Up to that point, Neil Gaiman's main credit as a writer was on the mysterious but well-received* Black Orchid *mini-series, and apart from the quality of his writing, he had no reason to believe the fickle comics market would sustain his new baby for more than a year.*

*Well, along the way,* Sandman *caught on big. So big that people who didn't read comics started reading* Sandman, *and the buzz made it as far as* Rolling Stone. *So big that Gaiman began to get more writing assignments, both as a regular and guest scripter (*Miracleman, Taboo, Spawn, Secret Origins*), which, when seen as a cumulative whole, gave him a reputation as one of the most consistently intelligent and innovative writers in mainstream comics.*

*All this has combined to make Neil Gaiman a very big fish in what is still a fairly small pond, and brought to him a fame that could be taken either as flattering and exhilarating, or bewildering and frightening. For the moment, he refers to it simply as "bizarre."*

*Sometime in the next year and a half,* Sandman *will come to a close, which for many fans, to extend the metaphor, is a little like getting advance news of the Beatles' breakup. With his newfound adulation approaching critical mass, Gaiman may find himself at a crossroads—in more ways than one.*

**Steven Darnall:** I guess the first thing I should ask you is what you're sick of being asked. I want to save some time for both of us.

**Neil Gaiman:** (laughs) "Where do you get your ideas?" That's the one I'm genuinely sick of being asked, and also genuinely fascinated by. What fascinates me is not that people ask the question, but what kind of answer are they really looking for? Because if I tell them the truth, which is "I make them up," they seem very disappointed. They want to know about the trek I do once a year to the mountain.

**SD:** Why do you suppose that's the question that comes up the most?

**NG:** I don't know. Probably because that's where the magic is. People seem to think that they can't come up with ideas, and they're wrong. They can and they do, but they just think of it as daydreaming, or wasting time. You know, kids get told not to make things up, and I think in my case, nobody told me long enough, or it just didn't stick.

**SD:** I'd like to touch upon what you've done with *Sandman* over the last five years. When you went into it, did you know at the start where you'd be at the finish?

**NG:** When I started I plotted the first eight issues of *Sandman,* and I did that for a fairly specific reason, which was I figured that we wouldn't sell anything. We'd be a minor critical success, and around about issue 8, I'd get the call from DC saying, "We're not selling anything. We're a minor critical success. We'll cancel you at issue 12. That way, you've done a full year." That was what they used to do with things.

So I plotted through to issue 8 with some ideas of where I wanted to go. When we got to issue 8, and we were surprisingly—at least to me, I don't know about everyone else—not canceled, that was the point where I basically sat down and figured out what I wanted to do for the rest of it.

**SD:** Which is going to wrap up in the next year?

**NG:** Year-and-a-half.

**SD:** There are characters who pop up in the first few issues who show up in later issues—in some cases, *much* later. Did you know when you created characters in the early issues that you'd be using them down the line?

**NG:** A lot of it is the equivalent of being a juggler who tosses a ball into the air, knowing at one point or another he can retrieve it. Yes, I knew a lot of what I was doing. There were balls that were tossed into the air in the first eight issues that still haven't come down.

**SD:** And will they?
**NG:** Yes.

**SD:** Whose idea was it to give Elvis Costello a cameo appearance in *The Doll's House* story? Was that yours, or were you as pleasantly surprised when you saw it as I was?
**NG:** Elvis Costello . . . Well, let's put it this way. You remember the title of the very first episode of *The Sandman?* It was called "The Sleep of The Just" [the title of a song from Elvis' *King Of America*].

**SD:** Well, as I read more of your work, and listen to more of his, it's obvious that there's *some* kind of connection there.
**NG:** I love what Costello does; he's a genius. And I love what he does to, and with, words. Songs, for me, have to be about something. Probably why I love what Lou Reed does. You get these songs that are sort of three-minute novels.

**SD:** Have you an opinion on *The Juliet Letters*?
**NG:** I love it. These horrible little people writing these horrible letters to each other. (laughter)

**SD:** It's the sort of thing that made me think, "This is like something out of a comic book!"
**NG:** Sure. You could do "Don't send any money." [from *Juliet*'s "This Offer Is Unrepeatable"]

**SD:** It seems like the term "Gaiman-esque" has become as overused in comics as "Python-esque" or "Fellini-esque."
**NG:** Let me put it this way: I remember sitting at the Atlanta convention, the Diamond sales thing, last month, listening to various companies announcing what they had coming up, and suddenly I knew how Alan Moore and Frank Miller felt when "grim and gritty" became a catchphrase. (laughs) There's all this stuff that sounded like me on an off-day.

**SD:** Have you read any of Marvel's "Gaiman-esque" titles, such as *Morbius* or *Hellstorm*?

**NG:** I don't read it. Somebody told me that Tom DeFalco had decided that they were going to do *Sandman* right, so they did *Sleepwalker.* He said it was all people talking to each other, and they were going to have lots of super-hero cameos and fight scenes. I read a couple of issues of *Sleepwalker . . .*

**SD:** And that straightened you right out, I'll bet . . .
**NG:** I thought "Well, boy, if they're doing it right, I'm just going to have to keep on doing it wrong, then."

**SD:** Your fans are known as serious gift-givers. Jill Thompson says you've probably gotten more tapes than any writer at *Musician* magazine.
**NG:** Most of the tapes I'm given are *terrible.* You know, Scandinavian death-metal or whatever. You know: [sings in a deep, slightly American voice] "Oh, Morpheus, come down from the sky and give me good dreams CHA-DUNG CHA-DUNG CHA-DUNG" or one guy accompanies himself on a harmonium or whatever.

**SD:** Well, that last one sounds interesting . . .
**NG:** It wasn't. But I still play them. I had a tape given to me in San Diego a couple of years ago by somebody who said "A friend of mine is a huge *Sandman* fan, she's just recorded this, she wants you to have it, she talks about you on one of the songs." About three weeks later I got around to playing it, and it was *terrific.* Absolutely stunning. There was an address on it, and I wrote to her and said, "I think it's wonderful, and thank you very much for mentioning me on the song," and that was Tori Amos, and that was the tape that later became a number of tracks on *Little Earthquakes.*

**SD:** That's one of the nicest stories I've heard about a fan *ever,* I think. Supposedly, Grant Morrison said he'd been getting tapes from fans, and he found it depressing to realize exactly *what* he'd been inspiring all this time.
**NG:** I don't. I get lovely fans, and I get inspiring people like Tori. I think it's wonderful.

**SD:** One of the things that seems to show up in a lot of your work is the *price* of being an artist. What do you think that price is?
**NG:** I don't know, I'm still paying it. What is weird is a lot of it goes back to all that stuff about "Be careful what you wish for; you may get it." For example: I like comic conventions. I genuinely *like* comic conventions. I like wandering around from table to table; I like wandering up and down

Artist's Alley and saying "Hello" to people. I like hanging out on the DC booth. I can't do that anymore. I'd like to, but I *can't.* I physically can't. If I stop moving, somebody will come up to me with something to sign, and if I sign it, somehow it's like ants sensing sugar. There will be fifty or a hundred people around me and then fire marshals will come and then I'm trapped in a crowd. It's bizarre.

**SD:** Then you get blamed for causing a commotion.
**NG:** Yes, and that's no fun. But yes, one of the things that does obsess me is the cost. You don't get anything for free, and there is definitely a cost of creation.

**SD:** But is there a cost beyond merely being in the public eye?
**NG:** Yeah, that's easy. That's one of the things you can point to, because it's an easy thing.

Sometimes I think if I were starting all over again, I'd go the Thomas Pynchon route. Create an identity, create a name . . . I can stand up there in front of a crowd of five hundred or one thousand people and chat to them quite happily and field their questions and do all that kind of stuff, when I know that I'm on. It's a lot harder when I get recognized in the street, and these days it happens more and more.

**SD:** In *Signal To Noise*, the main character is a terminally ill filmmaker who looks back at his work and thinks, "Nothing I ever created was as good as it could have been. Should have been." None of it came out the way he'd intended it.
**NG:** None of it ever does. One of the things that will occasionally keep me up at night is wondering whether . . . There is this small, still voice in the back of your head at all times that suggests that possibly the act of making up stories is not a fit occupation for a grown man. It makes you wonder whether or not you're doing it for a reason. Whether that reason is of any worth. Then, occasionally, people will come up to you and say, "*Sandman #8* got me through the death of my best friend," or "Through the crib death of my baby," or they'll tell you about what an issue of *Sandman* did to their lives. And at that point, it does sort of become worthwhile.

But on the whole, it's just you at home, trying to tell stories nobody's ever done before. And I'll see fan mail that says "Oh, you haven't done anything as good as 'Blah.'" "Blah" is always something I did five years ago: Great, thank you. Most of what I want to try to do is continue to go places with fiction that I've never gone before, and tell stories I've never told before, and one of the problems you rapidly discover about fans is what fans want is the last thing they liked. They want more of that.

**SD:** If your most recent *Sandman* story had been "24 hours," they'd happily go for more of that.

**NG:** They'd like "48 Hours," followed by "72 Hours," followed by "A Week of Horrible Maiming." And the point where I had to come up against that was at the end of *Sandman 1–8,* when I knew the one I'd done that people really got off on was the Hell one. That was the one where people really went "Wow," and I thought "Well, I've got this story line—'Season of Mists'— and I know they'll love that. Now do I do that next, or do I go off and do this story called 'A Doll's House'?" You know, the Sandman's hardly in it. And I did "The Doll's House." I figured if I didn't, that way lay the X-Men. You wind up in the position of continually giving them what they want, and that's not the bargain I signed. What I'm doing is telling the stories I have to tell, whether people want them or not.

**SD:** That's interesting. I'm sure a lot of fans might assume that you created these stories in the order in which they appeared. You're saying that some of them were mapped out months in advance.

**NG:** Actually, *Sandman 19* is the only one that was ever written out of sequence, just because it was going to take two months for it to be done, rather than one month, because Charles Vess had to pencil and ink it. He's not the fastest. I think I wrote that before I wrote "Dream of A Thousand Cats." Other than that, they had been written in sequence, but there are shapes in there. I had the idea for a serial killers' convention a year before I got there, and at that time I thought, "Boy, it's really a pain in the neck to have to wait a year to do a story." Little did I know that I was then going to have to wait three and a half years to bring Destruction on stage!

**SD:** Is it possible that the act of creating is somewhat masochistic?

**NG:** There have to be easier things to do. My old school got me in a few times to do "careers advice." I was the token writer, and people would come up to me and say, "How do I get to be a writer?" and I said, "Well, first of all, if you can do anything else, do that. You know, there are lots of other things you can do that are an awful lot more fun, pay a lot better, will let you sleep far easier." [laughs]

**SD:** Have you done any of those other things, or is this as fun as it's gotten for you?

**NG:** This is what I tend to do. What I do is I write things.

**SD:** So, no dark past as a school teacher?

**NG:** No, I almost wish I had done those things. Do you remember in the 1950s—it doesn't happen so much now, but in the fifties—you pick up books from the fifties and they all have author biographies on the back, and the guy's always panned for gold, been a bodyguard, been a tuna fisherman, worked on a ranch in Argentina, worked as a guard in a prison, and was wanted for three years by the FBI for a crime he didn't commit. What I think somebody should do is "Author Biography Holidays" for back jackets. You go on holidays for two weeks, during which you pan for gold, work as a bodyguard [laughs], and then you have all this stuff to put on your biography.

**SD:** Getting back to "the price": Maybe by committing something to paper, or canvas, or whatever an artist does, it's frustrating as well as liberating, because you end up sort of condemning an idea to remain fixed. Elvis Costello, for example, has written scads of brilliant songs, but he's also written some terrible songs with great lines in them.

**NG:** What is actually really interesting with Costello is every now and then you'll find he's written a song two or three times; the same set of lyrics but with a different tune, until he gets it right, or whatever.

It's one of the things that I find fascinating about writing. I can take ten–fifteen days on the first five pages of something and take two days on the last ten pages, because all the decisions have been made by that point. What I love about starting is the sense of infinite potential, and what I hate about finishing is how far short I probably fell of what I had in my head and how I wanted to do it. But occasionally you get lucky. Sometimes you get stuff that's better.

**SD:** And this is not even taking into account that you're predominantly a writer, rather than a writer/artist. You've had some wonderful artists, and in my opinion, you've brought out the best of some artists on occasion, but it must also be a little like playing the telephone game, where you're bound to lose something in the translation.

**NG:** Yeah, but sometimes you gain something. One of the reasons I love comics is that I get to work with artists. I get to work with all these different artists. I get to play to their strengths. I get to make them *do* stuff.

One thing that's fun is seeing an artist and going, "He's really good at that. I bet he'd be good at *this*." Everybody thought of Michael Zulli as an animal artist. He was "the good animal guy." I met Michael and talked to him and thought he'd be great on a historical. He has that sense of detail. And we went off and did *Sandman 13* together, as a result of which, Michael Zulli is now known as "the historical artist." [laughs] You want to do a period piece, you get Michael.

**SD:** Right. And with Kelley Jones, an artist associated with weird horror stories, you did "Dream of A Thousand Cats," which was probably not only a nice surprise for him, but for his audience as well.
**NG:** I think for everyone, because it showed that Kelley was an absolutely terrific artist, and we went on and did "Season of Mists," and all of a sudden, Kelley had this huge following.

And Jill [Thompson]. She's being mobbed at the convention, and I remember telling her two years ago, when we were about to start work on "Brief Lives," "You are going to be a hot artist by the time this is finished" and she laughed at me, because she was the one who gave away her *Wonder Woman* pages because nobody ever wanted to buy them.

**SD:** When you deal with other people's characters—you've done it in your own book, and also in books like *Miracleman, Hellblazer, Secret Origins*— do you ever go in with an agenda, other than to tell a good story?
**NG:** I'm rarely comfortable—I'm quite *good*—but I'm rarely comfortable at doing other people's characters, because I always feel like there's a responsibility there. It still goes on through *Miracleman*. You know, I want these characters to be the characters that Alan [Moore] created. I would like Alan to be happy with what I'm doing on *Miracleman*. There's rarely an agenda other than seeing a character who has been poorly used, or underused, and wanting to do them right. I was talking to Paul Dini last night, who's the script editor on the *Batman* animated show, and he was saying he still goes back to the Poison Ivy stuff that I did for *Secret Origins* and *Black Orchid* as the definitive Ivy stuff, and that's nice.

**SD:** Do you find it sort of a busman's holiday, since part of those characters has already been sketched in for you?
**NG:** No, no. I have the kind of mind that puts things together in sequences, and in story possibilities and permutations. I try to look at what's interesting about something, so I can quite happily go back to the first four issues of

*Prez* and go, "There is something strange and powerful in here. I think I'll try to do a twenty-two-page story and see what happens. Boss Smiley as God."

**SD:** It's amazing, because twenty years ago, I don't think anyone would have thought there was anything to *Prez*.
**NG:** Well, three months down they may still not! [laughs]

**SD:** You've had the good fortune to write *Sandman* with virtually no corporate interference, which is pretty rare these days. Are there any stories you wanted to tell, but found you couldn't—or wouldn't—because of your own mental checks and balances?
**NG:** The only one I've ever put aside would have been a story a little bit like "Dream of A Thousand Cats," but it would have been about fetal dreams. You know, the dreams of a fetus, and it would have been absolutely heart-rending, and, you know, it would have ended in abortion, and it would have been horrible, and so on and so forth. And I thought, "No, I'm not going to do that story." I might have done it if *Sandman* were an English comic, seen only in England, I might have felt quite happy about it. But I didn't want to do a story that somewhere in middle America, someone was going to grab a fourteen-year-old girl who'd been raped by her uncle and say, "Look! See that? Read this! *This* is why what you're doing is murder!" I didn't want to do that.

I think that what we are doing is creating responsibly. I tend to be more surprised at the amount of controversy we *don't* generate. We do something like . . . the AIDS insert, where Death talks about AIDS: a six-page comic where you are told what AIDS is, where you get it, and how not to. What do we get? We get fifth-grade teachers writing to us, asking for permission to Xerox it and hand it out to their class.

**SD:** Do you suppose the lack of controversy stems from the fact that comics have had this sort of gutter reputation, almost from day one?
**NG:** I don't know. I think it's probably more because *Sandman* as a whole needs to be read and understood before you realize what's wrong with it. There may be things we do that would offend. But mostly you have to be bright enough to *read* it, and understand what we're doing and why.

We got one letter when *Sandman 50* came out, for example, accusing me of pederasty, because there's a line in the sequence in the Arabian Nights story in the harem about the beautiful boys in the harem. One other letter came in, accusing me of having anti-Christian beliefs, because there's that line about the dried dung of the Pope. In both cases, those are things that I took directly from *The Arabian Nights*. It's an Arabian Nights story. Those are Arabian Nights things. The actual bit in *The Arabian Nights* about the dried Papal dung is all about how the dung of the Pope is dried out and sent around, but there isn't enough, so the parish priests add their own dung, and send it out, purporting it to be the dung of the Pope. And mainly that was in there to show how little the Islamic world knew of the Christian world, which I think allies with how little the Western world knows of Islam. During various signings over the last few months, people have come up with a copy of that and said, "I'm Iranian, and I want to thank you. This is the first positive portrayal of Islam or the Arab world I've ever seen in a comic."

**SD:** Of course, even if you had thought of those lines yourself, and not taken them from *The Arabian Nights*, it amazes me that people would assume . . .
**NG:** That they're the opinions of the author.

**SD:** Exactly. "Neil *must* be a pederast! Ice-T *must* have killed a policeman!"
**NG:** I personally have a great deal of respect for readers. I have a great deal of respect for the human race. I think most people can tell the difference between fiction and fact. I think that the action of writing about something does not condone it. *Sandman* doesn't provide answers; it isn't meant to provide answers. The best thing I can ever hope to do is provide good questions, and I think I do that. I hope I do.

**SD:** Should we ask about the future, and the last story line?
**NG:** Well, around about September or October, we wrap up "World's End." Then we take a month off. During that month, for the people who need some kind of *Sandman* fix, there will be a Death gallery coming out, with portraits of Death by various artists, by Moebius and various wonderful artists.

**SD:** May I interrupt long enough to say it was a nice coup getting Scott McCloud to contribute to *Sandman 50*?
**NG:** Thank you. It's a beautiful sketch, and it's also a comic. It was an entire story in one panel.

In December, "The Kindly Ones" starts. "The Kindly Ones" is going to be a huge, thunderous, bloody, smoke-filled storyline, and it's the last big *Sandman* story line. Lots and lots of characters that people probably think I've forgotten about will be back, including the three witches in various aspects, the resolution of the little Daniel Hall story line, The Corinthian will be back.

It will be huge, full of action, and very strange. Marc Hempel will be drawing it. There will be some other stuff after it, but that is the last of the big arcs.

**SD:** Will those stories that follow "The Kindly Ones" be of a resolutive nature?
**NG:** Well, a lot of resolutions will appear in "The Kindly Ones," and not all of them pleasant. The story that follows "The Kindly Ones" is going to be called "The Wake." Then there are a couple of short stories, then there's Charles Vess' "The Tempest," which is the end of it all.

**SD:** Are there any artists who've approached you about doing work whose work might be of an inappropriate nature for *Sandman?*
**NG:** There are a lot of artists who've said they'd like to work with me. To be honest, I'm not sure there is such a thing as an inappropriate artist. The trick is matching the artist with a story. Very often they have to wait quite a while. Marc Hempel asked me in Philadelphia in 1990; he's had to wait three years. There are a few artists I'd love to work with, who I'd think I'd do a wonderful *Sandman* story with, who Karen [Berger, *Sandman*'s editor] thinks are inappropriate. Bernie Mireault, for example. I love Bernie's work, I think he's great.

**SD:** You two did a story for *Secret Origins* a while back . . .
**NG:** We did the Riddler story. I'd love to do a *Sandman* story with Bernie, but Karen thinks he's too cartoony. Which is fair enough; she's the editor of the book.

**SD:** One last question: as a writer, you've been a journalist, and probably a number of other things. When all is said and done, what made you want to write comics, and what made you think that you could?
**NG:** What made me think I could? Arrogance. [laughs] It's got to be arrogance; I can't think of anything else, looking back on it. But it's also something I wanted to do ever since I was a tiny kid. I was a voracious reader and I could never understand why comics were of any less merit or importance than any other way of writing. I think the thing that keeps me with comics is there's still so much to be done. There's still this huge unplowed field, this huge unexplored wilderness, and as long as I can keep doing new things and coming up with new things, I will. Whereas there are lots of good novels out there; there are a few good movies out there. People have been writing great poems for years, but there aren't a lot of good comics. I like trying to write them.

# Neil Gaiman: A Man for All Seasons

## Stanley Wiater and Stephen R. Bissette / 1993

From *Comic Book Rebels*, published by Plume in April 1993. Reprinted by permission.

Most of the creators identified herein as "comic book rebels" have bucked the status quo of how comic books are published and the role creative people are relegated to in the traditional business structure of the industry. Yet Neil Gaiman continues to regularly work with established publishers like DC Comics. How, then, is he a "rebel"?

Gaiman was chosen as being representative of a new order of creators. Cosmopolitan and nomadic, they successfully maintain their creative autonomy while demanding the respect of their chosen publishers through a clear sense of who they are, what they are worth, and a canny blend of independence and diplomacy. In short, a creator plying the sharpened skills of both a seasoned professional and shrewd businessman, able to freely move between all media, and work with any publisher.

Born in 1960 in Portchester, England, and growing up in Sussex, Gaiman left school purposely to become a writer. His first professional work in the early eighties was as a journalist, meeting and interviewing many authors and cartoonists whose work he admired. Alan Moore showed him the rudiments and structure of how comic scripts were crafted, and in short order he chose to abandon his early company-owned comics work to collaborate with artist Dave McKean on their first graphic novel, *Violent Cases* (Escape, Titan, 1987; reissued in color by Titan/Tundra, 1991).

Soon after, Gaiman and McKean completed the painted comic *Black Orchid* (1988) for DC, prompting an invitation to write a monthly title for the company. Resurrecting the name of a character created for DC by Joe Simon and Jack Kirby in the forties—but completely creating his own incarnation rooted in the Dream-lord of myth and folktales—*Sandman* was launched in 1988 and continues as one of the finest mainstream comics ever created. He was Alan Moore's choice to continue *Miracleman* (Eclipse, from

1990 to the present), and his other comics projects include a number of short tales for anthologies like *Taboo* (SpiderBaby/Tundra), and the graphic novels *Signal to Noise* (Gollancz, 1991, US edition from Dark Horse), *Mr. Punch* (Gollancz, 1993), with Dave McKean, and *Sweeney Todd,* a work in progress with artist Michael Zulli. Outside the industry, he has authored or coauthored several books, including the best-selling collaborative novel with Terry Pratchett, *Good Omens* (1990). He is presently developing a television series for England's BBC-2.

So how is he a comic book rebel? Gaiman grew up seeing how previous generations—and his own peers—allowed themselves to be badly used by the industry. Along with others of his generation, he is determined to take better care of himself. Just consider *Sandman*, which is owned under work-for-hire law by DC Comics. Gaiman's accomplishments and negotiations after the first year of its run led to DC's granting an historically unprecedented (and retroactive) creative coownership and share of the character and title, including all licensing and foreign sales—rights and revenue DC had always denied creators. Having already alienated key creators like Alan Moore, who had at one time earned considerable money and prestige for the company, DC has finally begun to realize it is in their own best interest to nurture better relations with certain creators. Very quietly, a revolutionary change in how business is done has occurred, a vital precedent set for this and the succeeding generations to come. While working within the existing system, Neil Gaiman continually expands the possibilities of both the industry and the medium.

**COMIC BOOK REBELS:** What were the building blocks as a reader that brought you to comics as a creator?
**NEIL GAIMAN:** The main one was that I never discriminated—in the racial sense of the term—between comics and anything else I read. I was a voracious reader as a kid; I read anything and everything. And one of the things I read was comics. I couldn't understand why there was any kind of prejudice against them; why we weren't allowed to bring them to school; why was it something everyone sort of frowned on? Books were considered cool, and yet there was as much thought and artistry in a lot of the comics that I was reading—some of Archie Goodwin's work, some of the early DC horror comics. So I never discriminated; I never felt that comics were in any way a "lesser" medium. They seemed to me a *more* exciting medium: I always figured I would be a writer when I grew up, and one of the things I always wanted to write was comics. And here I am.

**CBR:** With your ability to now pick and choose between various mediums of prose—from short story to novel to screenplay—why are you still apparently most enamored with this medium?

**GAIMAN:** As a creator, I get more of a buzz from comics than I do from anything else. I cannot go back and look at a short story or a novel that's come out with pleasure. Rather I look at it and think, "Oh God, I should have fixed that." Whereas I can look at a comic I've done and get a real buzz off it and have a real feeling of pride. It's always a feeling of surprise to me when something that I wrote as a script comes out and it actually *works*. And it's a very pleasant surprise because I didn't really do it—all I ever did was *write* it. Knowing that the script for a comic is *not* the comic. The comic is the comic.

**CBR:** *Violent Cases* and *Signal to Noise* are driven by memories and meditation, *Sandman* by dreams, and even your work on the superhero title *Miracleman*, in a genre traditionally composed of larger-than-life actions is by nature intimate and reflective. Do you find comics an inherently introspective medium for storytelling?

**GAIMAN:** I don't think comics are an introspective medium. *They are a medium.* That's all. But, by nature, I *am* an introspective writer. My stories tend to be as much about what goes on inside people as what goes on outside people. I don't want to sound naïve, but I'm telling *my* kind of stories.

**CBR:** But don't you consciously reject the traditional comic book exploitation of action and violence in your work?

**GAIMAN:** *Black Orchid* is very much a conscious rejection of the traditional approaches to these themes. In *Black Orchid* I wanted to do a pacifist fable in which acts of violence did occur, but were unpleasant—a fable in which meditation and beauty played a very important part. *Black Orchid* was sort of a look at all the things I *didn't* like in comics, and then do the kind of comic I would like to be out there.

In a completely different sense, it was the same reason I did *Violent Cases*. *Violent Cases* was something we did for people who don't read comics; *Black Orchid* was something that we did for people who do. But having said all that, I don't think anything I've done since then has been done as a "reaction to" what's out there. What's been done since then has been done mostly as a combination of terror and desperation to find the way to the next panel or to the next word or to the end of that story. And there was never anything in *Sandman* where I said, "Okay, now I'm going to do a comic book like nobody else has ever seen!" It was much more of, "Okay, *that's* where the story went," so I followed.

I figured sooner or later DC would turn around and say, "You know, you really can't do that," and they never have.

**CBR:** You're currently best recognized by the public as the writer on *Sandman.* Considering you own most of your comic book material, why did you initially agree to work on a character you did not create?

**GAIMAN:** But *Sandman* very much *is* my own creation. Is it my own ownership? No, that's due to strange antediluvian business practices of a gigantic Engulf & Devour style corporation. But is it my own creation—sure! The idea that I'm probably best known for it has more to do with the fact that one gets known for the largest and most easily followable body of work. And if you line it up against everything else I've done, *Sandman* is very obviously the largest body of work.

**CBR:** You've said before that *Sandman* for you is a finite story. How is DC handling that, since comic book companies never allow a commercially successful character to be purposely taken out of circulation?

**GAIMAN:** This has been already dealt with, pretty much to everyone's satisfaction. About two years ago, I raised the issue with my editors at DC, and each of them went pale and said, "Well, this has never been done before, um, maybe, no, um . . ." But they've had a chance to let the notion sink in, and now realize that when I'm done with *Sandman,* that *Sandman* is done. But just because it may be the end of *Sandman* as a monthly comic book, it does not mean—as far [as] I'm concerned—the end of *Sandman.* There are stories outside of the monthly continuity that I would quite like to do. There's a story that begins before *Sandman* #1, which would be the storyline for *Sandman* #0. There're a number of myths and legends I want to write that I'll probably do in a few years' time. So there are a number of *Sandman* stories yet to be done. Basically, I've agreed to come back to the character so long as DC leaves it alone in the meantime.

**CBR:** Any downside to the acclaim that *Sandman* has brought to you? Creators often get pigeonholed to keep working on the same series, or at least remain in the same genre.

**GAIMAN:** I don't know; there is a level that I tend to get pigeonholed as a horror writer. But, then again, anybody who knows anything about my body of work knows that isn't *all* I do. And *Sandman* isn't even particularly horror. So I can't really think of any way it's affected me adversely. It generates an interesting body of fans, ninety-nine percent of whom are quite wonderful. And one percent of whom take it all a little too far and assume that I am privy to a body of wisdom denied to the commonality of mortals. Now that's a little difficult to deal with . . .

**CBR:** You've worked with an impressive procession of artists—particularly on *Sandman*—but your most frequent collaborator is Dave McKean. What is the bond, and how do you work together?

**GAIMAN:** Dave is one of my best friends in the world, and simply put, a remarkable artist. He's also a remarkable writer, as his own series, *Cages*, demonstrates. It's been a very interesting and rewarding relationship; comics is just one of the many things we do, and there are things we do apart. We work with other people, but we still ring each other up every day. I love the fact his mind works differently from the way mine does. He sees things I wouldn't see and I tell him things he wouldn't think of. By now, we must have worked in every conceivable way that's possible to work in collaboration.

With *Violent Cases*, I wrote it essentially as a short story and handed it over to him and said, "Okay, now run with it." With things like "Hold Me" [*Hellblazer* #27], or the story I wrote for *Outrageous Stories from the Old Testament*, they were written as formal scripts. You know, "Page one, panel one." While *Black Orchid* was scripted like a movie, and *Signal to Noise* was written in some strange bastard form that only myself and McKean could understand a word of. The script would be completely meaningless to anyone else, because they would ignore the fact that we'd been talking on the phone about this for a month and a half, and are, in a way, telepathic.

It's a relationship in which we trust each other implicitly. That's why I love working with Dave on the covers for *Sandman*. I trust him. What he wants to do is okay by me.

**CBR:** You mentioned *Violent Cases* being written in short story form. Any plans of adapting your short stories or novels into comic book form? Clive Barker, for example, has done quite well with the adaptations of his prose work into the comics medium.

**GAIMAN:** Mostly I would look at the material and say, "Well, I already wrote it once. You know? Why should I write it again?" If somebody came to me and said, "We would like to adapt *Good Omens*," I would say, "Okay, here it is. Go do it. Have fun! Send me the comics when they come out."

I'm not convinced that you can simply transliterate something from one medium to another. I remember when I was watching the stage play adaptation of *Violent Cases,* which was incredibly faithful—and didn't work. The dramatic highs and lows were all in the wrong places. They took the words of the comic book, but in terms of theater, the one bit of theater magic they did was during the sequence where the character is talking about the wonderful light in the sky. And at that point the director flooded the stage with this wonderful light. Which means that became the central image, and so became the center of *Violent Cases*—which it isn't! So the stage adaptation became kind of mushy and soft-centered, and the center in *Violent Cases* is about Al Capone beating these guys to death with a baseball bat while a birthday party's going on, which is something which was covered in two lines of dialogue on the stage—pretty much as a throwaway. It was at that point I realized that faithful adaptations very often miss something.

You need to recreate your story, you need to retell it.

What is interesting is that I did "A Murder Mystery" for the publication *Midnight Graffiti*, as a short story. And about twenty-five percent of the people who read it noticed that there was one incredibly obvious story, and beneath it, one much, much less obvious story going on at the same time. And a lot of people don't even notice that there's anything beneath the surface story to read! Whereas I know that if I did it as a comic, there would be two or three little visual clues running through it, which would have meant that perhaps ninety-five percent of the readers would have picked up on the other story.

That's why I find comics so interesting. The way that people read comics and the way they read prose is a different experience. I believe a lot of people don't read prose with the amount of attention and effort that they give to comic books. In a comic book they will read *every* picture, and *every* word, and be forced by the juxtaposition to look at how these things relate to each other.

**CBR:** What was the experience of adapting *Good Omens* into a screenplay? Was that an enriching experience?

**GAIMAN:** Not particularly, for a number of reasons. First time we tried to make the book into a ninety-minute movie, and it didn't fit. You remember the old story about the guy who goes into the tailor to be fitted for a suit? And the tailor fits him really weirdly, so the suit hangs on the guy with the arms being four or five inches too long? So the tailor says to him, "Just raise your arms." And then the guy says, "Well, look at the way the back hangs."

So the tailor says, "Fine, just curve your back and hunch over." And then the guy complains, "Well, look at these trousers!" The tailor says, "Fine, just lean that leg forward." Finally the guy walks outside, looking like Quasimodo, and this man comes up to the guy and demands, "Who's your tailor?" And the guy asks, "Why do you want to meet my tailor?" So the man says, "If he can fit somebody like you, then he can fit *anybody!*"

Which is sort of like the process of writing a film script from a novel. You're chopping off limbs, and trying to put things in that fit. So that aspect of it wasn't a particularly pleasant experience.

**CBR:** In other words, "Screenplay by Procrustes."
**GAIMAN:** Exactly! On the other hand, it *was* a pleasant experience to take everything that I've learned from doing these adaptations of *Good Omens*—the one I did with Terry Pratchett, and the one I did on my own— and using it for developing this TV series for the BBC. It has the working title of *The Underside.* So that was very interesting because I was working on something that was *meant* to be filmed, and meant to have actors floating around a sound stage. And I could do all sorts of neat things that I never would bother doing in comics. For one thing, rather than an artist drawing word balloons, here I could see actors speaking my words, and using their own expressions.

**CBR:** You touched earlier upon the concept that people literally have to read comic books more intensely than prose. In what sense?
**GAIMAN:** People skip when they read prose. People skip words, they skip pages, sometimes they skip thoughts. Or they flip through pages. Or they read it faster and less attentively than they read other sections. A writer has no control over how somebody reads. In comics, you have a lot more control over the experience of reading. Over what and how the person reading it reads. You are doling out pieces of information to them with an immediacy that they otherwise might not have.

**CBR:** You often draw upon world mythologies to either deliberately dissect them, and/or build upon them. Do you have a conscious game plan for using mythologies in the comic medium?
**GAIMAN:** No. I remember speaking to a woman who had been a friend of Joseph Campbell, and she said that Campbell believed that superheroes are the mythologies of the twentieth century. I don't actually think they are. Mainly because they don't have stories attached to them—they are simply

characters. You've got this strange division in twentieth-century mythology right now, in which you've got stories floating around with no people attached, like the urban legends: the vanishing hitchhiker, the death cars. And you have characters like Tarzan and Superman and Batman—but with *no* stories. I think all I wanted to do was to create people with stories.

I love and am fascinated by religion. And I love and am fascinated with myths. I love and am fascinated with history. So all of these things come out in my fiction. Were I someone interested in physics, hard science, and bioengineering, you'd be getting hard science fiction from me. But those are the subjects which fascinate and obsess me: mythologies; how people see the world, how the world sees people; what stories people create to allow them to cope with and interpret the world. Myths are almost like the rules of the game. They tell you rules and truths, even if the truths are not necessarily what they ought to be. Which is the same function that has evolved for the urban legends.

Myths are my favorite subject. I think if I wasn't writing comics there probably wouldn't be a career for me. Unless somebody came up with Personal Religion Designer. You know—people would come up to me and they'd say, "Hi. I'd like something that was strong in the sin department. I'd like a whole pantheon, and I'd like really neat holy days, and a great creation myth." And I'd say, "Okay, that'll be twenty-thousand dollars and five percent of your poorbox takings." I could do that.

**CBR:** In *Violent Cases* and the serial killer story in *Sandman* you explore violent American lore, while in *Mr. Punch* and *Sweeney Todd* you draw from murderous archetypes of European folklore, as if exploring both sides of the same dark street of human nature. A darker side than *Sandman* chooses to explore.

**GAIMAN:** Well . . . yes. [Pauses] *Sandman* is an entertainment. It's a delightful entertainment, even though I've had to work harder and longer and it's given me more headaches than anything else I've had to do. But I think it's something to do with choosing your targets, who your audience is. And yes, my audience is me. That is, at the end of the day, the person I'm writing most to please is myself.

But *Sandman* represents to some extent my preoccupation and fascination with America, with a sort of mythic take on American cities and institutions. The New York in *Sandman* is probably not the real New York, but the one I remember seeing on my first day there. With these magical manholes spouting steam, and this mad old woman rushing past me going,

"Fuck! Fuck! Fuck! Fuck! Fuck!" And standing before these buildings that just went up forever . . .

*Violent Cases* was a way for me to talk about America as well as violence. It germinated from the fact that a lot of the incidents in the first few pages are, in effect, true. It is quite true that my father sprained my wrist when I was about four, grabbed my arm trying to get me to go to bed and something went. He took me to a gentleman who, I was informed a few years ago, had been Al Capone's osteopath. That much is true. But other than that, the rest is not. Beyond that, I've always been fascinated by America. I always figured America was kind of like Oz—it was a country where, for only ten dollars, you could buy your own submarine and set it up in your bedroom! I knew we didn't have anything like that in England, so America has always been a "myth" that I've been fond of, and a myth I like building on and newly creating.

Your statement about there being a difference between my American work and my British work is partly to do when you think of the old saw that in England a hundred miles is a very long way, and in America a hundred years is a very long time. I have this theory that you can find anything in America. Absolutely *anything.* You just have to drive far enough. Sooner or later you'll find the guy with the seven-foot-high ball of string. Or the guy who makes furniture out of cheese in his garden. You just have to go far enough.

In England, you just have to look far enough back. And whatever you're looking for is going to appear sooner or later. So *Mr. Punch* and *Sweeney Todd* are looking back, if you will. It's significant that in *Violent Cases,* the osteopath character is European. He went to Chicago, and then he came back. In *Mr. Punch,* you're looking again at a childhood incident that happened to me around the age of seven or eight, partly real, partly imaginary, built up from family myth and from the inside of my head, and from Punch and Judy.

The patterns in *Mr. Punch* go back to the medieval mummers' plays and possibly before. It's buried in that. *Sweeney Todd* goes back to the mythical founding of London. That is the starting point for *Sweeney,* to some extent where the story will lead and end. Someone once explained about the "desks" of London, saying, "Well, about twenty feet down are Roman times." It's true: civilization *is* lower. You can calculate the time periods from the strata, how the ground has risen and so forth. *Sweeney Todd,* and to some extent *Mr. Punch,* involve just getting in there with our spade, and digging in particularly bloody ground.

**CBR:** How do you think your work in comics has changed the field?

**GAIMAN:** There is a level of work being done today that is more graphic in violence and sex. Yet I don't think that has very much to do with any-thing truly significant; it's a superficial "pushing of the envelope." The only way I can really reply is to remember what it was like when Alan Moore was doing *Swamp Thing*, and that was the mythical archetype around which everything revolved, coming out of the monster cycle. And you look at the comics that never quite got into it even that far. Yet, for example, there were no gay characters in *Swamp Thing*. There were no nipples, as I recall. Now mainstream comics have both. But these days, somewhere in all that, we've since come to think we have done something.

I think *Sandman* #6 to some extent is a watershed. Because it went far-ther in terms of extreme and graphic horror and sex than anything anybody had ever done previously in comics that I can think of. *Sandman* #8 was a watershed because it went farther in "nothing happens in this issue" than anybody had ever done in mainstream comics to date! But other than that, I don't know. I can't see a huge influence that I've had on the field. I confess that if I have had an influence, it's probably not anything you'll see for at least ten years. Well, maybe eight years . . .

But what I'm now interested in is the thirteen to fifteen-year-olds, who are reading their *Sandman* and *Black Orchid,* and who are sitting in class and arguing with their teachers. Saying, "Look, look—see this? This is litera-ture! It's every bit as good as the literature you've been teaching us! When I grow up, this is what I want to do for a living."

**CBR:** Which of your series are you personally most satisfied with?

**GAIMAN:** I have individual favorites. One of my favorites is *Miracleman* #19, the Andy Warhol issue. And *Miracleman* #22, which ties earlier episodes together. I love *Sandman* #19, "Midsummer's Night Dream," because that was such hard work. And I'm really proud of it. I'm proud of the fact you can't see me with my desk, covered with tiny pieces of paper, trying to keep the action backstage, frontstage, back of the audience, front of the audience, and the play, all moving along in three dimensions, and getting it all down saying everything I have to say. I'm terribly proud of *Signal to Noise.*

**CBR:** Any major encounters with censorship along the way?

**GAIMAN:** No, not really. I had one script about a serial killer in *Sandman* where I was asked to change a McDonald's into a Burger Joint. Things like that. I was told I couldn't use the word "masturbation" in my serial killer script. Having said that, I probably could use the term today. But I have been relatively uncensored in the industry.

There *was* one story I decided not to write. It would have been sort of a little complement to "Dream of a Thousand Cats." It would have been a story about fetal dreams. It would have made a lovely story. Had it only been published in England, where abortion is not really an issue, I would have quite happily written it with no problems. But I chose not to write it, because I suddenly thought there would be some fifteen-year-old girl who's been raped and wants an abortion. And somebody would come up to her and show that story, and say, "How can you even *think* of getting an abortion after you read that story?" So I decided not to write it, which in a way tears me apart.

I know I had enough people come up to me and say that *Sandman* #8 got them over the death of their child, or the death of a best friend or someone like that. But you know that your stories *can* change people's minds, and hearts. So that was a case in which I decided to censor myself; I didn't want to be responsible for the consequences of a living soul. But for the most part the censors leave me alone, for reasons not adequately explained.

# *Writers on Comics Scriptwriting*: Neil Gaiman

## Mark Salisbury / 1999

Infused with mythology and magic, horror, and humor, Neil Gaiman's epic *Sandman* saga elevated comics to a literary art form. The sprawling, wildly ambitious tale of Morpheus, Lord of Dreams, *Sandman* presented an intense, intellectual alternative to the more typical comics vision of caped superheroes duking it out with masked supervillains above city streets, and helped find the medium a place on bookshelves alongside more conventional fantasy fiction. People who hadn't previously looked at a comic found themselves inexorably drawn into the world of Dream and his extended family, The Endless, and the series received serious and positive critical evaluation from academics, mainstream publications, and literary giants alike. Witty, barbed, sly, and superbly spun, the *Sandman* stories, together with Gaiman's other work—including *The Books of Magic* and his many collaborations with the artist Dave McKean: *Violent Cases, Mr. Punch, Black Orchid, Signal to Noise*—revealed the former journalist to be a sublime storyteller on a par with Angela Carter and Clive Barker. While the Hampshire-born, Minnesota-based Gaiman has, of late, made the transition into other forms of writing—novels, movie scripts, and the television show *Neverwhere*—his influence on the comics medium remains undeniable and still reverberates today.

**Mark Salisbury:** You were a journalist and short story writer before you began working in the comics industry. Why the change of tack?
**Neil Gaiman:** I was a journalist to make money and short stories were something that I did on the side. If I sold one, I was happy. Journalism did

teach me a great deal, though: how to write to deadline and, more importantly, a certain economy of words. In an average comics speech balloon you need to be able to capture a whole personality and/or indicate vocal patterns in maybe a dozen words. From that point of view, it was tremendously helpful, but I never wanted to be a journalist. I wanted to write comics.

**MS:** Had you harbored such ambitions from an early age?

**NG:** As a kid, one of the biggest mysteries to me was how you wrote comics. But I knew they were written by someone, and I knew that was what I wanted to be. When I was fourteen or fifteen my literary heroes were Roger Zelazny, Samuel R. Delany, and Harlan Ellison, but also comics writers like Len Wein—I was a fan of his *Swamp Thing* and *Phantom Stranger* stuff— and Archie Goodwin. And at the top of my list was Will Eisner. I remember at school in Croydon, an outside careers advisor came in to discuss what we wanted to do, and I said, "I want to write American comics." I might have well said, "I want to be an astronaut." In fact, if I had, he probably would have had some kind of idea of how to reply. This was obviously something that no one had ever said to him before, and eventually he said, "How do you go about doing that then?" And I said, "I have no idea, you tell me."

**MS:** Many of today's comics writers grew up reading the characters they've subsequently gone on to write. What kind of comics were you interested in as a child?

**NG:** If I list my favorite comics you can begin to triangulate the genesis of *Sandman* somewhere in there. They were the Len Wein/Bernie Wrightson *Swamp Thing* issues, *The Phantom Stranger,* and maybe Jack Kirby's original run of *The Demon.* Plus all of the old *DC Witching Hour, House of Mystery, House of Secrets* . . . though these also kind of disappointed me, because I felt there was some wonderful potential there. Also, Barry Smith's *Conan* and Eisner's *The Spirit.* The superhero stuff I enjoyed but even as a little kid it felt kind of fundamentally pointless, in that if it's a hero versus a villain I know who's going to win. I figured that out early on. I liked *The Brave and the Bold,* where they'd team Batman up with someone unlikely. They'd be weird, and that was definitely the stuff I liked. It was all well-written and all a little odd. Mostly it was about storytelling, it wasn't about the costumes.

**MS:** When did you finally crack the mystery of how to write a comics script?

**NG:** If I'd had any idea exactly how to sit down and write a comic script I might well have started writing them at fifteen or younger. That was how they finally talked me into printing the script to *Sandman* #17 in [the graphic novel collection] *Dream Country*. On the one hand, I didn't like the idea of taking people backstage and showing them how it was done, but on the other I thought, "What if there's the equivalent of a fifteen-year-old Neil out there going, 'How do you do this?'" In the end I learned because Alan Moore showed me. We met at a convention, and after we'd been friends for a while I said, "I've always wanted to know how you write a comic script," and he just pulled out a piece of paper from a notebook of mine and said, "Well, I start with page one, panel one and put everything in it that you could possibly want an artist to know." He basically went on to show me how it was all done and I went home and wrote a short comic story. I sent it off to Alan, who said it had some problems but it also had potential. Then I wrote another one and he said it was good, that he'd be pleased to have written it himself. Then I more or less left it for a couple of years until fate plunged me back into the wacky world of writing comics.

**MS:** So how did the big break come?

**NG:** I was sick of journalism and I ran into a man in a pub, a friend of a friend, who asked me what I did. I said, "I'm a journalist, what do you do?" And he replied, "I write comics." I expressed my own interest in comics and he called a couple of days later. He was working on a new comic and was interested in working with fresh young talent. It never came out, and the reason the guy was interested in working with fresh young talent was because nobody who had been around the block would work with him. But through it I met Dave McKean, who was a young art student, and we were introduced to Paul Gravett from *Escape*. He liked what I was writing and what Dave was drawing and asked us if we were interested in doing a five-page strip for him. It is much to Paul's credit that when we went to see him a week later and said, "Would you mind terribly if instead we did a forty-eight page graphic novel called *Violent Cases*?" he thought about it for a minute and said sure. That's how I wound up working with Dave, which was easily the most important thing that ever happened to me.

**MS:** Didn't you also do some work for *2000 AD?*

**NG:** I did about five "Future Shocks" and was not impressed. One time I got saddled with a Spanish artist who didn't speak any English, and had obviously had some kind of rough translation of the script placed in front of him, and he hadn't quite drawn it as written. And then the people in the *2000*

*AD* office went back over it and rewrote what I'd written to try and make it match what the guy had actually drawn. And then they took out all the jokes.

**MS:** Not long after that you made the move to American comics with DC's *Black Orchid* and *The Sandman.* How did that come about?

**NG:** [DC editors] Dick Giordano, Karen Berger, and Jenette Kahn came to London on a talent scouting expedition, the one on which they recruited Grant Morrison and Pete Milligan. Dave and I walked in and pitched a *Phantom Stranger* idea, and they said no. I got desperate, picking forgotten characters, but somebody was doing everybody, it seemed. Finally I said *Black Orchid,* and Karen Berger looked up and said, "Blackhawk Kid, who's he?" And I thought, "Yes, I've got one they don't know." We did an issue of *Black Orchid* and the people at DC really liked it. But then I got a phone call from Karen, who said they were worried because they'd got two people nobody had ever heard of working on a character that nobody had ever heard of, and a female character at that. So she said, "What we're gonna do is put Dave on this *Batman* book that Grant [Morrison] is writing and give you a monthly comic. That way we will raise your profile, so by the time we release *Black Orchid* people will know who you are." And that was why, at the end of the day, Dave got to do *Arkham Asylum* and I got to do *Sandman.* Six months earlier I had mentioned to Karen and Jenette that I was thinking of reviving the seventies *Sandman,* the Joe Simon one, because I loved the idea of someone who lived in people's dreams, and Karen suggested I go ahead and do it. Then the next day she phoned up and told me, "Roy Thomas has already revived that character for *Infinity Inc.,* so can you make up a new *Sandman?* Just keep the name and go have fun."

**MS:** Do you consider what you write to be literature, as opposed to just comics?

**NG:** I would hope so. The lovely thing about comics, because it's words and pictures together, is that people come to them from different traditions: from the written word, from films, and from comics. What I was interested in most of all was words, because they were the one thing that I had complete control over as a writer. I sometimes worry, looking at some of the comics that are now on the stands, that I may have done some bad things there. I see comics that are desperately overwritten, where you never get a silent panel and everything is captioned almost to the point of redundancy. They'll show something in the panel and then there will be a long caption explaining it in florid, sub-literary terms. That may be my fault, and if so I'm really sorry. It certainly wasn't anything I set out to do.

I came from a very booky tradition. I love words and the things you can do with words. And it always seemed to me that, with the exception of a very few writers like Alan Moore and Will Eisner, words always seemed to come in second in comics. I wanted to get them up there so they could come in at least equal. And it was interesting to see some of the things you could do if you decided to break the rules and just play. Like in *Season of Mists*, in the opening chapter, just to stop and do these little pen descriptions of each member of The Endless. That was enormous fun and worked terribly well.

The thing about *Sandman* was at the end of the day my intended audience was me. I remember the thrill of discovering Alan Moore's *Swamp Thing*. There I was, twenty-four or twenty-five, and every month I'd go down to my comic store and get the new *Swamp Thing* and it was wonderful. It was a great feeling to be twenty-five and have somebody writing a comic for you, something that was as well-written as anything you were going to find in the prose section or the poetry section or the play section of a bookstore. So what I wanted to do with *Sandman* was write a comic with me as the target audience; the kind of thing that if I wasn't writing it, I'd like to go down and read every month.

**MS:** Your work has always been steeped in mythology, magic, and fairy tales. Are these particular obsessions of yours?

**NG:** Oh yeah. You can probably write about something you're not interested in, but not with any level of conviction. It's like writing *Star Trek* books, you have to care or at least be interested in those characters or else the magic isn't going to be there and the readers are going to know. There was a science-fiction fan and occasional writer whose real name I've forgotten, but who wrote under the pen name of David McDaniel. He wrote two, maybe three *The Man From U.NC.L.E.* books. There were dozens of these books that came out during the sixties and early seventies, but the only ones that anyone who has ever read them remembers are titles like *The Vampire Affair* and *The Dagger Affair*, which were written by David McDaniel. They were the only ones where the author obviously cared about adding to the mythology and was having this wonderful time with it. I think that's true with more or less anything; you follow your obsessions.

**MS:** So are you incredibly well read or do you tend to make stuff up?

**NG:** There are areas where you know your shit and there are areas where you fake it. The art of writing is the same as the art of convincing a teacher that you really did do your homework or you studied something that you didn't. It's the art of lying convincingly and it's amazing how much you can learn from a little. Having said that, it's also huge quantities of stuff that one simply knows. If you are a writer, you tend to have sort of a magpie head. You store away all sorts of weird and wonderful trivia, which pops out when you need it. A lot of the mythology stuff, maybe ninety-five percent of it, I know fairly well and I'm interested in. And then there's stuff that you'll read for pleasure. I remember this book called *Funeral Customs Around the World*. It was wonderful. I kind of picked it up on a whim and started reading and got completely fascinated by the different ways different cultures—based on different environments—have of disposing of unwanted corpses. There are cultures in which you can't bury them, so what do you do? Sometimes you drop them in a river, to be eaten by crocodiles. In Tibet, where they don't have any wood to burn them with, and don't have any rivers to throw them in, and the ground is too hard and rocky to bury them, they wind up grinding them up and feeding them to the birds mixed with a little corn as a way of getting rid of them. It's called sky burial. I remember reading that and going, "That's an issue of *Sandman*," and doing my funeral issue set in a necropolis, with this huge graveyard and all the different burial methods get demonstrated and discussed, just because I thought that was so cool.

I also think that if you're writing magic, anything that sounds right is right, or it may as well be. In fact, I figure that on the whole you're better making it up convincingly than going out and researching it, because I always find the real magic that you research is always so unconvincing. I also remember very early on in *Sandman*, I put in some genuine Enochian magic words, really just to spice things up, and a number of times over the following couple of years I was taken aside by people who needed to know where I had been initiated and how dare I betray the profound secrets of the Order by using words that are not to be written down.

**MS:** How much of you is in the character of the Sandman?
**NG:** They're all me. The mistake that people tend to make with any of this stuff is, "Is this character you and the rest of them not you?" No, no, no—when you think that way you've lost it. Is the Sandman me? Yeah, he's kind of me-ish. He doesn't have a sense of humor, which I think I do, and he's thinner and taller and much, much older. But I gave him my dress sense just because it made it easier for me to write him as a more sympathetic character. But Death is me too, and Delirium, and Merv Pumpkinhead. In fact, Merv very often wound up being almost the voice of the author. Writing *Sandman* I'd get to the point, looking at a certain character, where I would go, "I can't believe you're doing this. Come on!", and that's normally the point I would bring Merv on and have Merv say, "I can't believe you're

doing this. Come on!" The way you make up characters—for me at least—is you very rarely go and find them outside. Normally you take a little bit of you, even with the bad characters—the Corinthian, say—and you go and find that side of you in them. And if you find it with any conviction, you'll be writing something that will convince.

**MS:** So how much of your life have you documented within the pages of *Sandman*?
**NG:** A lot of it is not exactly one-to-one correspondences. But things would happen and I would put them in the comic, but I would put them in the comic probably in a form that only I would ever recognize. If there is a code, it's private and normally they become starting-off points for things.

**MS:** Yet that's you narrating *Violent Cases,* isn't it?
**NG:** Definitely, but that was Dave McKean's idea. I wrote the story and I remember Dave saying, "I think I'm going to make you the narrator." At the time I was very kind of, "Hang on, but then people will think this is true," and he said, "Oh shut up, I don't have anyone else as a model so it may as well be you."And I said okay. It's kind of cool and a lot of the memories in *Violent Cases* are mine anyway. Just as a lot of the memories in *Mr. Punch* are mine. Those books are very unreliable works of autobiography.

**MS:** I remember an interview in which you said that in a comic the writer is the director and the screenwriter, while the artist is the cameraman. Does that still hold?
**NG:** Yep, and in Dave McKean's case it's normally a lot more than that. I'll write scripts for Dave that I don't write for anyone else in terms of their looseness. Very often with Dave I'll just give him the words and occasional little stage directions. With anyone else I'm going to be very, very precise. I'm going to tell them exactly what I want and hope they can basically get something out of my head and onto the paper. I look at Dave's work and as far as I'm concerned he has a better storytelling sense than I do. In fact, he has a better storytelling sense than pretty much anyone I've ever met. So I tend to give him very much a free rein.

Normally if we're doing something, we've probably been talking about it for six months to a year first. *Signal to Noise* was slightly less than that, just because it leapt out at us. With *Mr. Punch,* we'd been talking for two years about doing this book, gathering reference material together. So when I finally wrote it—and *Mr. Punch* went through three very solid drafts—there was a level where I felt all I had to worry about was the words and the story. I knew that the pictures would take care of themselves, that was all Dave. I knew the kinds of things he would be doing with puppets, with photos, and with art, but I didn't dictate and I don't think I even suggested. When I came to write it, I simply sat down and wrote the words.

**MS:** Have you ever had a situation with an artist where you've had to ask them to do something again? Or do you trust the artists you've collaborated with?
**NG:** I trust my scripting and writing skills enough. I know my storytelling skills are not the greatest in the world. On the other hand, I also know that what I suggest will work, so what I always say at the beginning of any script when working with a new artist is, "Look, I'm the writer here, you are the artist, if you can see a better way of doing it then do it that way. Not a different way, but if you can see a better way, then do it that way."

**MS:** Do you think working that way gives an artist enough leeway?
**NG:** Well it depends. It depends on the artist and what I'm doing. On *Sandman,* with a very few exceptions, I didn't want to give people leeway. I wanted to make sure they got it right. I feel when you're telling an artist, "Do this," or, "This will work," what you want is for them to do that and for that to work. And mostly it does. When you give an artist leeway, unless you trust them implicitly and know what you're going to get, you can very often wind up with something that bears no relation to what you did. I've heard too many horror stories from too many friends of mine who write comics, where what actually came out bore no resemblance to anything that was in the script and then they had to desperately try and cover it over by rewriting.

**MS:** So is there ever any interaction between you and the artist?
**NG:** Oh sure. For a start I won't write a script unless I know who's drawing it, and then I'll want to talk to them. Sometimes you really hit it off with an artist as friends, sometimes you don't. Working with Bryan Talbot was wonderful, because Bryan would always fax me stuff as he was doing it and very often what he was drawing would find its way immediately back into whatever I was writing. I've never been able to understand how writers can write scripts not knowing who's going to draw it, because you write for the artist. The most important thing to know about that *Dream Country* script is, at the end of the day, it's a letter to Kelley Jones, telling him what to draw and how to do it. But if you compare the script and the finished comic you'll also find places where he went off on his own and did something that wasn't what was suggested.

**MS:** Stylistically, you're closer to Alan Moore, who also describes in detail what he wants in a script, than, say, Garth Ennis, who favors the stripped-down approach. Do you agree?

**NG:** I suppose. Philosophically I think the place I'm coming from is closer to where Alan is coming from but also to some extent closer to where Grant Morrison is coming from. An Alan script for a twenty-four page comic will probably be about eighty pages long. A Grant script for a twenty-four page comic is normally twenty-four pages long. With me, a script for a twenty-four page comic would normally come in at about forty-eight pages, maybe ten thousand words. I think part of it was influenced by Alan, yes, but I think mostly it was wanting to be able to call the shots. If I say, "Dredd comes in room," I want to know what kind of room, what kind of angle is he coming in at, is this important, and what else do we need to know? Very often with artists I've been working a long time with, or I trust and who have obviously got it, I may well be giving them panel descriptions that are no longer than, "Dredd comes in room." With an artist I don't know or haven't worked with before, you'll get much, much longer panel descriptions because I'm trying to cover all the bases.

What was fun with *Sandman,* though, was that if it was anything, it was a kindly dictatorship. In that it was my story, dammit, these were my people and the artists were playing in my sandbox. I was also trying to work it in such a way so everybody had the most fun, and make sure the artist had a cool experience they could look back on. But at the end of the day I wanted it to be my thing. This was not a "plays well with others" kind of thing. No. You're playing my game, you have to play according to my rules.

**MS:** Do you think that's why, despite the fact you had many different artists working on *Sandman,* with differing styles, it still feels like a coherent whole?

**NG:** I think so. The storytelling, the panel-to-panel storytelling, is mine all the way through. It's the way I tell stories. There are only two episodes in the whole of *Sandman* where I didn't do them full-script. One of which was "Ramadan" in *Sandman* #50. Because I wanted to get that "Arabian Nights" effect I wrote the first half of the thing as prose, because I wanted to get that sweep. I thought I'd go back in and break it down into panels later, and when the time came I phoned [P.] Craig Russell and said, "Craig, what kind of panels do you like? Big ones? Little ones? How many panels do you like putting on a page? What are you comfortable with?," the kind of stuff I normally ask an artist. I always like to ask an artist first what they like draw-ing, which very often nobody's ever asked them, but which can make an enormous amount of difference to the story. They can say, "I always wanted to do a blah," and you go, "That's a great idea for a story." In Craig's case, he answered, "What have you written so far?" and I read it to him and he said, "Let me do this, please, just give me the story as is and let me do it." And that's how we did it. I had read Craig's adaptations of Rudyard Kipling and operas in the past, so I knew he'd do a wonderful job. The other time was with John J. Muth, who did the penultimate *Sandman,* which I wrote more or less as a poem. I just wanted to see what he'd do with it.

**MS:** How long does it take you to write a script?

**NG:** When I started writing it was about a week and a half to two weeks at the most. Occasionally I'd get lucky and write one in a weekend, even at the length my scripts run to. Then, as I went on with *Sandman,* it got harder, mainly because there was so much that I'd done before. I'd go, "Okay, I've done that panel transition already, I've done that scene, so think of another way of doing that." When you're starting out there's a huge gulf between one panel and the next. How do you get from this panel to that panel? There comes a point where it stops being very hard and becomes very easy for a little while. Then, for me, it started getting hard again because I really don't like repeating myself. If there's anything that characterizes me as a writer, it's probably that. By the time an audience turns up I've already gone and decided to do something completely different. In the beginning I could write a *Sandman* script a month and have half a month left over to do other things in. And by the end of it I was taking eight weeks to write a twenty-four page script. The last two *Sandman* arcs, *The Kindly Ones* and *The Wake,* took ages to write, and the book only maintained a vague semblance of schedule because I started *The Wake* while I was still writing *The Kindly Ones,* in order for [artist] Michael Zulli to get a head start. Even then it must have taken two years to bring out the last thirteen or fourteen issues.

I remember being told off by one writer who writes a comic in a day. We were talking and I was saying, "I've just finished this last *Sandman,* and it took me about three weeks to write," and this person looked at me and said, "I bash them out in a day. How can you afford to do it?" Because at the time we were only making $1,500 to $2,000 a script. On the other hand, the ten volumes of *Sandman* are still in print, and they still sell more than anything else does. We've done roughly a million of them in the US alone and well over a quarter of a million in the UK, and over the years they've paid me back for the amount of effort I put into them. There was no guarantee that they would in the beginning, it was just how I felt they had to be done. Looking back, I'm not sure why I was doing it. I definitely wasn't doing it for the money. It was partly the fun, the joy of creating art, and a lot of it with *Sandman* was just the joy of doing something I didn't feel anyone had done before, which is not something that you get very often in any field of art or literature.

**MS:** Is it true you make a mini version of a comic before you begin writing?
**NG:** I take twelve pieces of paper and fold them over so you have the cover, and everything including the ads. I'd irritate DC because I'd always want to know where the ads were going to be placed. They hated that, but it's kind of useful for knowing where to put double-page spreads. I'd draw a little cover for it and then turn it over and on the back page I'd write the numbers one to twenty-four. I'd jot down the high points; the things that I knew were definitely going to have to happen at some stage, roughly where they were going to happen, and more or less on what page. Then I'd probably draw page one for myself and sometimes I'd draw and write as I went along. Sometimes I'd draw the whole thing and then I'd write it. Often I'd know I had four pages of conversation and I'd just note "page of conversation here." I'd use the little booklet almost as a problem-solving device. If I was stuck, I would just sit and draw something. If it got to the point where I couldn't figure out a way to make the story seem interesting, I'd go in there and just draw it. It would also stop me doing silly and irritating things which I would occasionally do when I was writing on the road, like accidentally writing a twenty-five page comic without noticing and then have to try and talk everyone into letting me have my twenty-five page comic and only do twenty-three pages in the following issue, which occurs at one point in *A Game of You.*

**MS:** I understand that you listen to music when you write, and that issue three of *Black Orchid* was heavily influenced by Frank Sinatra. Was that the case with *Sandman* as well?
**NG:** Very definitely, and very often I'd have to figure out what the right music was. The worst time was during one of the "going to hell" episodes where I just had Lou Reed's *Metal Machine Music* on in the background and kept it there for three days while writing. Not something I recommend for anybody's health. Lots of *Sandman* was written to Iggy Pop and Talking Heads. I like having appropriate music. When I was writing *Stardust,* which is not actually a comic, I wound up loading the CD player up with English folk music, which I don't normally listen to, but seemed completely right for the mood. It's the magic of mood and you want to be in the right kind of place and have the right kind of stuff. It's one of the reasons why, when I'm

writing a lot of fiction, I don't read fiction. Instead I read nonfiction, because you want to keep your palate clear. If I'm reading an author you'll find them in what I'm writing, the flavor of them. It's like milk in a fridge takes on the flavor of whatever it's sitting next to. I'd also choose music that will keep me sitting there, because when you're writing the easiest thing in the world is to stop writing and find an excuse to go and do something else instead. I remember the joy when random play came into my life, because there were all these albums that I couldn't play anymore because as each track finished I'd start humming the beginning to the next one.

**MS:** You've written a number of screenplays for both television and film. Was comics a good training ground?

**NG:** Probably. It's definitely harder writing a comic script than writing a movie or a television script, because in those there are decisions that will be taken by the director, the cameraman, or the editor that you don't have to worry about as a writer. Say you have a scene where somebody rings a doorbell and your guy gets up and answers the door. If you're writing that in a movie script you say, "The doorbell rings, Joe gets up and answers the door." In a comic you say to yourself, "I have two panels to do this door answering scene, so how I am going to do it?" You have to decide essentially where you are going to shoot it from; are you going to shoot it from outside? Are you going to have a shot of him walking down the corridor? Is the door going to open from outside? Are you going to cheat and have a very small panel of a finger pushing a bell and the door opening? These are problems you're going to have to solve while you're writing a comic. Having said that, I get very puzzled watching people move or fail to move from one medium to another. It seems to me so natural that anybody who writes comics could also write novels, television, or movies. And yet one watches famous novelists coming to write comics and running badly aground, and comics people are likewise going off, trying another medium and making an unholy mess of it.

**MS:** Do you still see a future for yourself in comics?

**NG:** With comics right now I'll do occasional little things if somebody waves an artist at me that I've always wanted to work with. I did this little Vertigo story because Jeff Jones wanted to do his first comic in twenty-five years. I loved the idea and I didn't even care if it was any good or not. I will probably go back one day and write some more, but the thing is, I feel now like I've written a few good comics—*Mr. Punch,* maybe three or four issues of *Sandman* I was fairly satisfied with—whereas I feel there's lots of things out there that I haven't done to my satisfaction. I haven't yet made a movie I'm pleased with. I haven't made a television series I'm happy with. It's quite possible in five or ten years' time I'll do some stuff that has to be comics, and I'll come back and spend a few years just doing more comics. But I did comics because I loved them and I stopped because I felt it was right to leave while I was still in love. I never got to the point where I had to get up in the morning, stare into the mirror gloomily and go, "Oh God, I've got to write a comic today." I'm pleased, proud, and slightly baffled that comics seemed to have brought me a modicum of fame and a modicum of fortune, but I didn't go into it to do that, because when I started writing nobody got famous and rich from writing comics. Do it because you love the medium. Do it because there's stuff to be said. Do it because it's fun.

# Words, Words, Words . . . A Glimpse inside the Mind of Neil Gaiman Parts I and II

## Hannah Kuhlmann / 1999

From the *Minnesota Daily*. Reprinted by permission.

Author Neil Gaiman has been churning out fantasy and horror fiction for well over a decade, in both comic book and prose form. Born in 1960 in Portchester, England, he now resides in Wisconsin with his family and uses Minneapolis as a metropolitan headquarters. In addition to his ten volume graphic novel opus, *The Sandman,* Gaiman has also written two novels, two short story collections, a number of other graphic novels and a children's book called *The Day I Swapped My Dad For Two Goldfish.*

While the writer in residence keeps a relatively low local profile, his status as a hot creative commodity was recently confirmed when Miramax magnate Harvey Weinstein personally recruited him to adapt *Princess Mononoke,* the highest grossing Japanese film of all time, into English.

In a characteristically wordy and sharp-witted interview with A&E, Gaiman reveals his desire to scare and disturb his readers, his own fear of Hollywood, and his pride over the newest Sandman book, *The Dream Hunters.*

**Hannah Kuhlmann:** First of all I wanted to ask you, out of all the places in the world to settle down, why were you drawn to the Midwest?
**Neil Gaiman:** The main one is simply that my wife is American. She was American when we married and has remained so ever since. All of her family is from Minneapolis, originally. And, I kind of like the Midwest. There's a not-in-Hollywood, not-in-New York quality to it. You know, three hours and forty minutes away from LA, and two hours and whatever it is minutes away from New York, which I have to visit much more than I would enjoy. I think

everything about it is terrific, except the winters. I've never actually understood the concept of a Midwestern winter. If you're English you figure when water goes hard, it's cold, and that's probably about as cold as things get. You know, that's sort of it. I didn't realize how many acres below water going hard there were. The sheer concept that you could take a step outside, take a deep breath, and the hairs in your nose would freeze was something completely alien to me. But on the other side, the flip side, I'd come through Minneapolis a lot of times on book signing tours and I like the area. I like the houses, I had a lot of friends out here and still do. There are a surprising number of good writers in the area, and good writers who are friends of mine.

**Q:** Let's talk about *Princess Mononoke.* What goals did you try to achieve with your English adaptation?
**NG:** Mostly, that people wouldn't sit there going, "I'm watching a Japanese film," all the time. One tried to, to whatever extent one could, feed little bits of information in, make it feel like you were watching something that could have been American. I was probably happiest those few times that people who didn't know that it was a Japanese movie didn't realize [it was Japanese] till the final credits.

It was to get a level of naturalism into the dialogue, and also a level of beauty into the dialogue, wherever I could. The beauty wasn't actually the easiest thing to get in there, I have to say, if only because you were forever limited by the fact that these mouth movements were recorded long ago. The mouth movements were made, so it doesn't matter how beautiful the line you've come up with, you're still limited to those three or four openings and closings of the mouth. I'm proudest of the Gillian Anderson stuff, some of the Moro stuff. Yes, one still had to match up the beginning of the conversation and the end of the conversation, but because Miyazaki wasn't worried about giving the animals lip movements, there was a little more room. Which was wonderful.

**Q:** What does "Mononoke" mean? How does that fit into the story?
**NG:** Mononoke is a word that does not translate. You can, let's see, translate it a number of different ways. "Having to do with the spirit of things" is one. "The intangible quality that makes something itself," is another. Concerning things that do not exist, ghosts, and goblins and the spirits of the wood, and those things in the woods that actually have power. Those are all mononoke. The giant wolves are mononoke. The little Kodama people would be mononoke. You could translate it as phantom, or ghost, or whatever. Princess of

goblins, princess of beasts. It really is an intangible word, and in the end they decided to leave it untranslated.

**Q:** The film's protagonist, Ashitaka, refuses to punish anyone or choose enemies at all, and I've noticed that in your other work, especially in *Sandman*, you're always exploring the nature of revenge, retribution, and judgment. What's your take on the film's nonjudgmental attitude?

**NG:** I think what makes that story work so well is the fact that you have a bunch of different sides going on, and they are all grey-shaded. Everybody has a motivation, everybody has their back story and everybody's complicated. If Lady Eboshi had turned up in a Hollywood movie, let's say Lady Eboshi was in a Disney movie, she would be evil. She would be evil all the way down to the sheer core of her soul. The fact that she is building this iron works would be indicative of how evil she is. The animals in the forest would be good, and it would be *FernGully*, and that's how it would work. But you stop and you look at Mononoke, and you go, "Well actually Lady Eboshi, here she is creating this place, in order to be able to feed and house and so forth the dispossessed, the lepers, the outcasts, the brothel girls." All of these people are alive and have a world because of her. And meanwhile, the battle that is being fought between the animals and Lady Eboshi is a battle that was long since lost in Japan. I think one of the reasons why *Mononoke* was such an obscenely huge success in Japan is because it's talking about a battle that was lost. It was won by the equivalent of the iron worker people. It's an overcrowded island. These forests are gone, the Emishi people are gone, pretty much.

**Q:** What appeals to you about Japanese mythology?

**NG:** I think partly just the alien-ness. The fact it's not a mythology we're brought up in. There are oddnesses to it, there are weirdnesses, there are little things that don't fit. And also I like the way that the stories don't follow Western patterns in the way that they end. Very often they just sort of end in the middle, or they don't quite end in the way that we would end them. When I wrote *The Dream Hunters*, the Sandman book, once I finished that I sent in to Maya, Mr. Amano's assistant. She phoned me up and she said, "You know, it's an awful lot like Japanese stories, only it ends better. It ends so much more neatly and it makes so much more sense than the traditional Japanese stories." I don't know whether that's just because Maya and the Japanese have been corrupted by Western storytelling patterns—and "corrupted" there is used very ironically—or just whether it's that we are so used to story shapes. These old story shapes that never quite work in one's head, or leave one hanging or have weird inexplicable bits, that are just sort of odd, I love them. I love the foxes. When one's reading some of these stories, I love the areas that are unexplained. I tried to get some of that in, too. I really wanted that sort of slightly inexplicable quality to some of the stuff going on, into *Dream Hunters.*

**Q:** How is *Dream Hunters* different from the past *Sandman* books?
**NG:** The most important way that it's different is that it's not a comic book. I'm not sure that it goes much further than that. People say to me, "How is your version of *Princess Mononoke* different to the Japanese version?" And I say, "Well, it's in English." How is this different? It's not a comic, it's a prose story, beautifully illustrated with a painting per page by Yoshitaka Amano, one of Japan's finest artists. And, beyond that . . . it's definitely a *Sandman* story, it feels like a *Sandman* story. I mean, the thing about *Sandman* is, you have to bear in mind that you're talking about something that covers well over two thousand pages, spread out over ten volumes, so . . . um, *The Dream Hunters* is a particular kind of *Sandman* story. There were stories like "A Dream of a Thousand Cats," or "Ramadan," the *Arabian Nights* story, it's one of those kind of ones, in which the character of Morpheus himself, seen here as the King of All Night's Dreaming, has in some ways a widely tangential, deux ex machina quality to him. Because it's not his story, and on the other way what you are seeing does help define him and help define his story. I thought it was fun in this one, seeing the [Sandman's] story was over, to build in echoes into The Dream Hunter that would echo back into books like *The Kindly Ones*, where you see choices that the Sandman himself made, had made later on in the story, being echoed by what happens to the Monk and the Fox.

**Q:** Tell me more about Yoshitaka Amano's illustrations for *The Dream Hunters.* What in particular did you love about them?
**NG:** Um, I think the thing that drew me first of all to Mr. Amano's work was the sense of confluence. I saw his first book, *Think Like Amano,* and he sent me several other books, his illustrations for *The Tale of Genji,* and some fairy tales and so forth. And what I loved was, the way that on the one hand you can see his western influences, and they are all over the place and wonderful. Everybody from Arthur Rackham and Tenniel to Whistler, and Klimt and Schiele. All of these people are there, but it's all being filtered through a point of view that is uniquely Japanese, and a set of techniques that are

uniquely Japanese. And I really liked that, I liked the idea that one was going to be doing a book here that would be in no way faux-Japanese.

Let's back up a little. The first thing of Amano's really that I saw, or that I knew that I saw—I'd actually seen a lot of his work it turned out in 1989 and loved it—was a poster that he did for the *Sandman* tenth anniversary. *Sandman* itself finished three and a half years ago. The last story, *The Wake,* was told, and I stopped writing *Sandman* and went on to do other things. And when I saw this poster, I looked at it and two things happened. One of which was going, "You know, I've never done a Japanese *Sandman* story," and the other was going, "And, I have all this myth and legend knocking around in my head right now, from researching *Mononoke* and from childhood reading and stuff, that I'd love to build into a story." So, the joy of working with him was a very, very explicit fun of knowing that it wasn't going to be Japanese-ish. I wasn't going to have to worry about working with an artist who might accidentally put this ancient Japanese monk in jeans or whatever.

When we started working together, Mr. Amano went back to Japan and actually visited fox temples, and went to the ancient imperial city and wound up researching this stuff, and was very, very happy and grateful to have researched it. He said he found an awful lot of his Japanese heritage, stuff that they don't teach you. So we were both made very, very happy by this. I just loved the, as I say, the kind of strange, true Japanese quality that he brought to it, which gave me a lot more confidence in writing it. It was fun, they'd pick up on mistakes I'd make, and they'd go and research little things for me. I'd say, "Okay, I want a character here with a concubine, is that right for the period of Japan we're in right now?" They'd phone three different professors in ancient Japanese history and get three completely different answers from them. Or I'd say, "I want a chair here, it's important to me the *Sandman* has some kind of throne. Were there actually any chairs in Japan at this time?" And eventually, we'd come back with yes, there were. There were three chairs in Japan at this time. The emperor had one, and the emperor's eldest son, and the minister of the right hand or whatever had chairs that had been brought in from China. And I thought, "Okay, if the emperor can have a chair, then I can give the *Sandman* a chair." If there hadn't have been I couldn't have done, he would've had to have been sitting cross-legged on the floor.

**Q:** I want to address the buzz about *Sandman* movies. In an ideal situation, if you were given complete artistic control over a film version of *The Sandman* and the best possible conditions, even then would you want to translate it to film?

**NG:** No, not really. I mean the thing about *Sandman*, from my point of view, is that it was huge. Every now and then people come up to me and say, "Tell me in a couple of sentences, what is *The Sandman* all about?" I say, "Look, if I could've said it in a couple of sentences, it wouldn't have taken me seven years of my life and three million words of script to have written it out." If somebody came to me and said, "Ok, HBO is willing to do a 75 episode, half an hour each episode Sandman, do you want to get involved?" I'd say sure, because at that point I think you might have a chance of telling that story in strange and interesting visual ways. But films are about one thing, and *Sandman* never was. *Sandman* moved from horror to fantasy, high fantasy, dark fantasy, mainstream, magical realism, historical fiction. So the first question you come to talking about a *Sandman* movie is, what do you throw out? What do you get rid of? And, then of course, you're dealing with Hollywood. I don't want to be there when the phone rings and someone says [sleazy California accent] "Okay, Neil, you sittin' down, guy? 'Cause we got great news for you, okay? Well . . . we got Arnie!" [Switching to Schwarzenneger voice] "Pleasant dreams, motherfucker . . ." I don't want to be there for that conversation. I really hope it's good, I would love them to make a good film, if they make a good film I will be very proud and hold my head up high, but it's not something that I feel I want to get involved in. I want to get involved in things that I can have influence over, feel like I'm doing the right thing on. The *Death* movie, the story of *Death*: *The High Cost of Living*, is a small story. It's all about one thing, which is a young man who wants to kill himself, who doesn't think he has anything left to live for, who meets a girl who claims to be Death on her one day alive every hundred years, and discovers that he has an awful lot to live for. It's just nice and straightforward, and simple, and I can tell that story.

**Q:** Let's go back to what you said just a second ago about horror and fantasy in *Sandman*. In your mind, what's the difference between horror and fantasy, and where do you like your work to fit within the two?
**NG:** I think they're kind of like the Twin Cities, really. It's a Minneapolis/St. Paul kind of thing. You just sort of cross the river and everything gets a little bit weirder and less reassuring.

**Q:** Which city is horror and which is fantasy?
**NG:** Can I plead the fifth on that one? (laughs) I think it depends a lot on my mood, to be honest. They are very, very similar and the view is the same. But horror is reassuring. You know, in horror, the street lights are out. I've never

been very good at frightening. I've never been the kind of author who's particularly good at getting something to jump out at you and go boo. Some authors are, I'm not. But if I'm going to write something disturbing, I'd like you to wake up three or four nights later screaming from it. Not to some boo at the time, just . . . scream later.

**Part 2**

**Q:** On a totally opposite note, are you planning on writing more children's books?

**NG:** There's a new one that is all written, that is just waiting for Dave McKean to draw. You know, *Goldfish* was written about four years before it was published, and one reason why it took so long is we were waiting for Dave McKean to find a month to draw the pictures in. The new one was written about eight, nine months ago. This one is called *The Wolves in the Walls,* and it's about a little girl who is convinced there are wolves living in the walls of her house. Her parents tell her no, no, no, it's rats, or mice or bats, and they are of course wrong, and she is of course right. There are wolves living in the walls of her house, and one day they come out. They take over the house and the family has to flee, and it's sort of how the family gets their house back really.

And then there's a book called *Coraline. Coraline* is a really, really creepy little book for little girls, probably little girls of all ages and sexes. I started writing it for my daughter Holly, when she was about seven. One day, I turned around and Holly was thirteen, and Maddy, my littlest daughter was four, and I thought you know, if I don't write this book soon, Maddy will be too old for it. So I sent the manuscript to my editor at Avon and said, "Here, read this." She phoned me up the next day and said, "It's wonderful, it's really creepy and weird but wonderful. What happens next?" And I said, "Ah ha. Send me a contract, and I will tell you." I've written another nine thousand words or so of it, which is every bit as creepy as the bit before it. It's about a little girl named Coraline who goes through a door in her house that ought not to exist, and meets her Other Mother. Her Other Mother looks like the mother that she left behind, only she has big black buttons for eyes, and long white fingers, and she wants Coraline to stay with her forever. After a while we discover there are other little children, the ghosts of various children who she shut in the cupboards who also stayed with her forever. So it's fun, it's really spooky. I just have to finish it, which I will do when I finish the current novel.

**Q:** What are you working on right now?
**NG:** Currently working on a couple of things. I'm working on *Neverwhere*, the movie, and writing a novel, called *American Gods.* It was weird; I moved to America and started writing stories set in England, being *Stardust* and *Neverwhere.* I thought, it ought to be a nice idea, living out here, to write a story set out here. So I am. And, I'm just about to go off for a meeting with some people who desperately want to do a computer game, write a computer game. While on the one hand I think this might be fun, it's also true that every time in the last five years that—longer, God, about eight years now—that I have agreed to write a computer game for somebody, they've gone out of business. These are well-financed companies with giant offices, and the next thing you know, once I agree and we get to the point of signing a contract, all of a sudden there's somebody in the office who says—I'm just worried, you know, these are nice people with homes, they have children to support.

**Q:** They're braving the odds for you.
**NG:** They really are! It should be fun, it's taking a very strange concept, a science fictional idea. I said, "I have this one weird, weird SF thing that might be a peculiar kind of game." So, going to do something with that.

**Q:** It's evident, at least to me, that you're extremely well-read. My question is, if you magically gained control over Oprah Winfrey's book club—
**NG:** (laughs)

**Q:**—and you suddenly had the power to directly influence the reading public of America, what books would you choose?
**NG:** Oh, God . . . what a lovely question! I love the idea that I could actually send the people of America scuttling, lemming-like towards certain authors.

**Q:** She has that power, you know . . .
**NG:** I know, she has that power. I think that if I had that power, it would last one book. They'd be stumbling around going, "Woah, what is this thing? Ok, let's see what's on Jerry Springer, see if he's got a book for us." Um, what would I send people? I don't know, it would be a strange sort of

mixture of people currently writing. I think I'd love to send people towards Jonathan Carroll, just because I think he is one of the best kept secrets in America, or American literature. I don't even believe that all of his books are in print, which is a crime. He's absolutely brilliant, this American author currently living in Venice. Books like *A Child Across the Sky, Outside the Dog Museum, Sleeping in Flame, Kissing the Beehive,* the new book is called *The Marriage of Sticks,* gorgeous books. Elegant, honest and strange, and practically unknown. I'd love to send people to read Jonathan Carroll if I had that power. Um, I'm just about to do a thing for Amazon.com. [They] got in touch with me and said would I write a little essay on three books that I could recommend, two current ones and something old. I was planning to recommend a Peter Straub book, [Lynda] Barry's wonderful new novel *Cruddy,* which is just one of my favorite books of the last couple of years, and a novel by a man named Gene Wolfe, an amazing Chicago author, named *Peace,* which I think may be one of the finest novels of the twentieth century, and completely overlooked. It won a bunch of book awards, but the impression I get is the people who gave it the book awards didn't really understand it. And what else? I'd love to bring back some forgotten authors, James Branch Cabell. In 1921, *The New Yorker* in an essay said, "Well, there's only one American author currently writing who we all know his place in the world of literature is completely assured, and that man is James Branch Cabell," who by 1929 was practically a forgotten figure. G. K. Chesterton too, I'd make people read lots of Chesterton.

**Q:** What did you think of Tori Amos's new album? I know you're an admirer of hers.

**NG:** I love it. I first heard its unmixed form. England in June I went and stayed at her little Cornish farmhouse studio, played me all the tapes, or tracks. I think it's astonishing, I think it's lovely. One of the things I like best about Tori is, she keeps moving. It's, you know, I don't think you could take any track from any of her albums and put it on the previous album. She said to me, when she'd finished, "Well, do you like it?" I said, "Yes, I like it very much." She said, "Well, what is it?" I said, "It sounds to me like a greatest hits album from an alternate universe." You know, you took the best track off the hip hop album, the best track off the—you know, "Suede" and "Bliss" and "1,000 Oceans" seem to come from three completely different worlds, taking three tracks at random. It's wonderful stuff. I think "Suede" is my favorite. I like the creepiness of it.

I was writing, working on the novel *American Gods,* on the train to San Diego back in July, early August. I love taking the train in America, it's a very good thing to take the train because you get three or four days of peace and quiet, and nobody phones you and nobody gets in touch, you can just sort of get things done, eat a little too much. It's not actually the eating too much, it's the fact there is no exercise of any kind; you're having three, four meals a day and putting on incredible quantities of weight, and going off and writing. I just have this little CD-R that they burned for me, have the album playing over and over. And I liked the creepiness of "Suede."

**Q:** Of all your characters, who do you think you have the most in common with?

**NG:** Hmmm . . . Let me ponder this one for a moment. I don't think anyone's ever asked me that. If a character is going to work, they work because you take something of yourself and put it into all of them. So, you try and go and find those little bits of yourself. I don't think I've ever consciously written me into a story. Richard Mayhew in *Neverwhere,* if you look at him . . . They say, "Oh, he's you, isn't he?" and I say, "Well, no, not really. But he's bits of me." Just as the Marquis de Carabas in *Neverwhere,* who is his completely opposite, is bits of me. And I kind of hope that characters like Mr. Croup and Mr. Vandemar are bits of me too. In *Stardust,* there may be bits of me in Tristran, but there's as many bits of me in the Witch Queen. There was an interview that they did with me and Tori, in the English Independent newspaper [October 10th], and at one point she's talking about my characters. "Well, they're all Neil, of course," she says, "the girls are just Neil with good silicone."

© 1999 Minnesota Daily via U-WIRE

# Weird Tales Talks with Neil Gaiman

## Darrell Schweitzer / 2000

From *Weird Tales*. Reprinted by permission.

Interviewer's note: This was recorded at the World Horror Convention in Denver, May 11–14, 2000. Neil won a Stoker Award for the *Sandman* comics, but the real tribute to him and to his talent came the previous evening, when he conducted a *three-hour* reading of the entirety of his new children's book, *Coraline,* about 28,000 words. It's a beautiful, eerie story, somewhat reminiscent of the best work of John Bellairs, author *of The Face in the Frost.* But what was most astonishing was that Neil, who is undeniably a good reader, held the audience completely spellbound for that long, when they normally would have been at the Friday night parties. It was an amazing experience, comparable to the best Harlan Ellison readings, or the time Fritz Leiber read "The Haunter of the Dark" in Providence at the first World Fantasy Convention in 1975, only blocks away from where the events in the story "actually happened." Neil's three-hour reading is probably not going to start a tradition, because very few other people could actually do it. This interview was recorded in the Green Room on Saturday afternoon, a much calmer and more ordinary time for such things.

*Weird Tales*: Our readers may know you less well than comic-book readers—
Gaiman:—the guy who wrote the introduction to the Lovecraft Dream Cycle book.

**WT:** Something like that. Or they've seen a pirated American tape of *Neverwhere* by now. So, could you give a brief outline of the high points of your career up to the moment?
**Gaiman:** My career to date, by Neil Gaiman, age thirty-nine and a half. I started out in England as a journalist. While working as a journalist, I

collaborated with Kim Newman on a book called *Ghastly Beyond Belief,* a book of science-fiction and fantasy quotations, the worst of. I then did a biography of Douglas Adams, while still supporting myself as a journalist, called *Don't Panic.* Then I threw my lot in for fiction, and did mainly graphic novels and comics for the next ten years. I started with a book called *Violent Cases,* then did a monthly comic called *Sandman,* which won the World Fantasy Award and sundry other awards. But the best book I did during that time was one with Dave McKean called *Mr. Punch,* which is a fantasy about Punch and Judy and memory and childhood. I also wrote a bunch of short stories. I won the International Horror Critics Guild Award for *Angels and Visitations.* I have been nominated for various World Fantasy Awards and Stokers and suchlike along the way. I did a TV series called *Neverwhere,* then turned that into a novel in England and rewrote it as a novel for America. I then did a fairy story called *Stardust,* and am now hard at work on a novel called *American Gods,* which is late; and I just handed in a very, very creepy, scary children's story called *Coraline.* That's pretty much my career to date. I've done a few other things along the way.

**WT:** You may be the best-known comic-book writer in the world. There aren't a lot of them who actually become *famous* in any case. So you must be doing something special.
**Gaiman:** I think Alan Moore may be the best known of us. I was very very lucky because the period in which I was writing mainstream comics happened to coincide with the period in which Alan Moore wasn't, which meant that I got to win every best writer award in everything, which was great fun. But, yes, I suppose I am. The odd thing right now about being me is that there are people who have discovered me from different places and different directions. There are *Sandman* people who have no idea that I have done anything else. There are people who found me through *Neverwhere.* As far as they are concerned, that is my first novel. There are people who discover me from one place and not another. To some of them I am the guy who wrote the introductions to the Dunsany books, or who wrote *Stardust,* so to them I'm a Dunsanian scholar and fantasist.

**WT:** There are people who probably know you as a Lovecraftian humorist, for "Shoggoth's Old Peculiar."
**Gaiman:** That was so bizarre. It was nominated for a World Fantasy Award last year, which was very nice, albeit very, very puzzling. Luckily it was up against "The Specialist's Hat" by the lovely Kelly Link, which was a story I

much preferred. I was very, very happy when it won. It was one of those nice occasions, because I couldn't think of what I'd do if I did get the award except get up and say, "I think this is really Kelly Link's," and hand it over to her.

**WT:** But yours is a story of great charm. Lovecraft somehow readily lends himself to humor.

**Gaiman:** Lovecraft was the inspiration for the very first piece of fiction I remember writing and being pleased with. I'm not saying that it was any good, but the first thing that I wrote that I was pleased with was an attempt to write Cthulhu's autobiography, as dictated to Mr. Whateley. I gave it to a fanzine called *Dagon* and they published it in the mid-eighties. Horror and humor are so close anyway, but Lovecraft lends himself because he takes it so seriously and his readers take it so seriously. You only have to twist half a turn to the left and the material becomes screamingly funny. Witness that wonderful—

**WT:** *Scream for Jeeves* by Peter Cannon?

**Gaiman:** No, I wasn't even thinking of *Scream for Jeeves,* which is also wonderful, and is coincidentally based, oddly enough, on a gag that I must have come up with about the same time as Peter Cannon did. I'd written a letter to *Dagon* afterwards and said, "I'm glad people liked this Cthulhu biography so much. When I get around to it I will reveal the letters that have come into my possession, the Wodehouse-Lovecraft letters." I started talking about the musical they collaborated on, because Wodehouse actually was in New York and, I believe, a *Weird Tales* reader during the twenties. He was out there working on musicals. Wouldn't it have been fun if he'd written to Lovecraft and said, "Would you like to collaborate?" And I talked about "Cthulhu Springtime," which was the musical they collaborated on. Let me see if I can remember some of the lyrics. I quoted a few:

> Although I'm just a bird in a gilded cage,
> kept captive like some parakeet or love,
> when a maiden meets a giant lipophage,
> her heart gets chewed and broken like that old
>       adage.
> I'm just a fool who thought that Cthulhu could fall in
>       love.

I explained how there was only one performance of the musical, the dreadful thing that happened to the theatre, and how nothing has ever been built there since. I had an enormous amount of fun with it. I was going to say that coming into this convention [the World Horror Convention in Denver], there was that wonderful table in the dealer's room full of Cthulhupoid stuff, jokey stuff, including a Cthulhu to go on the back of your car instead of a Darwin or a fish, that sort of stuff. It's very Cthulhupoid.

**WT:** Were you warped by Lovecraft early in life like everybody else?

**Gaiman:** Oh yes. I was eleven or twelve. I was very lucky. Grafton books, or Granada Books had just brought the whole Lovecraft corpus back into print, about 1972 or 1973 in England. The first story of his I ever read was "The Outsider." That is such a great story. You know, the thing coming up into the light and then discovering it's the ghoul after scaring everybody. But yes, I discovered HPL and thought he was great. And then I picked up Clark Ashton Smith and thought, I don't like you. You don't do it for me. Whatever it is I'm reading Lovecraft for and getting off on, I'm not getting from Clark Ashton Smith. It was really disappointing because the Smith books had these gorgeous covers. There was *Averoigne* and *Zothique* and all that. I'd buy all the Smith books and I loved the ideas behind them. A couple years later I discovered Jack Vance and *The Dying Earth,* and thought, yes, this is better. But probably I am a philistine. Probably if I went back and read Clark Ashton Smith now I'd go, "Oh what a fine and beautiful writer." I was missing it all. But possibly not.

**WT:** Other than to supply quotes for *Ghastly Beyond Belief,* did these inform your sensibility and influence what you wrote?

**Gaiman:** Definitely. Everything you read as a kid is important. Everything you read as a kid is shaping you, particularly if you're going to be a writer. When I look back now, there are some things that are just key books. Judy Merril's *SF 12.* It had "The Star Pit" by Delany. It had Lafferty's "Narrow Valley." It had Aldiss's "Confluence." It had some William Burroughs in it. I read that when I was eleven or twelve. I didn't understand half of it. It didn't matter. It was shaping things inside my head. Running into Roger Zelazny mattered. Moorcock when I was nine was deeply, horribly important. Zelazny and Lafferty and Harlan Ellison and all those guys by the time I was ten or eleven, again, awfully, awfully important. I would be a very different writer without them. What is odd is that I expected that I'd be a science-fiction writer. When I was a kid, if you'd asked me what I was going to do, that's what I would have said. I expected to be Larry Niven. I figured I'd write cool, hard-science things, despite the fact that I never actually wrote SF for pleasure. When I turned around somewhere in my early thirties and found that I seemed to be a fantasy and horror writer, I was almost surprised.

**WT:** I think that the reason for that, for most Baby-Boomers, is that when we were kids science fiction was much more predominant. There was very little fantasy and horror available. Therefore when you encountered fantastic fiction, it was under the umbrella of science fiction. I also thought I was going to be a science fiction writer, and look what happened.

**Gaiman:** I think that's exactly right. The stuff that actually was the drug we were responding to—not even that, the true awe. When you hit the true awe, it all came under the SF rubric. Books were packaged with spaceships on the cover. You go back and reread Zelazny now, and it's very obvious that he's not writing SF. He's writing fantasy. What is "A Rose for Ecclesiastes" anyway? It's a fine and beautiful fantasy.

**WT:** In those days, indeed, fantasy was something you had to sneak in, either as a children's book or as science fiction.

**Gaiman:** Yes.

**WT:** Now we may have the opposite problem. Not only is fantasy predominant, it's expected to be published in ten fat volumes. I wonder if somebody really could get a fine and beautiful *short* fantasy novel published now.

**Gaiman:** I don't know how fine and beautiful it is, but that was my intention with *Stardust.* The joy for me with *Stardust* was that it is a hair under sixty thousand words. People say to me, "When you get to the end and you do that stuff where they're coming home, all of the sudden you take half a page and you list some of the cool things that happen to them. Why didn't you take five chapters to tell that?" And I reply that it would have turned it into a different book. I wanted to write a Dunsany book. I wanted to write something that came in at sixty thousand words, that was a small, elegant book in which everything happened.

**WT:** I think the reason you got away with it is that you're famous and you have clout. You have to have clout nowadays to get a short book into print. Anybody can have a long book, but if it's short, the publishers and bookstore buyers are going to have to be really convinced that it's going to sell, even if it doesn't weigh in by the pound.

**Gaiman:** Oh, I think so. And even then the publisher did some very peculiar things. And bless them. They want to maximize their sales and so forth. But they put this enormous typeface in, so they could get it to 350 pages instead of the two hundred pages that it probably would have been much happier at.

**WT:** How did you make the transition from writing comic scripts to writing novels? They are very different media, after all.

**Gaiman:** One of the things I did was that, all the time while I was writing comics, I still kept a foot in the prose camp. I didn't get to write a lot of prose, but I wrote "Chivalry." I wrote "Troll Bridge" and "Murder Mysteries." Some solid short stories that got anthologized and picked up for Year's Best anthologies, that kind of thing. So I was always writing the shorts. By the time I had finished *Sandman*, *Neverwhere* was happening. I had been working on that for five years, and I was then able to send the scripts off to Avon and say, "I'm going to be writing this novel. It's going to be based on these scripts." So I think that from that point of view, nobody was in any doubt. But a lot of people have real problems moving from medium to medium. I don't know why that is, but I've watched it happen. There were some people, like Harlan Ellison, who are storytellers. If you say, "Tell it as a thirty-minute episode for TV," and they can, and you say, "Tell it as a big-budget movie" and they can. If you say, "Tell it as a piece of stripped-down prose" and they can. You say, "Tell it as a comic," and they can do it. There are many, many more people who are fine novelists, but when you say, "Good, now write me a fifteen-page comic," and it's appalling. Or they cannot write screenplays. They cannot make the transition, or they cannot bring the magic from one medium to another.

**WT:** One of the differences might be—correct me if I'm wrong because you have written comics and I have not—that in a comic or a screenplay, you are expecting someone else to supply the visuals and much of the atmosphere, and therefore you concentrate on dialogue. By contrast, the worst screenplay writer ever would have been H. P. Lovecraft, because he was all visuals and atmosphere. He did, in his prose, all the things that art or photography would do, and less of what the script would do.

**Gaiman:** I disagree with you, and I think that one of the problems we get with people moving from one medium to another, especially into comics, is that's what they assume. They think that the artist is going to put in all the detaily stuff and all they have to do is worry about writing cool dialogue. What you have in comics that you don't have in prose is control over how the information is received. You have control over the rhythm of the information, just putting it down, beat by beat, in panels. When I'm writing a script, I'm writing a letter to an artist, telling him what I want, what I'm trying to do, what I want in each panel, what effect we're trying to do. The thing that I miss in prose more than anything else, that is like a piece of the toolkit that you have in comics that you don't have in prose, is the silent panel. Just the beat after somebody says something, or you just, pull back and somebody is standing there on their own without saying anything. You don't have to describe them anymore. You don't have to add anything else in. You just have a beat. I keep trying to do that in prose. How can I get that exact effect? I still haven't figured it out.

**WT:** You could skip a space. Or you could vary the rhythm of the prose drastically, as in a long, screaming tirade followed by a one-sentence paragraph that says, "Nothing happened."

**Gaiman:** It's one of those things that you can do in comics and you can approximate and move around it in prose. And there are things you can do in prose that you can't do in comics. You can really go into someone's head and start mucking around behind the eyes.

**WT:** I am reminded of a comment Lord Dunsany made. He saw a script which had a gorgeous description of a sun setting over a landscape, and this had to be crossed out, so that it just said, "Sun sets, left." This is what I mean by the visuals being supplied by somebody else, in that case the stage designer and the director.

**Gaiman:** Yes, that's very true. The advantage in doing a comic is that I can describe that sunset to an artist and see how close I can get it. If I just say, "Sunset," I might get anything. But one of the media that I love most is radio plays. There you can do both. You can do all the things you can do in prose and all the things you can do in comics, strangely. You have control over timing and beat, and you have the immediacy of films, but the audience is still building the pictures in their heads.

**WT:** You've got the visuals.

**Gaiman:** Exactly. I did an adaptation of my story "Murder Mysteries," which is about a murder committed in Heaven before the Fall, and about the angel investigating this murder. I adapted that for the Sci-Fi Channel, SciFi.com. We put together a wonderful cast starring Brian Dennehy as the angel private eye. It is lovely listening to it because you can do things on the radio. At one point they're walking around this city of angels and they come into this hall in which the universe is being constructed. At one point the hero falls through the universe as it's being built. How many millions of dollars would it take to achieve that on the screen?

**WT:** Someone made the comment that there are some things you just can't do in any medium other than radio. It might have been Robert Bloch who said it. The example given was a scene in a radio play in which they filled up Lake Erie with whipped cream and a fleet of helicopters lowers a giant maraschino cherry on top. If you did that in a movie, it would just look silly, but the mind's eye can produce it effectively.

**Gaiman:** Exactly. You're doing it in people's heads. The one that really didn't work, I remember was from *The Hitch-Hiker's Guide to the Galaxy.* When they did the line in the radio play, "Ford, you're turning into an infinite number of penguins," it was marvelous. But when they did the TV show and tried to show Ford turning into an infinite number of penguins, it was one of the most embarrassing moments in the whole show.

**WT:** Horror also works this way, and often does better on the radio.

**Gaiman:** Horror always exists as this wonderful balancing act between showing the monster and not showing the monster. What Clive Barker did that was so brilliant when the *Books of Blood* came out—it really felt like a breath of fresh air—was not only did he show the monster, but the monster that came on was cooler than the one that you'd imagined. That, I think, was lovely. Then everybody started showing the monster. Unfortunately their imaginations and their descriptive powers were not up to Clive's. I think that mostly monsters are best kept in the shadows.

**WT:** There is the basic aesthetic problem that once you've shown everything, you've shown everything and there is nothing more. I am sure we have all seen any number of movies that play all their cards early. Then unless they have a strong plot, they're dead.

**Gaiman:** Completely. The weird thing right now about *American Gods,* my new novel, is that it is probably a fantasy novel. I don't think it is horror, though it has enough horror in it to upset some people. I got some lovely letters from ladies who were romance fans. They were big fans of *Stardust.* They have their newsletters and they have their websites, and they praised them to the heavens. And I cannot see them liking *American Gods* at all. So word fifteen is "fuck." You're not through the first sentence before you get the word "fuck" because I just want to tell everybody that this is not a sweet book, and it's not a friendly book, and it's not a nice Victorian love story. If you have any trouble, *put it down now*. You have your out in the first sentence.

**WT:** So you'll get a different audience with every book. Do the *Neverwhere* readers like *Stardust?*

**Gaiman:** I don't think so. Some of them did and some of them didn't. The wonderful thing about my time in comics was that I did train a core readership in understanding that what I was going to do next was not what I did last. If you don't like it, that's probably okay, because there's a good chance you will like what I do after that. And I'm not going to do the same thing over and over and over again. So I trained people. Except, of course, that all the *Sandman* people went out and picked up *Neverwhere* and said, "Uh, it's not *Sandman*. We don't like this." The *Neverwhere* people said, "We love this. We've never read anything like it." Then they picked up *Stardust* and said, "Oh, this isn't *Neverwhere*. We don't know if we like this or not." Meanwhile, most of the people who picked up *Smoke and Mirrors*, my short-story collection, liked it, because even if there are short stories or whatever in there that you don't like, there's enough stuff in there that you probably would. It keeps them happy.

**WT:** Sooner or later you get the publisher offering you five million dollars for another *Neverwhere* sequel, and another, and another. You can get trapped that way, as Frank Herbert did with *Dune*. We all should hope to have this problem that people keep offering us millions . . . but what do you do in the face of this Faustian temptation?

**Gaiman:** I don't know. The big problem with me in *Neverwhere* is that I'd love to do another *Neverwhere* novel. I have at least two or three stories in the series going on in my head. But there are other things that I'd like to write first, which is why they aren't getting written. What I might do— I'm thinking that when the current novel is finished, I could do a book of three novellas. One would be a *Stardust* novella, one would be a *Neverwhere* novella, and one would be an *American Gods* novella. This is not an attempt to cash in on my audience, but because I have these bloody stories floating around in my head.

The *Stardust* one is really peculiar because they get to go to Hell in a hot air balloon. There's a *Neverwhere* story called "How the Marquis Got His Coat Back." They're all nineteen to twenty thousand word stories, which is a really irritating length to write anything at all, because nobody really wants that. So I will probably end up doing three in a book. But, yes, the financial thing is horrible. You can really get trapped into what Joe Straczynski calls "The velvet trap," the Rod Serling thing. They give you an awful lot of money, and then your standard of living goes up to that awful amount of money, and then they've got you. Somebody who is earning twenty-five thousand a year, go and offer them a million and they can turn you down with a clear conscience. I turned down a ten million dollar deal a few years ago with a clear and easy conscience, because I didn't want to do it. I didn't like the amount of things I'd have to give away to do it. Once you get trapped at a certain level, I can see how the whole *Dune* thing would come in. Roger writing more and more Amber books. You look at them, especially the last batch of *Amber* books, and they really weren't very good. They didn't read like he was writing them because he wanted to write them. Then all of a sudden he did *A Night in the Lonesome October* which he really did want to write.

**WT:** Then someone could come to you and ask you to do an on-going weekly series of *Neverwhere.* Has that happened?
**Gaiman:** There's a movie that's happening right now, that is being directed by a guy called Richard Loncraine. I wrote about eight drafts of the script until I got very tired of writing drafts of the script, and I stepped aside, and I believe they've got Andrew Birkin writing the script. Then I will either come back or not come back at the end to give it a dialogue polish.

**WT:** To get back to an interesting comment you made before we started this interview. . . you said that one of the things you really wanted to read was all the works of Robert Aickman, cover to cover. This will probably surprise some of your fans. It's a different sensibility. What do you see in Robert Aickman that makes him essential?
**Gaiman:** I think that Aickman is one of those authors that you respond to on a very primal level. If you're a writer, it's a bit like being a stage magician. A stage magician produces coin, takes coin, demonstrates coin vanished. [Gaiman is doing this as he speaks, quite capably.] If you're a professional stage magician, you're not going, "Oh boy! He vanished the coin!" You're thinking that was a smooth or a not smooth French Drop. Or, "Look, he did that sleight. I haven't seen that one done in a while." Or, "Look, there's a reverse French Drop." That tends to be what you do as a fiction writer, reading fiction. You'll go, "Oh, look. He's setting that up." You're in the position of a stage magician in the audience. You may admire the way something is done, but you never worry if that woman is going to get cut in half. Reading Robert Aickman is like watching a magician work, and very often I'm not

even sure what the trick was. All I know is that he did it beautifully. Yes, the key vanished, but I don't know if he was holding a key in that hand to begin with. I find myself admiring everything he does from an auctorial standpoint. And I love it as a reader. He will bring on atmosphere. He will construct these perfect, dark, doomed little stories, what he called "strange stories." I find the same with Lafferty. We were talking about Lafferty earlier as somebody who I'd love to read. I am hoping someone will do the complete short stories of R. A. Lafferty. What is interesting is that when you read the early Lafferty, the closer he comes to what one might consider a normal story, the less successful he is. I think that with Aickman, that the closer he comes to something that somebody else could have written, the less successful he is.

**WT:** What I find curious about both of these writers is that they are authors one admires very much but you don't really understand. Does anybody really understand either Lafferty or Aickman?
**Gaiman:** God? Certainly, if there is one. But no, I think that the joy of Lafferty and the joy of Aickman is the joy of people who exist completely independent of everything else. I love Stephen King. I think that Steve is an astonishing storyteller. And I also think that he's a really good writer. I think that he's written books that were sloppy and I think that he's written books that were really good. But I think that he's a really good wordsmith. I think that he's a better wordsmith than he gives himself credit for. But Steve is comprehensible. That is one reason why he is a very popular writer, because you understand what he is talking about. You can connect to it. You can draw the dots. You can see where it works. I can understand why Peter Straub responded to Robert Aickman, because Straub loves jazz. Steve loves rock. Stephen King is rock & roll. Aickman is jazz. And Lafferty is something played in an Irish bar on an instrument that you're not quite sure what it is and you're humming the tune but you don't remember the words as you walk out.

**WT:** Another thing about these writers is that you can tell they're not faking you out. There are many writers who will just plop down a mass of almost random words and say, "Well this is really very profound, and if you don't understand it you must be an ignoramus." You somehow know with Lafferty or Aickman that this is not the case.
**Gaiman:** Avram Davidson is another one of those. You're not being faked out. And Gene Wolfe. If you're going to put together four people who belong on the same page, I would have said Lafferty, Aickman, Gene Wolfe,

and Davidson. If you don't get it, it's your fault somehow. Go back and read it again. You'll get there. I remember Aickman's "Mark lngestre: The Customer's Tale." I wound up researching. Who was Lord Lovatt? What is his tie-in to Mrs. Lovett? What is the significance to all this stuff? How does it tie in to Sweeney Todd? I finally got to the point where I went, "You know, I do understand this." I don't think I've ever put as much effort into any other story by Aickman, but one assumes that it's there for the repaying, in the same way that a good Gene Wolfe story tends to return what gets put into it.

**WT:** These are all brave or oblivious writers. They are taking risks. If you do what they do, you run the risk that lots of lazy readers will take their money elsewhere, and lazy publishers will anticipate this and not publish you.
**Gaiman:** I don't think I am one of them. I may occasionally visit from time to time, but at the end of the day I am probably in the Stephen King camp. I'm a storyteller. The coolest thing for me is the telling of a story. The moments that matter are the moments when I get to surprise myself, the giving to people points of view they haven't had before. A very strange thing caught me with *American Gods*, because I needed a prose style which was really meat-and-potatoes, very straightforward, very, very basic. And I got very tired of it very fast. So I started writing short stories to go into the body of the text, set in the past. For each of them I can write beautiful, elegant prose, and not worry about the stripped-down, Elmore Leonard stuff that the novel is in.

**WT:** I think that you have to keep your readers in mind, but ultimately you have to take these risks for the sake of the book. But many people won't notice anyway. It's always been my theory that the reason that many really bad books get published is that a lot of readers are completely style-deaf. They just skim it. So somebody whose prose is like fingernails on the blackboard can get published and become a bestseller.
**Gaiman:** I think that's true. I'm not really one of those people. I tend to write for very small audiences. My audience can be me. If I am writing a short story, the audience can be the editor who solicited the story.

**WT:** The downside is that if most people are style-deaf, they'll never know if you're writing beautifully.
**Gaiman:** That's very, very true. But I also figure that there are enough people out there who can tell the difference. James Branch Cabell once said that a man crafts a beautiful sentence for the same joy you get from playing a

good game of solitaire. You don't craft a beautiful sentence for the multitude. You craft a beautiful sentence for your own satisfaction.

**WT:** You've somehow managed to become very popular. You've had your cake and eaten it too.

**Gaiman:** I guess I have. I don't quite know how, and I don't necessarily want to investigate too hard. I think I'm very lucky. There are two kinds of saying "I think I'm very lucky." One is a self-deprecating way, and what you're actually saying is that I think I'm very clever and I think I'm very good, so I'm going to say I'm very lucky and you can all go, "No, no, no! He's not lucky. He's brilliant." I think I'm very lucky, just because the stories I like to tell happen to be the same stories that people like to read. I don't think I could change the kinds of stories I like to tell. So if public readership tastes did not happen to coincide with what I like to write, I would still be writing the same stuff, and I would simply not be selling anything. [Laughs.] I am fortunate that at this juncture, I'm telling stories people like to read. Whether or not this will continue, I don't know. There is a wasteland in literature which is filled with authors, good authors, and bad authors, who told the right story at the right time, and briefly were famous, briefly were popular.

**WT:** One example I can think of is Joseph Hergesheimer, who most people know from dedications and introductions in James Branch Cabell books. He woke up one morning in 1929 and he had no audience.

**Gaiman:** Completely. But Cabell himself was a minor writer, with some critical acclaim, who wrote *Jurgen*, had one line in some New York newspaper saying, "This guy Cabell is getting away with murder; all the chorus girls are reading this filthy book he's written." The New York Society for the Suppression of Vice under Mr. Sumner busted *Jurgen*, took the plates, sued the publisher. Cabell and the publisher won the case, and Cabell was now a best-selling author. There was a line in *The New Yorker*, if memory serves, saying that "while the literary laurels of the future are all in doubt, there is one name from our time that will ring out forever into the future and that is the name of James Branch Cabell. And by 1950, everything except *Jurgen* was out of print and he was writing for tiny university presses.

**WT:** Even now there are only occasional reprintings.

**Gaiman:** They reprint the fantasies, but there are Cabell books which are finer than some of his fantasies that have not been back in print since 1929.

**WT:** Another one the critics of that era were certain would be one of the great novels, if not the greatest novel of the twentieth century, was Walter de la Mare's *Memoirs of a Midget.* It didn't happen.

**Gaiman:** It didn't happen, but that was the one they all pointed to. Like *Messer Marco Polo* by Donn Byrne. Yes, but tastes change. You write for your time. I write for me, at the end of the day. I am my audience. I write to amuse myself, in the very, very fundamental sense that it passes the time, it staves off boredom, and I don't know that there's anything else out in the world that I am actually any good at. And I have too much of a work ethic to sit and watch television all day, or else there isn't enough good TV, and I get bored. So I've got myself a little cabin now, twenty minutes from home, overlooking a lake. I get in my car and I drive my twenty minutes, and I settle down, and I write. There is no phone in there and there is no TV in there, and all the books are books that relate to whatever I am working on. And I write, or I make cups of tea.

**WT:** Thanks, Neil.

# CBLDF: Neil Gaiman Last Angel Tour Interview

## Shawna Gore / 2000

Courtesy of the Comic Books Legal Defense Fund. Reprinted by permission.

In the last ten years since concluding the award-winning comic book series *Sandman*, writer Neil Gaiman has stretched his literary legs to write a number of popular and critically-acclaimed novels, a children's book, the English-language screenplay for the Japanese film *Princess Mononoke*, a television series for the BBC, and too many other things to name. Gaiman has also expended a considerable amount of time and energy raising money for the Comic Book Legal Defense Fund (CBLDF), a nonprofit organization which defends the First Amendment rights of artists, retailers, and other comic-book professionals.

Despite a busy schedule completing his next novel (*American Gods*, HarperCollins), developing his next comic-book project with painter John Bolton (Dark Horse Comics), and beginning work on the forthcoming *Death* movie (Warner Brothers), Gaiman agreed to take time out this October to barnstorm the country for a series of live readings to benefit the CBLDF.

Gaiman will appear for one night only in New York City, Chicago, Portland (Oregon), and Los Angeles in what is being billed as THE LAST ANGEL TOUR. Since 1993, Gaiman's readings have generated over one hundred thousand dollars for the CBLDF. As the title suggests, this will be his last reading tour for a very long time, and Gaiman is committed to making the most of it. THE LAST ANGEL TOUR is projected to raise over fifty thousand dollars to benefit the Comic Book Legal Defense Fund.

The following interview was conducted by Shawna Gore in August 2000.

**Shawna Gore:** Let's start by talking about the Fund itself. Why do you support the Comic Book Legal Defense Fund?

**Neil Gaiman:** Because I come from a country that has no First Amendment. I don't know of any other country in which freedom of speech is guaranteed, legally. And I also don't know of any country—most other countries treasure what freedom of speech they have—that is so gifted and appreciates it so little. In America, where you have guaranteed freedom of speech, I don't particularly feel like it's treasured and treated as the miracle and really cool thing that it is. A lot of people seem very uncomfortable with it, and because of that you will have things happen like the Mike Diana case.

**SG:** Mike Diana is the cartoonist in Florida who was taken in by the police because his work was deemed "offensive," right?
**NG:** Yes. This is a case where somebody is found guilty of drawing offensive comics and is sentenced to a three-year suspended jail term, must seek psychiatric treatment at their own expense, and are not allowed within ten feet of anybody under the age of eighteen; ordered to take a course in journalistic ethics, one thousand hours community service, three thousand dollar fine and forbidden to draw—forbidden to draw!—with the local sheriff's office empowered to make twenty-four-hour spot searches of their abode to make sure they are not committing art and flushing it down the toilet.

**SG:** That is truly amazing, and yet it happened not too long ago.
**NG:** At that point, you realize what a fight this is—and that was a case that we fought and lost! And what you don't hear about are the ones we win and the ones that never go to trial. Without the Legal Defense Fund, things would be so much worse. Which is why I am out there fighting for it continually, because I consider freedom of speech and the freedom to be able to read things that people have written an incredibly important one.

**SG:** Is that one of the reasons you moved from the UK?
**NG:** Not in particular. But it was one of the delights of coming out here. But it is a brief, frustrating delight. It is a very bright double-edged sword. Because on the one side, you guys have this really cool thing, and on the other hand . . .

**SG:** What happened to Mike Diana is always a possibility.
**NG:** Yes, it is taken for granted and things like Mike Diana happen. So, my attitude is that I should be doing something about it. I don't think it is coincidental that some of the biggest funders, you know, supporters of the fund, in the last seven or eight years have been Canadian, English,

Irish—an awful lot of people are supporting the fund, both American residents and people who live outside of America.

**SG:** Let's talk about your Guardian Angel tours. For a number of years, you have been participating in reading tours to benefit the CBLDF, and these are engagements where you do live readings of your comics work and short stories in a theater-like environment. "The Last Angel Tour" is coming up in October. How many have you done before this?

**NG:** We have been doing them since—well, I believe the first of the gigs was in '93, and we've done one or two a year from there on. It wasn't until about three years ago, that it sort of solidified into a real tour. Up to that point I was just doing an occasional gig, like we'd rent a theater somewhere and just do it. One of my very favorites was in Boston, Massachusetts, which is near the headquarters of the Legal Defense Fund. There's a beautiful old theater there that we have rented for these performances. I was doing one a year, maybe two a year, and then we decided life might be easier if I went out and just went on the road, as part of an actual tour.

**SG:** What happens on these tours? I think it's hard for some people to understand that you, or any writer, would read their work aloud as entertainment.

**NG:** I think it is just hard for somebody to understand that it can actually be an enjoyable experience listening to somebody read, which is even weirder. This is something that people used to do a long time ago, and it hasn't been done for years and years and years. You know, Charles Dickens used to go on these huge reading tours and so forth.

**SG:** And that's how writers used to really earn their income, right?

**NG:** Oh, completely. That was how a writer made his or her living; it was the way that Oscar Wilde and Dickens and any writer for many years was able to earn an income. They'd come out to America and do American reading tours. When I was about ten or eleven, I went to a local theater in Sussex to watch an actor who, if memory serves, was Emlyn Williams, do a recreation of one of Dickens' readings. It was amazing. This actor stood up in front of an audience, reading passages from Dickens, and some short stories, and he held an audience utterly spellbound for a solid theatrical evening.

That was the place I realized one could do it. And years later, I'd never actually done much reading out loud or anything like that. And then, The Beguiling in Toronto—which was probably the best comic store in the world—said, "We are going to rent a theater for you. Come up here and do an event for us, and raise money for our legal fund." The idea had not really

occurred to me before that. It certainly wasn't something that had me thinking, "Oh, my God—this is what the world has been waiting for!"

**SG:** Before that, had you given any thought to performing your work?
**NG:** Nope. I was terrified. But somehow it ended up working. We figured
out the basics of what we have done ever since at that same show. A format
for these readings has evolved, and that first one helped determine it. We
said, "Okay, how do we run this?" And we came up with something like this:
start off with a thoroughly enjoyable short story, do some shorter pieces,
do another solid short story, break for, oh, twenty or thirty minutes, so the
people can (a) go to the toilet, (b) stretch their legs, and (c) write down any
questions they might have. We do a portion of each reading as a Q&A, and
it works much better if the audiences writes the questions down on a slip of
paper, so we can go through the questions backstage and pick the best ones
to cover. That way, when the reading starts again, I can run through as many
of the questions as I can do in however much time we have got. It helps prevent repeat questions, and we get to be selective about choosing questions
on interesting topics.

  After we've covered the question, we then do a couple of show pieces
and one big one to end with. I usually try to do something special. That
brief first show, I had just finished writing the story "Snow, Glass, Apples,"
so I read it to the public for the first time. And the next one, which I think
was Northampton, I had just written *The Day I Swapped My Dad For Two
Goldfish.* I read that to an audience for the first time. And on this tour, I am
sure that I will do something very, very similar.

**SG:** What is your experience while you are doing these readings? Do you
find yourself getting more lost in the stories or thinking about your performances as a reader?
**NG:** Mostly, I just enjoy it. I mean, it's a lovely experience. There have been
a few that weren't great, like when we did one on the Queen Mary in Long
Beach. That was frustrating because the acoustics were really weird. From
where I was I could never quite hear myself, so it was a little bit weird. But
mostly you are just watching a bunch of adults with the kind of rapt expres-
sion on their face that you normally only see in a room of five-year-olds.
And they are sitting there incredibly happy, maybe never having realized
that they could enjoy themselves with somebody reading to them.

**SG:** I think people forget about that pleasure. The moment it stops when
you are a kid, nobody really reads to you again.

**NG:** Oh, exactly. And all you tend to meet as an adult are really boring read-ers—they put you off for life! That's one of those things I have never quite been able to understand. I'll go to readings, you know, occasionally, with a major author reading where I have also been invited to come read. And you will be up there and you will finish telling your story and then the next guy is there, and all of a sudden you are listening to something like this: [feigned monotone—ed]: "and the door opens and the sultan's men came all bran-dishing their swords. I said please get out of my way, none of them did, and one of them slashed at me with his swords so I leaped for the drapes and jumped over his head and then I got out of the room and don't stop don't stop she shouted as I laughed." And you are just listening to these readers droning on and on—and I'm thinking, "Can't you hear the music when you write this? Don't you hear the voices?" That's something I do—the voices, which is part of the fun. I used to think I had no desire to act, but that's not true, I guess. It's not that I don't want to act. I discovered something when I was in *Signal to Noise*, the radio version. I wrote a part for Dave McKean [artist on *Signal to Noise*—ed.]. And then, when it came time to record it, Dave had chicken pox. And our lead actor, the older actor, Warren Mitchell, had not had chicken pox, so Dave couldn't go into the studio. And that meant I ended up acting with Warren as a place-holder. It was enor-mously fun, because I got to go out there and act, do my bit, and I never, ever have had to be embarrassed by people listening to me because eventu-ally the producers went in and filled in my parts with Dave's acting. But I love performing. I could never do it, and I need an excuse to do it, and these readings are that excuse for me.

**SG:** Have you documented these readings at all?
**NG:** I did, a few years ago, a CD called *Warning: Contains Language*, which Dreamhaven put out, and it did fairly well. It had some problems through Diamond, its distributor, because we could never actually convince them that the name of the CD was *Warning: Contains Language*. They thought this was some sort of warning. They kept putting it in their catalogue as "Neil Gaiman's CD Contains Bad Language." I thought it was a really cool, clever, funny title, but it confused at least a few people. The other prob-lem with it was the fact that nobody knew it was a double CD. It had a thirty-dollar price tag on it, so everyone must have thought, "My God! This is expensive." It was actually two CDs, and at least a few people have it. That bit of me performing is out there.

**SG:** So you've dabbled in performance, then.

**NG:** I dabble occasionally with doing readings in the studio, and I'm thinking of doing another one. But we're looking right now at taping or filming much of the upcoming tour, partly because it's the last one, and partly so that we have actually got something that the Legal Defense Fund can have to sell after it's all done.

**SG:** Now that you're more of a popular media figure, I guess that makes your public appearances a bit more of a "to do." How do you feel when you hear that there are people, presumably fans of your work, who have paid, I think $1800 at an auction to get VIP tickets to your readings?

**NG:** That was one of these spur of the moment things that I decided to do with the CBLDF, and of course it's flattering. We also auctioned off my leather jacket for the Legal Defense Fund. I was talking to Chris Oarr from the Fund, and he had this big auction going, and I suggested we auction VIP tickets, and maybe throw in a nice dinner and a backstage pass. And I think Chris was expecting to get maybe two hundred dollars for each ticket. When they started crossing one thousand dollars we were blown away. But for people who have been to these readings before, and if they support the Fund, I think these events might actually be the most fun you can have without a partner and a little privacy (laughs).

**SG:** I think your role—as far as your fans are concerned—is more like that of a storyteller rather than a comics writer or a novelist.

**NG:** Yes, I think so.

**SG:** How old were you when you started telling stories?

**NG:** Oh, let me think. I was a kid. I mean, my first stories were what my daydreams were. When I was a kid, my daydreams were the kind of daydreams where you would be tumbled into a parallel universe with the only copy of *The Lord of the Rings* in existence—a universe just like this one but they hadn't had *Lord of the Rings.* So I'd bring a copy along and get it published under my name, and that way I'd be the guy who wrote *Lord of the Rings.* That was one fantasy. And there was another that was really kind of fun where I kidnapped all of the writers that I liked through space and time and imprisoned them and made them work on a giant fantasy novel just for me. I had the plot for this twelve-book series based on this one daydream. I must have been eleven at this point.

**SG:** This must have been before you realized that you possessed the talent to actually create the stories yourself?

**NG:** Completely. That was when I was sort of a kid, and before I had any concept that I could write. But I knew that was what I wanted to do. I just couldn't see at the time that I was going to be good enough. I knew I couldn't sit down and write a great novel, so that was my solution at the time. And as I got older, I still loved telling stories. This is what I am; it's what I do. I make stuff up. I have the kind of head to make stuff up.

**SG:** Did you just discover your talent for throwing all the words together and making it sound pretty, or is that something that developed once you started taking writing assignments in school?

**NG:** I was always one of these kids who did incredibly well in English, but it was what I loved doing. It wasn't work. You get to sit down and make up a story, and I could never think of anything I'd rather do.

**SG:** You just mentioned *Lord of the Rings* and a few other books. I am assuming you were really inspired by other people's stories when you were a kid. What other works inspired you?

**NG:** Depends which age. When I was seven, it was the *Narnia* books. When I was nine, it was Michael Moorcock. It was fantasy and science fiction that always struck some kind of deep chord with me. It wasn't that I didn't read everything, I was the kind of kid who did read everything. But it always seemed to me that fantasy is a very, very useful tool. It is a very useful mirror—very useful way of seeing the world. You can say things in fantasy that are difficult to say in any fiction that's meant to resemble the real world.

Plus, I always felt that as a writer, you get to be God, and as the storyteller you get to be God. And, if you're going to be God, you may as well have the power to do absolutely anything you want, you know. Whether it's to have a small boy be able to swap his dad for two goldfish, and bring him back. Or to create a world underneath London, or to decide what cats dream about. You have that power as a storyteller. The act of storytelling has always seemed to be supremely exciting.

**SG:** Is there a format you prefer? You write graphic novels, and you write novels, and you do some poetry. Which of these feels more comfortable for you, or is it all part of the same process?

**NG:** Well, it's really all part of the same thing. However, radio plays are probably my favorite.

**SG:** Oh, really?

**NG:** Yes. I did a radio play for the BBC a few years ago (*Signal to Noise*), which was just brought out on CD. And I did a similar thing last year for the Sci-Fi channel website, adapting my short story "Murder Mysteries." In each case, I loved it. It's like comics that you are actually creating inside somebody's head, because as they're listening to the words, the images are forming for them. But it's not a medium that people sit still for very long, which is kind of why it is fun to do these tours for the Comic Book Legal Defense Fund.

**SG:** I know you have a new book coming out next year. You've written a number lately—*Stardust, Neverwhere, Smoke and Mirrors.* I heard the next one is called *American Gods*?

**NG:** This is true. *American Gods* got started almost a year ago—I started it just before San Diego [The San Diego International ComicCon—ed.] last year. So over a year ago. And I swore a mighty oath when I really started it seriously that I wasn't getting a haircut until it was done. (laughs)

And now, I am this appalling mess. I look more and more like Howard Stern.

**SG:** It's been a while since I saw you at the Small Press Expo—I guess about a year.

**NG:** Exactly. Then I looked completely human. Now, I am—I am faced with the bizarre—definitely Howard Stern territory. So I will be enormously pleased to finish the novel. The novel has got much too long and so has the hair.

**SG:** That's the story on the hair. What about the book?

**NG:** I guess I would start by saying it's the closest thing I have done to *Sandman,* since I finished *Sandman.*

**SG:** Other than that comparison, how would you describe *American Gods?*

**NG:** Well, it is either a fantasy novel or a theological thriller. Or a murder mystery. Or a short story collection, depending on which way you want to see it. It includes all those things in its makeup. And its also a horror novel. And has some—you know—some congealed blobs of sex in there as well.

I like the concept of a novel also being able to be read as a series of short stories. There are a few writers who have pulled that off successfully.

What I did in this is one central narrative that goes through the whole novel. There was a lot of stuff that I needed to do that was outside the frame of the novel. So I just started writing them as short stories, and I ultimately decided that they actually belonged in the novel. So every few chapters you stop and you get a short story, illuminating an aspect of America's history.

**SG:** Is this focusing on any particular period of American history?
**NG:** The novel is set in the present day, but the first of the stories is set 14,000 years ago. The first short story has people coming across the land bridge, the Siberian land bridge. Although I love the fact that just as I get into the novel, it changes. I go heavily into fictional ways that different races have turned up in America. One must admit that it becomes desperately, hugely archaeologically, and scientifically arguable and there are theories that maybe the Ainu people came down this way and we think maybe the Polynesians came up this way, and actually lots of people were turning up in America all the time. Which is lovely. I love all the mad theories that are coming in and they all, every mad theory, helps the novel.

**SG:** And you are still exercising a sort of fantasy aspect with this novel, too?
**NG:** Oh, sure. It's a novel about God—an abandoned God. A forgotten God. A blue-collar God. And it's a war story and it's historical. And the scientists, you know. And there is some crimes in there too. I mean its basically one of these things if I am hugely lucky that HarperCollins will be publishing as a bestseller, because it doesn't really belong anywhere else. Which shelf do you put it on? A big one.

**SG:** So other than *Sandman,* this is probably one of your more epic works?
**NG:** It is, and I was so hugely optimistic, I thought I could hash out a first draft of it in three months. Instead, it's closer to a year. I spent a few months noodling with it, but it has taken about a year. But I've had an awful lot of fun with it.

**SG:** What about film work? I hear you may be directing a movie?
**NG:** Yeah. Currently what I am spending most of my time doing is apologizing to people who were meant to have things written this year. But I am late with the novel, and I am not starting those things 'til the novel is done. So, the thing I am really meant to be working on now is the Death movie, which I am also meant to be directing. And there are some very pissed-off producers at Warner Brothers whom I would like to just take this opportunity to apologize to—and to promise they will get their script when the novel is done.

**SG:** So that's where the *Death* film is. Any insight into what story the movie will tell?

**NG:** It will be a lot like "Death: the High Cost of Living," only bigger. "The High Cost of Living" was an enormously fun story, but if you filmed it, it's probably about forty minutes long. I wanted to take that core—the idea of the boy with everything to live for—who doesn't want to live. He meets a girl who claims to be Death, and the film follows them around New York for twenty-four hours, seeing what kind of scrapes they get into and watching them learn things.

**SG:** So, you have done radio broadcasts, but have you ever dealt with a film before?

**NG:** Not exactly. I did a TV series with BBC—the original version of *Neverwhere*. And, of course, last year I did the English script of *Princess Mononoke*, so it's not entirely virgin territory.

**SG:** Is this really the last "Angel" tour?

**NG:** Probably. We may follow up at some point, but I don't have as much time on my hands as I did when we first started. To do these tours, we give up two weeks and go off and do L.A. and San Francisco and Seattle—or last year it was Washington and Boston and so forth. And that's two weeks that I don't get to do other work. I have too many more stories to tell right now. So it's time to call it a day, but this will be one fun last tour, and I think we're really going to make an impact.

# Dreaming *American Gods*:
# An Interview with Neil Gaiman

## Rudi Dornemann and Kelly Everding / 2001

From *Rain Taxi*. Reprinted by permission.

Neil Gaiman's writing career began in journalism, that most reality-oriented of approaches to the word. He first made a name for himself in comics, a genre that isn't usually connected all that closely to reality. But Gaiman's writing blends and balances things that aren't ordinarily combined: reality and fantasy, humor and horror, the fairy tale and the novel, the personal and the cosmic.

Gaiman's alchemy was amply evident in his influential *Sandman* series for DC Comics, which was remarkable not just because it was so well done, but because it was done so much on its own terms. As opposed to the reimagining of older heroes that was the trend, Gaiman gave us a whole new imagining, inventing the saga of "the dreaming" and its denizens as he told it. Certainly, he wove in connections to older comics and even older stories and myths, but his *Sandman* went its own way. Some of this uniqueness came from the central character of Morpheus, neither hero nor anti-hero, who had the ring of archetype, but remained an original creation. Some of it came from the variety of kinds of stories Gaiman wrapped around the character—everything from horror stories to historical vignettes to wonder tales.

Since bringing *Sandman* to a close, Gaiman has written several novels, a collection of short stories, and even, with frequent collaborator Dave McKean, a children's book (*The Day I Swapped My Dad for Two Goldfish.*) His new novel, *American Gods,* follows the story of Shadow, an ex-convict who becomes mired in the machinations of pagan deities brought to America by immigrants and then abandoned for the newer gods of technology, drugs, and money. In picaresque fashion, Gaiman interweaves the broader story of a brewing storm, an all-out war between gods, with shorter tales of different people who came to America as indentured servants, slaves, and prosperity seekers. The amalgam explores America's spiritual center and centerless spiritualism through the timeless archetype of the mythical hero.

Sipping on a tall cup of chai, Gaiman spun animated and eloquent answers to our questions. A shorter version of this interview appears in the Summer 2001 print edition of *Rain Taxi Review of Books*.

*Rain Taxi*: You dedicate *American Gods* to "Kathy Acker and Roger Zelazny, and all points between." How do you view the literary continuum, and how do you see yourself in it?

**Neil Gaiman:** It's an interesting dedication because it's about three things. It's about absent friends, and it's about writing a book for absent friends. It's also about the literary continuum—there's this thing that runs from here to here and very elegantly and peculiarly, it runs from A to Zed. In the nineties I lost a number of friends, but the two big friends I lost who were also writers were Kathy and Roger. Roger was someone who I had not known as well as I should have done. We'd see each other at conventions and things and talk on the phone, and we'd always have long conversations about how sooner or later I had to come down to New Mexico and hang for a week . . . it was always something I figured I had plenty of time for. When he died it really shocked me, and I did wind up going down to New Mexico for the memorial. Kathy was somebody who I was very good friends with in London from 1985 onward. I remember I got an email one day saying she was dying, which seemed a little odd because I had spoken to her six months before. I phoned some friends of hers in England and was told: No, no, she's just being a drama queen, she's fine, she's got flu, whatever. I sent back an email to these people saying, "My people say she's just got flu." "No, she's dying in a hospital in Mexico, here's the phone number." She was in room 101—I thought, there you go, there's a literary reference. It was good, I got to say my goodbyes, tell her I love her, tell her to hang in there. We said a few words and she was dead a couple of days later. That one hurt. So I wanted to write something for them. In many ways, I have no idea if Kathy would have liked it. I think she would have done. I know she would have liked chapter two with the extreme sex in it—that was there for Kathy. But I sent a copy of the book to Jane Lindskold who was Roger's partner in his last few years. She wrote back and she said, you know, Roger would have loved this book. I felt very happy about that. It was interesting because I wasn't trying to write a Zelazny-ish book. I think Roger was probably the best fantasy/SF writer of the sixties and seventies when he was on form. I really wasn't trying to emulate him. I was just trying to write a book that I thought he would have liked.

In terms of where *American Gods* fits on the literary continuum . . . I'm not sure. I'm enjoying not being sure. With most of them I can tell. *Neverwhere* is an urban fantasy adventure novel.

*Stardust* is a fairy story. *Sandman* is a giant sequence of ten graphic novels. *Mr. Punch* is a magical realist memoir. *American Gods* is a thing that will probably be read by science fiction people as SF, by the fantasy people as fantasy, by the horror people as horror. We'll see whether the mainstream and literary people read it as literature. For my part it was very much a way of trying to use the tools of fantasy and some of the tools and engines of horror to try and describe the world.

**RT:** Representative of the mix of cultures making up America, *American Gods* tells the many tales of immigrants who came to this country and brought with them their gods. Little by little, the gods become dysfunctional and their mortal manifestations turn into prostitutes, grifters, criminals, and the forgotten elderly. Is this a political fable for you—is this the story of the decay of values, American or otherwise?

**NG:** I would not describe myself as a political writer except in the sense that the personal is political, which is something that I do strongly believe. And in that sense *American Gods* is a very personal novel and a political novel. I was trying to describe the experience of coming to America as an immigrant, the experience of watching the way that America tends to eat other cultures. It's very interesting going to Canada because that doesn't happen. If you're wondering around Toronto, whatever, you feel that there's no attempt to turn any of these other cultures into a Canadian thing. As a result of which, you have a much more interesting, to my mind, mixture. In America, to quote Michael Moorcock, "Art aspires to a condition of muzak"—everything homogenizes, it blands. I think I was trying to talk about both the blanding of other cultures, the way the rough edges get knocked off very quickly and the way the things that make them special and unique get forgotten or lost or abandoned or subsumed into the "American Dream." In addition to that I wanted to talk about future shock: the way that we are currently slamming into the future incredibly fast and what that means, and what it means that the future that we were heading for in 1984 now feels incredibly dated. For that matter, 2001 feels incredibly dated. Where does that come from? So trying to take all of that and put it into a framework that would also let me write about the House on the Rock, and do these little historical short stories as well, which were such a joy to write.

**RT:** What about place? Most of *American Gods* takes place in the Midwest and the South, in sparsely populated places. You identify sacred places and ones of "negative sacredness." How does place fit into your vision of American spirituality?
**NG:** I think what was for me the most interesting thing was not necessarily what I did there but
how it's been received by readers on the East and the West coasts. The reaction is sort of, "Gee, you're making those fly-over states sound almost interesting. Who knew there was anything going on there?" There's an awful lot going on in all of these places. It's another convenient fiction that life exists on the West coast and life exists on the East coast, and there's a little life in Texas; that you could take a map of America and sort of color in the places where there's life. And someone would grudgingly draw a little circle around Minneapolis, which they've heard of. But this would be the only place with any life until you got to Chicago, which is the next place they heard of which has life. What I was trying to say is that there is an incredible amount going on in these places, and it goes very deep, and it's really interesting, and really cool. I try and define what it looks like and what it feels like.

I'm normally not an on-the-ground researcher. The point where I discovered the joys of on-the-ground research was actually after I had written *Neverwhere* as a TV series, but before I had written it as a novel. I spent a day on a location scout looking for places the TV series could be set, which meant that I actually got to wade through the sewers; I got to wander through some of these strange decaying backstage places. When I came to write them later it was incredibly useful having that knowledge of what it's like down there—stuff I made up became very solid. With *American Gods*, I wanted to use that, and I would actually do things like go on little road trips. I'd say if my characters are going from here to here, I need to sort of follow the kind of places they're going and see where they wind up. We get that wonderful chapter in Cairo, Illinois; it exists because I had to drive from here to Florida and thought I'd do it by taking back roads. I liked the sound of the name. When I got there I discovered it was this wonderful town that had once been full of history and that history had now passed by. The time when the Mississippi and the Ohio were trading rivers. Everything was happening on them—they were the arteries, the confluence, a wonderful place. Now it's sparsely populated, with a sign saying, "Welcome to historical

Cairo." That's about it. I walked through the customs house museum which was one of the saddest little buildings I've ever walked through. So what can you have in Cairo? The Egyptian gods seemed so perfect for that.

**RT:** Did you do other research to unearth the myths and legends that populate *American Gods?*
**NG:** To some extent, although a lot of that stuff was stuff washing around in the back of my head. I have a very functional knowledge of things like Norse myth. There were a few I ran across while I was doing the book that I wanted to learn more about. The most frustrating of them, of course, was Czernobog and the Zorya, the Slavic gods, because there's so little about them actually known. I ran across them while I was beginning the book, and I loved the idea of Czernobog the black god and his brother Bielebog the white god, and the Zorya, these sisters of the dawn—the morning star, the evening star, and the mysterious midnight sister. And then I spent weeks trying to research them more. At the end of three weeks of solid research I had nothing I hadn't had in some little Peterson's book of gods at the start. There's so little known about the Russian Gods. The Catholic church and the Russian Orthodox church stamped out most of it, and then Napoleon burned the rest of it on his way to and from Moscow.

**RT:** As an English writer living in the US, you're surrounded by American speech—from the people you encounter to the media you see, hear, and read. Do you find this influences the language you use as a writer?
**NG:** It influences the language I use to communicate. With *American Gods* I was trying very, very consciously—there was a level at which it was a little like trying to write a novel in French—you know, "This novel is to be written in American." I allowed myself Wednesday, who while very American, I allow some Anglicisms into his speech. I loved doing things like writing my little Essie Tregowan story, with the English girl getting transported from Cornwall to here. The strangest thing about doing it was actually the copyediting process. That was weird because I had the English edition and the American edition. An American copyeditor went through the book, and pulled words that were invisible to me, like "hessian" and "burlap." Where I described Johnny Appleseed as picking up a hessian sack, they said no, it has to be burlap. I kept it hessian in the English one and changed it to burlap in the American one. After eight or nine years out here my accent is just a mess. Americans still think I have an English accent, but English people are very surprised to discover that I'm actually English!

**RT:** Your writing has drawn upon material and subjects from several cultures: British, American, and recently—with your *Princess Mononoke* script and *Sandman: The Dream Hunters*—Japanese. Are there differences in the stories native to different peoples and different places?

**NG:** I think that the biggest, quickest, and hardest thing to learn for a writer is that what we think of as the unchanging verities of story are a load of bollocks. Absolute rubbish. There are no unchanging verities. Furthermore, the shapes of stories, which is what we're conditioned to think in—you know when something's a story because a set of things have happened—there is a very specific western one, and by Western I will take in all the way through Iran, Iraq, that kind of area. As soon as you've hit India, the shapes of stories change completely. Once you move into China and that whole area, the shapes of stories again change completely. Africa, again different story shapes—what constitutes or satisfies that moment of satisfaction. I remember reading a wonderful essay by Chip Delany and I unfortunately forget who he was citing, he was citing someone else, who flush with joy about the eternal verities of story was in the African bush. They'd been exchanging stories—he and some Africans. He told them the story of Hamlet. And he got to the end of the story, and they all expected him to continue. He said, "Well that's the story." And they said, "Did they find the witch? They need to find the witch and kill her." In their stories, the things that happened in Hamlet could only have happened because there was a witch—these kinds of events occur and the ghost comes in and you find the witch and kill her or him. And here is what we consider one of the great stories!

In *Sandman*, I happily gave the impression that these are the stories that continue forever. But the fact is they are very Western. With *Mononoke*, I remember talking to Miramax and saying all you really have to do to make this film move from being a wonderful art house film into something that Americans will take warmly into their hearts is you chop ten minutes from the end, you add a thirty-second sequence of Prince Ashitaka going back to his village with San as his bride and the villagers saying hurrah hurrah it's over and throwing confetti. I wasn't saying do it; I should make it really clear it was *not* something I was recommending. But that would have given the film the closure that a Western audience would have wanted. We know stories begin with the Hero having to leave his village and being sent away. If the prince is sent away from the village because evil has struck and so on and so forth, he goes out, he finds his bride, he comes back to his village. The prince comes back as the king, and in *Mononoke* that doesn't happen. It ends on a very ambiguous note: he's simply living in the town and helping the girl, and they'll be seeing each other, but there is no joining of cultures. He certainly isn't bringing her back to his village as his bride. He's not going back. That area fascinates me—the things that aren't part of what Campbell liked to think of as the unities.

**RT:** I'm glad you mentioned the theme of the Hero, because much of your writing is concerned with the meeting of mortals and immortals, that moment in which they collide for better or worse—like Michelangelo's Sistine Chapel painting of God and Adam touching fingers. This can be an explosive moment, a moment of self-realization and transition; the hero of *American Gods*, Shadow, experiences this moment and becomes a conduit between the supernatural and natural worlds. What inspires this tendency in your work?

**NG:** That's one of those questions that I'm useless at. It's like when people ask, "Why do you write about angels?" and I say, I don't know; I try to keep them out, and they crawl back in like cockroaches. In order to be able to answer that with any kind of accuracy, I worry that I would have to pin it too hard to the board, and it would never get up again. A lot of it is because you want to talk about humanity and you want to talk about people, but people are icebergs. So much of us is underneath. The imagination and the place that dreams come from is so huge and so important. I'm trying to write about the real world, in that I'm trying to write about whatever it is the experience that makes us human, the things that we have in common. I don't feel that writing about the real world means that I should be constrained to a version of reality that you see on the eleven o'clock news or read in the *New York Times.* I do not see why every single weapon in the arsenal of the imagination can't be mine.

In the case of *American Gods*, one of the things that really made it concrete for me—which I tip my hat to in the text—was reading Herodotus, which I did when I first came to America. The lovely thing about being an auto-didact (as all writers to some extant are, is you learn very quickly how to teach yourself cool stuff, learn cool stuff, read cool stuff, and get the meat of something out of it. And give the impression that you know so much more about it than you really do). In the case of Herodotus, and there are a few moments in Suetonius as well, you're reading about a world view in which you're being told who won this battle and the strategy and the tactics. There are people here who are obviously the grandchildren of the people in this battle, and you're getting all the information. Then, we sent a runner from here to there to tell the people in Marathon that we had won. On the way, the runner met Pan in a clearing, and Pan said to him, "Why don't you build me a temple? I want a temple and I want it built on this spot." The runner said okay and he kept running and he was almost dead when he arrived, and they revived him, and he told them that the Greeks had taken the battle and also that Pan wanted a temple. These days we would tell the event as: Greeks won the battle. That's the real thing that happened. The runner seeing Pan we treat as either apocryphal or as imagination or as an over-stressed mind. (On the wonderful list of barking-mad theories comes that nice gentleman with his origins of consciousness in the bicameral mind, who claims it was all the left brain talking to the right brain. The right brain is going, [making puppet motions] *I am Pan.* The left brain is going, *Oh, all right.* God knows how you'll transcribe that!). The point being that you had a world in which the gods were written about and treated as simply part of the world. And I thought wouldn't it be a really cool thing to try and put that into the here and now. If people did come over with their gods, what are their gods doing, *how* are their gods doing? That's really where the whole thing sprang from.

**RT:** It seems that despite our modernity and dedication to technology and progress, and the elision of the imagination you are referring to, Americans are still somewhat steeped in pagan ritual; vestiges of paganism have been subsumed by Christianity, Judaism, and Islam. Have we lost something by forgetting the history, etymology, and significance of these rituals?

**NG:** You guys actually have more of the weird shit ritual stuff going on than you would imagine. Coming over here from England, I was awe-struck by what Americans do at Halloween. I find it magnificent. In England, you get the occasional fancy dress party. One of the things I wanted to do in *American Gods* was remind people about where some of these things come from. One of my favorite sequences to write was when we meet Easter; you get this whole conversation in a San Francisco coffee house about the origin of the word. And I love that, the fact that Easter is somebody's name. Easter is a slight modernization of Eostre of the Dawn. She's the one you get the estrous cycle from. She was a fertility goddess whose high feast was at planting time in the Spring. She was worshipped with symbols of fertility—eggs chiefly, and rabbits, and flowers, and couples going off and copulating, and so on and so forth. All that stuff was completely subsumed which is why you get people today making jokes about whether the Easter bunny was crucified. I love that. This is something old that overlays something else. You had better be aware when you're getting your Easter eggs and doing your Easter hunt that this is for Easter, she was Eostre of the Dawn. And it's perfectly possible that that was a corruption of Astarte—God names wandering westwards.

**RT:** You've written in many different forms—comics, novels, film, and television—and quite a few of your books and stories have started out in one medium and then had a later incarnation in another. Which elements of a story translate well and which don't?
**NG:** It's always a learning process. What I tend to do is move stories from medium to medium because I'm interested in how it works. I just finished doing a movie adaptation of *Death: The High Cost of Living*—

**RT:** Oh, good.
**NG:** Yes, I'm really pleased with it, or at least pleased with where I got to by the end of it and really looking forward to doing the second draft. When I was a young man I sat in a theater audience and watched *Violent Cases*, my first graphic move, being done on the stage—good stage adaptation, intelligent director, good actor—and I sat there saying the lines under my breath along with the people doing it, and realizing that it didn't work. It didn't work because they had simply *taken*—there was no effort to translate it to the stage. It had been trans-literated. They basically took the graphic novel and put it on the stage, and the dramatic high points were not high points now that they were on the stage. Little things became huge. Huge things became small. That fascinated me completely, and taught me a great deal. The weirdest thing about *American Gods* is that, as far as I'm concerned, it's my first novel. I'd written *Neverwhere* first, but *Neverwhere* was very specifically my own adaptation of my TV scripts, so it wasn't really novel-shaped. It has beats that aren't novel-shaped, it has highs and lows, and there was nothing much I could do to it in the writing other than get the descriptions in and stuff like that. *Stardust* was a very interesting book, but *Stardust* was essentially something that I was writing as an illustrated project—with Charles Vess. *Good Omens* was enormously fun, but *Good Omens* was a collaboration with Terry Pratchett, and an enormous learning experience for me. Terry was by far the senior partner on that.

With *American Gods*, it was the first time that I had actually gone, okay here's a blank book—one of these big leather-bound black sketch books; some store was clearing them out, had a major sale on these big sketch books, five hundred pages. So I bought a bunch of them, and sat down and wrote the words "American Gods" with a fountain pen on page one and turned it over and started to write. That was a very, very conscious thing. I really wanted a second draft. It's my experience with computers that they do not give you a second draft. Computers give you an ongoing, ever-improving first draft, but there is no discontinuity there. I wanted that, so I wrote the book by hand, and after every few chapters I would stop and type up what I had done so far.

**RT:** You've written a lot of what, on the surface at least, are very different stories—ranging from kids with goldfish to young men looking for fallen stars to hidden worlds under London. Are there any themes you see yourself coming back to from one piece of writing to the next?

**NG:** The trouble with common themes is that they're things that people point out to you. Themes tend not to be things you notice yourself, and when you notice them or when they do get pointed out to you, they can freeze you. For example, somebody once said to me, that they always knew when they were entering the final act of whatever I was doing because there was always a kiss. And it was a terrible thing to be told. Up until that point it had been completely unconscious. And of course the odds are that it's probably there in *American Gods.* I haven't stopped to think about it. I kind of hope it isn't, but I'm sure somebody will be able to say, Oh look, here it is. What I try and do is to sit and go with the story, which is not a commercial way to write. There's that wonderful quote by Freud or Jung or one of those German gentlemen with beards, when asked how somebody could achieve fame and success, the reply was, "You shit all in the same place." Which I always took to mean you keep doing your thing until you have an enormous pile of it! I'm very, very lucky; I have nothing to complain about. But the people who go and live on the best seller list tend to do it by writing more or less the same book, more or less once a year. Do the same thing once a year and your bank manager will thank you. The last thing I wrote was a fairy tale. This is a huge sprawling, picaresque novel about America and its imagination. The next book of mine that will be published next May is a very short novel aimed chiefly at children and those who, in their hearts, remain children, about a very small, very brave girl who goes through a door that shouldn't be there, to a place that shouldn't be there, and encounters her other mother who is a very scary lady with black buttons for eyes, and who wants the little girl to stay with her for always. So everybody who loved *American Gods* is going to go, what the fuck is this?

The lovely thing about writing comics for so many years is that comics is a medium that is mistaken for a genre. It's not that there are not genres within comics, but because comics tend to be regarded as a genre in itself, content becomes secondary; as long as I was doing a comic, people would pick it up. And they got very used to the fact that I'm going to go where my inclination takes me and wherever that takes me is going to be wherever I go. So I kind of trained people to expect that. With the world of books I don't know if I've trained them all yet. The people who were with me back in the comic book days, they're much more forgiving. If they didn't like *Mr. Punch* they'd come back for the next thing.

**RT:** I think you've answered our next question—we were going to ask if you write with different audiences in mind or if you imagine an ideal reader who's generally genre-agnostic.

**NG:** My ideal reader is me. And yes, my ideal reader comes with me and is forgiving. And will *re-read.* I don't know in this day and age whether it's a quixotic goal or not. Gene Wolfe, one of my favorite writers in any genre, defined good literature as that which can be read with pleasure by an educated reader and re-read with increased pleasure. One of the delights of Gene Wolfe's fiction is that you can go back and read a book you've already read and knowing a little bit more about it you will find more there. I always try to do that with my stuff. Even the short stuff. There will be something else there you probably won't get on the first reading that will be waiting for you. If *American Gods* works, it's like a magic trick, it's like a sequence of magic tricks.

One of the great things about being a writer who gets read is that cool people turn up at your signings. Last week I was in Los Angeles, I was master of ceremonies at the Nebula awards. Great fun. The day before I did a signing at the LA book fair, and there was a man named Michael Ammar in the signing line. And he said, "Look I'm doing the Magic Castle tonight, would you like to come and see me as my guest?" I said, sure. I came and watched him, and the guy was incredible, one of the top sleight-of-hand magicians in the world. Technically flawless and a delight. He also gave me a video showing how he does stuff, teaching some basics. And he finished his act with the cup and the balls, which is one of the great classics. One of the moments that was most impressive was he had three cups and he's produced two balls for you and you're not quite sure how he did it. For the third ball, he twirls his wand [motions upward] and he says now, and you look down and the ball is already sitting there. And every single person in that audience gasped as they looked. Somehow it had appeared there. Watching the video, knowing that was what I was looking for, I took even more delight in the fact that as he waved his wand he simply put the ball on the table—no effort made to hide it—but secure in the knowledge that he was directing our attention well enough that he knew of the hundred people in that room there were two hundred eyes on that wand at the precise moment that he was just placing the ball on the table. As he directed our attention back to it, it was as if it had magically appeared.

There's a lot of stuff in *American Gods* where I'm directing your attention. If the novel is working, you are looking over here while I am putting something on the stage, setting something up, so when you get two chapters on, or ten chapters on, or in one case eighteen chapters on, you're going to go, Oh my God, I should have seen that coming. It's both enjoyable and frustrating. One of the nice things about doing that stuff is that next time through the book, somebody can actually enjoy watching my hand put that little thing there.

# *Voices of Vision*: Neil Gaiman

## Jayme Blaschke / 2002

From *Voices of Vision*, 2005. Reprinted by permission.

*One of the great things about Texas is that there are two well-established science fiction conventions that draw top-flight guests. Armadillocon is held in Austin every fall, while Aggiecon is held at Texas A&M University in College Station every spring. Both focus primarily on books and authors as opposed to television and movies, so they are comparatively relaxed and intimate.*

*That's not to say Neil Gaiman didn't attract legions of followers—he did— but those legions weren't quite as many as at other conventions, allowing Gaiman and his daughter Holly as close to a low-key weekend as they could hope for. In fact, conventions had gotten so grueling for Gaiman that he confused he would've passed on Aggiecon had not a former convention organizer, Dan Robb, bribed Gaiman's personal assistant with a crate of fresh mangoes several years prior.*

*Alas, such are the great stories that never make it into interviews. It wasn't until after the recorder was turned off that Gaiman began talking about his aborted DC Comics miniseries with collaborator Matt Wagner, in which onearmed Oliver Queen, many years from now, writes his Right Stuff-style memoirs in the New York Public Library. Or fired up his laptop to share the recently completed first draft of The Fermata script for director Robert Zemeckis, including a strange and funny scene involving Charleton Heston that will never make it into the filmed version. Or the salsa-making conversation where I commented that wiping your eyes after dicing habañero peppers is a bad idea, to which Gaiman replied that going to the bathroom and touching your privates is even worse . . .*

Interviewed March 23, 2002, College Station, Texas. Published in RevolutionSF .com, May 2002.

Best known for his groundbreaking work on *The Sandman* series from DC Comics, Neil Gaiman has quickly become one of the most important fantasists of contemporary literature. The best-selling author of several novels including *Neverwhere, Stardust, American Gods,* and *Good Omens* with Terry Pratchett, Gaiman has also authored the critically acclaimed children's books *The Day I Swapped My Dad for Two Goldfish* and the forthcoming *Coraline.* His short fiction has appeared in the collections *Smoke and Mirrors* and *Angels and Visitations.* A native of Great Britain, Gaiman currently resides in a Gothic mansion in the American Midwest.

**Jayme Blaschke:** Your *Sandman* stories were essentially complex, serialized epics in a marginalized medium. As your stature as a writer grows, I can't help but see a parallel with the career of another product of Great Britain, Charles Dickens. Have you ever considered the parallels between your careers?

**Neil Gaiman:** I don't know if I particularly considered parallels. I do remember, toward the end of *Sandman,* I was reading *Bleak House* for pleasure. There were points in there where I'd go, "Okay. You know what you're doing with this. You *don't* know what you're doing with this. This is just something that you're writing to fill in a few pages, but you're putting something in that may become important later. *This* is something where you *think* you've done something that isn't important, but actually it will become important to you later."

I recognized the beats. I recognized the technique, reading that. There's a level on which you know something when you're going into a story, but a lot of the stuff will turn up on the fly and you'll use it. You have to sort of learn to be open to the infinite. You learn to toss balls in the air, not necessarily knowing how they'll come down, but knowing they will be descending at the point where you'll need them.

Terry Pratchett had a character in a book recently—the Fifth Horseman of the Apocalypse, who quit before they became famous. His name was Ronnie Soak, and Terry had written him without knowing which horseman he was. He just named him Ronnie Soak, because it sounded like the right kind of name. There came a point where he was writing Ronnie Soak going past a shop window in which everything was reflected, and you'd see his name reflected in the window. And it said "Kaos." That was the moment where the penny dropped for Terry, who this character was. You can ask yourself questions: Did you know this unconsciously before? And when you're involved in serial narrative, you don't necessarily know.

**BLASCHKE:** So is that kind of subconscious, serendipitous writing unique to the serial form?

**GAIMAN:** No, what it does is. . . In the serial form, you realize early on you are locked in. In normal writing, if you're working on a novel, and you get to chapter eleven and you realize you need a gun in the desk drawer, you just go back to the desk drawer where we saw it in chapter two. You make sure that you mention there was a gun in it, and when people read the book, they go, "Ah yeah. Got a gun in the desk drawer." When somebody goes for it in chapter eleven, it's there.

You can't do that if people have already seen that drawer, and they've already seen that it was empty in chapter two. So you learn to make decisions without necessarily knowing why you've made that decision. You'll put a gun in that drawer because something *has* to be in the drawer, and then in chapter eleven you'll look around and go, "Oh my god, I need a . . . Oh, I've already put it there." That is a very weird and specific kind of thing.

If anything, the whole serial nature of fiction taught me not to go for perfection. You know, perfection—you're heading for the horizon. You'll never reach it. Get to the point where you've done enough, you're willing to let it go, it's as good as it's going to be. Let it go. Move on. Do the next one.

**BLASCHKE:** In a 1997 *Interzone* interview, you commented that once you accomplish what you set out to do in any particular medium, you would abandon it and move on to some other form. Have your thoughts on that changed any in the intervening years?

**GAIMAN:** I stopped writing comics feeling that I'd done a few good ones. Having said that, that was five years ago. I'm now starting to get interested in comics again as a medium. I'm partly going, I wonder if I could still do it? You know, there's that old gunfighter kind of mentality.

The flip side of that is, for me, the point where there's not challenge anymore, the point where I really don't have anything left to say. I stopped journalism because I was done. I stopped book reviewing because I was done. What's nice now is that every now and again I can actually pull out those old skills and use my journalistic skill when I'm doing an introduction or whatever. Once or twice a year I'll do a book review for the *Washington Post*. It's kind of nice. It's like revisiting old skills, speaking German when you haven't spoken German for a while.

Mostly, I'm simply aware of how good one can be and how good I'm *not*. I just finished a script for Robert Zemeckis. Everybody loves it, which is nice. And they love it for what it is, which is nice. But I look at it and I go,

"Yes, but . . . I couldn't really have done anything else. Most things film-wise, I look at and I realize I couldn't write that." I'm not terribly good at action-adventure. I don't care enough about the beats of action-adventure. If I did, *American Gods* might have been a different kind of book. If I did, it would've delivered a nice, satisfying hack-'em-up, cut'em-down war at the end, which I never had any intention of delivering.

**BLASCHKE:** The Zemeckis script you mention is an adaptation of Nicholson Baker's novel *The Fermata*. How does the experience of adapting someone else's work compare with doing your own material?

**GAIMAN:** Actually I *love* adapting other people's stuff. What I'm crap at is adapting mine. Adapting *mine* is horrible. I will never do it again—I've tried it a couple of times. The lovely thing about adapting somebody else's stuff is I can say, "For a movie, I like that, that, that, and that." I love *good* adaptations that other people have done of my stuff. Bad adaptations set my teeth on edge. I've seen some very good adaptations. David Goyer's script for my story "Murder Mysteries"—doing that as a feature film—I thought was brilliant. Henry Sellick's script for *Coraline* was terrific. And each of them took huge liberties. They changed things and they moved things, they rearranged things, and they added things. And they were all the right things to add to turn it into a film, to make it ninety minutes, to give it the ups and downs of where everything fell. I couldn't have done that to either of those stories. It's like a path that you walk, and you can't necessarily walk any other path. Whereas I think adapting somebody else's story, sometimes you can get a sort of helicopter view of it. You can say, "Well, there's another path over there that still hits those same high points, but just does it differently."

**BLASCHKE:** How does that compare with *Neverwhere*'s evolution? You started with a television script, adapted it into a novel, and from that into a feature film script.

**GAIMAN:** What was interesting with that was that turning it from a TV series into a book was not hard. I *still* have my doubts about how success-ful it was, but I know a lot of people love it. I still don't feel that the beats are right for a novel. I think it's too episodic. It was written as episodic TV. For me the novel was written essentially not as a novel, but as a correc-tive action to the TV show. It's like, this is the TV show, but it's not what I meant. *This* is what I meant.

The TV show . . . It was like standing up in front of an audience and being translated. You're standing there and you're saying, "Thank you very much for inviting me here, and I'm going to have a wonderful time." And your translator gets up there and says, "Mr. Gaiman is very pleased to be here, but his stomach hurts." There's a level on which you publish something like *Neverwhere* in order to say, "Actually no, I didn't say my stomach hurts—I said I'm having a wonderful time."

With *Neverwhere*, it was very much a corrective action. *This* is what I meant, *this* is the feel I wanted, *this* is the look I wanted. When people talk about *Neverwhere*, I want them to talk of the book. I want them to understand the book. The TV series has some stuff I'm proud of in it, and some stuff I'm not. But it wasn't my thing. I can't defend the TV series. I can't stand behind it in the way that I can stand behind the book. Everything in there is what I wanted it to be.

**BLASCHKE:** So is the movie script everything you wanted it to be?

**GAIMAN:** Turning it into a movie was nightmarish. I think I went through about eight drafts before I quit. The big problem was that it wasn't film-shaped. It really is absolutely episodic in six parts. You either have a three-hour-long story or then you must be cutting and pasting the movie around. Finally, I said, "Look, I've had enough." And I stopped.

**BLASCHKE:** So is the *Neverwhere* feature now dead?

**GAIMAN:** No. It's got a different writer. A young guy whose name I've forgotten did a couple of drafts on the script. I may come back for a final polish and try to make the dialogue sound more like me. I may not, I don't know.

It's got Vincenzo Natali as director, who did *Cube*, which was a lovely little science fiction film. *Neverwhere* may well happen. The trouble is, after ten years, I'm very cynical about film in a very easygoing kind of way. Some things happen, but lots of things don't. There's never necessarily a reason why some of them do and some of them don't, except for odd little circumstances that are completely out of your control as a writer. If I wanted to become a producer, that would be a different thing, but I don't. I'm happy being a writer, and I'm happy to let the producers have the ulcers.

**BLASCHKE:** But you're not averse to trying on the director's hat with the *Death* movie? How do you reconcile that?

**GAIMAN:** God knows. Let's just see what happens when I finish the script. I'd very much like to direct it only because I don't want somebody else to fuck it up. I'm not saying I won't fuck it up, but if I do fuck it up, at least it'll be the thing that I'm trying to make. I got very frustrated on *Neverwhere* with the director, who was trying to make something other than what I'd written. I figure you can do one of two things in film—you can write something for a director and you let them make it, or if you don't want them to do that, then you'd better direct it yourself.

**BLASCHKE:** Do you consider yourself a genre writer?
**GAIMAN:** No.

**BLASCHKE:** What kind of writer are you?
**GAIMAN:** I'm the kind of writer that tells stories. I don't think of myself as being in any particular box. If I had to "genre myself," I'd say, "I suppose I'm an imaginative writer." If you look at the body of my work, it's not even exclusively fantasy. You have problematic things like *Signal to Noise* in there, which is fundamentally mainstream fiction. It tends to wander over into the fantastic, just because that's the way my head works.

I love the fantastic, both as an agent and as a key. If you want to concretize a metaphor, the fantastic is a perfect way to do it. So much of fiction is an attempt to concretize a metaphor.

**BLASCHKE:** Each book you've done since redirecting your efforts toward prose has staked out new territory for you. What's the direction behind your newest work, *Coraline*?
**GAIMAN:** I started it just wanting to write a story my daughter Holly would like. It's an intensely personal book. It's a lot more personal in most ways than pretty much anything else I've ever written. I can point to almost everything from the real world that's in that book and tell you from where in my life it came. Coraline's house is the flat that we were living in in Nuttley when I started it, except for the drawing room, which is the drawing room from the house that I lived in when I was five, which had the door that opened onto a brick wall. The nice old ladies downstairs were a pair of magnificent theatrical lesbians with a bunch of Scottie dogs who taught me elocution when I was eleven. All of that kind of thing.

Stories of Coraline's life, bits of Coraline are . . . some of her is my kids and some of her is me. Very explicit. Some of her parents are me. It was a very weird little personal essay about childhood, and about the powerlessness of childhood. It started from this G. K. Chesterton quote: "Fairy tales are not true, they are more than true. Not because they tell us that dragons exist; but because they tell us that dragons can be beaten." That is the fundamental truth of the fairy tale.

**BLASCHKE:** *Coraline* has a very distinct Lewis Carroll air about it. Was this deliberate on your part?

**GAIMAN:** *Alice* was a touchstone book. *Alice* was one of those books I could more or less recite word for word by the time I was six or seven. And could still, now. I could probably still recite practically any poem from *Alice.* Um, let's see . . .

> Fury said to a mouse,
> That he met in the house,
> "Let us both go to law:
> I will prosecute you.
> Come, I'll take no denial;
> We must have a trial:
> For really this morning
> I've nothing to do."
> Said the mouse to the cur,
> "Such a trial, dear Sir,
> With no jury or judge,
> Would be wasting our breath."
> "I'll be the judge, I'll be the jury,"
> Said cunning old Fury
> "I'll try the whole cause,
> And condemn you to death."

That's "The Mouse's Long Tale." You know, it's hardwired into the circuitry, which means that *Coraline* is definitely, hugely influenced by *Alice.* Except that it has a plot. It's not just a sequence of events. And *Coraline* is very active, whereas *Alice* is peculiarly passive. Will Self observed that the key word of *Alice* is the word "curious." He said every book has a word, and the word curious—curiouser and curiouser, curiously—occurs all the way throughout. Alice's curiosity is what pulls her in. I discovered that when I did the reading for the audiobook that the word that Coraline seems to echo all the time is *asked.* It's a book about asking. I didn't know that's what it was until I just kept reading it and the word *asked* was there on every page.

And the answers are never satisfactory.

**BLASCHKE:** You've worked with prose, poetry, children's books, comics, songs, television, motion-picture scripts—does the same writer work on these different projects? Is the creative process the same for you regardless of media?

**GAIMAN:** I don't know that you tap different sources of creative energy. I have visions at that point of some little men down in some power room going, "Okay, well take it off diesel, on to fusion. Off fusion, on to turbine power." One of the drives, the impulse, to tell stories is the same all the way. What you tend to use is different skills. A completely different skill set. It's a very odd thing. I'm *finally* getting the hang of writing spoken dialogue, after having done it for ten years now. I think I'm actually just starting to get the hang of writing dialogue that will be spoken. I'm very good at writing dialogue that *looks* great on the page, but then some poor sucker has to speak it. We discovered doing *Neverwhere* that the only actor who had no trouble at all with my dialogue was Paterson Joseph, who played the Marquis. Paterson was straight out of the Royal Shakespeare Company. With Shakespeare, that's not how people normally speak, but that's how you learn to deliver.

I'm just finishing *The Fermata,* and it's the first time I've actually ever really been satisfied. I was catching rhythms that would deceive people, that would be enough like the rhythms of speech that they'd work.

But it's skill sets. So much of it for me is instinct, and so much of it is also . . . There's a weird level in which everything is equally hard, which can be frustrating. I wish some of the things were easy. I feel like it ought to be much harder to write a six-hundred-thousand dollar Hollywood film script than to write a short story that won't net me more than a hundred dollars. But it's not. It takes me the same sort of effort to do the short story as it did to do the film script.

**BLASCHKE:** *American Gods* is a book that involved a tremendous amount of research on your part. What good stuff didn't make it into the final novel?
**GAIMAN:** The biggest—this in terms of a *lot* of research, a real body of research—was the whole Japanese internment camp thing. I quote from Richard Dorson's "A Theory for American Folklore" in *American Gods.* It was obvious in reading him that he kept asking himself some of the same questions I kept asking myself about America. The thing that people seem to miss, the ones who didn't quite get *American Gods* . . . I don't think they got the significance of the opening quote. He begins:

One question that has always intrigued me is what happens to demonic beings when immigrants move from their homeland. Irish Americans remember the fairies, Norwegian Americans the *nisser,* Greek Americans the *vrykólakas,* but only in relation to events remembered in the Old Country. When I once asked why such demons are not seen in America, my informants giggled confusedly and said, "They're scared to pass the ocean, it's too far," pointing out Christ and the Apostles never came to America.

I'd come at it from a different direction, which is noticing how many folk stories, once they got to America, lost their magic. The magic fell out. There was a weird practicality that came in. The difference between the Jack stories, as told in England and the Jack stories told in Appalachia fascinates me. Because the magic's gone. A lot of that was what I was trying to get in to *American Gods*. The idea of fairies . . . fairies in America makes so much more sense if they've come from another country. It doesn't seem like something here. Yes, there are primal American powers, but they're not that kind of thing.

**BLASCHKE:** How does this relate to Japanese internment camps?
**GAIMAN:** Richard Dorson, in another essay, talks about the Japanese internment camps—or the American internment camps in which the Japanese were put—and how, several years in, with all these Japanese people in one place, you started getting cases of fox possession. You got people seeing Japanese shape-shifting badgers and so forth. There were all these odd phenomena reported, which were fundamentally Japanese magical phenomena. Which didn't happen until you put several thousand Japanese American people into a small part of America and made them be Japanese again.

I wanted to do a story about that. I think the thing that eventually dissuaded me was my slow realization, having done all the research on this, that I was probably looking at a fifteen-to twenty thousand-word story in a novel that was already way too long. So very regretfully I put it all on one side.

I *have* kept all the research materials. I may write it one day, I may not. I think it's going to be a very Bradburyish short story. It's going to have that flavor, at least in my head.

**BLASCHKE:** Currently you're involved in a very loud, very public, very acrimonious legal duel with Todd McFarlane over the Miracleman character as well as other properties—
**GAIMAN:** Actually, I take issue with practically everything you've said there. I don't think it's loud. I mean, it'd be loud if I was standing up doing a WWF thing. But I really haven't. I took exception, publicly, to one thing he said where he seemed to be attempting some kind of bizarre blackmail. I

just thought, "This is pathetic," and I put it up on my journal just as sort of, "I really don't take this seriously, but . . ." But apart from that, I'm letting the lawyers do the talking.

**BLASCHKE:** But within the fan community, you must know, it has commanded a great deal of attention. What kind of impact does this have on the industry in general? Creator's rights?

**GAIMAN:** Creator's rights are hugely important. A lot of people, people like Frank Miller, like Alan Moore . . . until the 1980s, workers in comics had no rights of any kind. You had no control over what you did, you derived no income from your creations, you had no reprint fees when stuff got reprinted. You did not get royalties. All of these things are things we have fought for very, very slowly. Comics publishing was being dragged kicking and screaming into the twentieth century.

And then you get publishers like McFarlane who, in his legal brief, had essentially asserted that by writing a comic for him, you have lost any rights in the underlying material. He contends that he does not have any obligation; he can reprint your stuff as much as he likes and has no obligation to pay you any royalties or to make any payments for any exploitation of stuff you've created in other media. It makes it worse that this comes from somebody who was loudly espousing creator rights.

The reason I did the work for him in the first place was he phoned me up and said, "Hey, creator rights!" Oh? All right. For creator rights I'll do stuff. Absolutely. Had he phoned up and said, "Hey, not only is it work for hire as far as I'm concerned, but I'm going to treat you worse than DC and Marvel," I would've said no. I would never have been in this mess.

**BLASCHKE:** What is it about *Miracleman* that makes you willing to fight this particular fight?

**GAIMAN:** It's just that weird old schoolyard bully thing. McFarlane had, as far as we can tell, legally no right to the *Miracleman* stuff at all, but he stood up there saying, "Hey, I'm going to publish *Miracleman*. I own it, and anybody who wants to take me on in court, I'll see them in court." He got up there, started beating his breast and saying this, and I thought, "You *don't* actually own it. *I'm* going to take you on." I'd like to see that material back in print. I'd like to finish the story I began with Mark Buckingham all those years ago.

**BLASCHKE:** Speaking of all those years ago, what do you see when you look back on works such as *Black Orchid* or *Violent Cases?*

**GAIMAN:** It's very odd. I look back at something like *Violent Cases* and think I did something really clever without knowing what I was doing. And that's okay. That's the joy, sometimes, of being a young writer. You're allowed to do the village idiot thing, of firing an arrow at a tree and then going and drawing your target around it to indicate you've hit the bull's eye. You don't actually have to draw the target first and then fire the arrow.

I like *Violent Cases* a lot. I think *Black Orchid* has some good bits in it. I think the Arkham Asylum scene in there is really cool. We did some things that worked there. I think its heart is in the right place. I think all that is good about *Black Orchid* comes from the fact that its heart is in the right place, and all that is bad about *Black Orchid* comes from the fact its heart is in the right place. We set out to do this feminist, ecological fable about a purple flower woman who could fly. And we succeeded. I'm not sure quite how laudable or valid a goal it was to set out to do it in the first place. But it was what we set out to do, and we did it very well. And I'm continually running into people—normally the wives of comic store owners—who basically say, "This is my favorite comic. It's my favorite graphic novel. It's the only one that he's ever brought home that I liked. Thank you so much for writing it."

**BLASCHKE:** You're best known for *Sandman,* but most people forget that you started the series very early in your career. Does it ever frustrate you that this one work casts such a large shadow?

**GAIMAN:** The point about *Sandman* is it's the single largest body of work I've done. It was about ten years of actual work. I started working on it in '87 and finished it in '96. That was a solid nine years, for eight of which it was coming out in the public, but for one of which was just me.

*Sandman* is two thousand pages long. It was four thousand pages of script. It was done over nine years and it came out every month. It's still ten volumes long. If *Neverwhere* was ten volumes long, and two thousand pages, and had come out in installments for nine years, *Neverwhere* would be the thing I'm known for. I've never done anything on that scale since. I may turn around when I'm fifty-five and go, "You know what, I've probably got a good ten years of really big production in me, I think I'll do something on that scale again." At that point, I'll turn around and do my equivalent of *Book of the New Sun* or something. But I don't want to do that yet. I'm very happy doing things that are smaller than two thousand pages and take less than nine years to do.

The only reason I survived *Sandman,* frankly, is that it was coming out every month. *American Gods* came close to driving me absolutely nuts, because it was about two years' worth of work. By the middle of year one, I actually stopped and finished *Coraline,* chiefly because if I didn't finish something I knew I was going to go mad. So I finished *Coraline.* At least I finished something. And then went back to *American Gods.* I continued writing this book that felt very much like walking toward the horizon. Only, finally, I got there.

# *Sandman* Comic Book Creator Neil Gaiman

## Neal Conan / 2003

**Neal Conan:** This is *Talk of the Nation*. I'm Neal Conan in Washington.

It might be hard to imagine needing *Cliffs Notes* to read a comic book, but if you're not familiar with the work or writer Neil Gaiman, his stories and characters are a little distinct from the usual tights-and-cape crowd. Gaiman's plots jump from history to mythology to everyday life. Cain and Abel, Orpheus, Shakespeare and Satan have all made appearances. Gaiman may be best known for his long-running comic book series *The Sandman*. The books revolve around the very dysfunctional personalities of a family of abstract concepts, everything from desire to destiny to dream, the eponymous *Sandman*. Like Greek gods, they tend to dangle up human affairs with their family infighting on a cosmic level.

Neil Gaiman is also a best-selling author of fantasy novels and children's books, screenplays, rock 'n' roll lyrics and radio scripts. If you have questions about his work or about writing comics in general, join the conversation. Our number here in Washington is (800) 989–8255. That's (800) 989-TALK. And the e-mail address is totn@npr.org.

A new collection of stories hit comic book shops yesterday. It's a hardbound book called *Sandman: Endless Nights*. Neil Gaiman joins us here in Studio 3A. And good to have you back on *Talk of the Nation*.

**Mr. Neil Gaiman** (Author, *Sandman: Endless Nights*): Thank you, Neal.

**CONAN:** As you go through life, you once gave—in the beginning of this book you give a wonderful less-than-25-word summation of *The Sandman* series, which it should be said ran for nine years once a month, more or less. Start us off with that.

**Mr. GAIMAN:** I think the summation that I give, which was given as a sort of very desperate attempt to summarize a 2,000-plus-page story that ran over ten volumes, was that the Lord of Dreams learns that you must change or die and makes his decision.

**CONAN:** Well. those of us who have read the comics know what choice he made. But tell us. this is now the second book you've done in *The Sandman* series since the comic book series actually ended. Why come back to it now?

**Mr. GAIMAN:** It felt like the time was right. When I stopped, I stopped still enjoying it. It was a very conscious decision. I'd finished the story that began in *Sandman* No. 1, *Sandman* 75, and I'd done these ten volumes and I still loved it. And I thought, "If I stop doing it now while I still love it. It'll be good to go back to. If I keep doing it until I'm sick of it, it'll be like one of these TV shows that everybody remembers fondly and just wishes that people would put out of its misery."

So I stopped and came back a few years ago for *Sandman's* tenth anniversary to do a book called *Dream Hunters*, which was a written novella illustrated by a wonderful Japanese artist called Yoshitaka Amano, where I completely made up an old Japanese folk story and had Amano illustrate it. For this, it's now the 10th anniversary of "Vertigo," the imprint that *Sandman* was the flagship of, I suppose. And my editor, Karen Berger, asked if I would do something for the tenth anniversary, and I thought about it and said yes. What I'd really love to do is go and get some of the European artists I love, go and get a bunch of artists I've always wanted to work with and never have, and I'll do a story for each of them.

**CONAN:** After all that time, though, were you afraid that maybe, you know, you'd been in these voices, in these characters for nine long years and, as you say, the first redux was not so long after that, but that you were afraid that maybe the voice, the feel for these characters had gone?

**Mr. GAIMAN:** Oh, terrified, absolutely. It was like going to a party with a bunch of your best friends from seven years ago and you haven't seen them in seven years and you really don't know what they've been doing and whether you'll have anything in common. And you get there and there's maybe two minutes of awkwardness and suddenly you realize how much you've missed them. And it was lovely. I really—it didn't feel like work. Again, going back and writing seven stories—I think there's about 160 pages—and it was just wonderful. And in each case I had the excitement of getting to work with a master artist, Milo Manara, the Italian.

**CONAN:** When you're working with an artist—we're going to be talking with one of your artists later in the show and we'll bring this up later, but when you write, you know, a storyline, do you write it with a particular artist and what he or she can do with his or her style in mind?

**Mr. GAIMAN:** Yes, absolutely, one hundred percent. And I won't write a story unless I know who's going to be drawing it because you're trying to play to the artist's strengths. You're trying to figure out, "What do they bring to something?" And normally if I'm going to do a long story line with somebody, find out what kinds of things they'd like to draw that they never have or what they don't want to draw. You can phone somebody up and they can say, you know, "I just don't want to draw cars," or whatever. You go, "OK. Then I'll do something with no cars in it. That's easy."

**CONAN:** Set that in Greek times.
**Mr. GAIMAN:** Yeah, absolutely.

**CONAN:** Ancient Greece. Yeah.
**Mr. GAIMAN:** So in this case, yes, for Desire, I got Milo Manara, who is famed across Europe for erotic comics and for beautiful historical work. For Delirium, there was an American artist named Bill Sienkiewicz, who I wanted to work with for fifteen years, and finally we got to do a story together and so forth. So you're imagining this story for that person.

**CONAN:** And you mentioned, obviously, the erotic content of at least some of the stories. Comic books, you have to point out to people who are not familiar with them, these days a lot of them are not for kids.
**Mr. GAIMAN:** That's absolutely true. What actually is harder these days is finding good comics for kids. I was very proud recently to have done a story for Art Speigelman and Françoise Mouly's *Little Lit* series, "It Was a Dark and Silly Night . . ." and the three. And it's got me and Lemony Snicket and people actually doing children's comics because people aren't doing many children's comics anymore.

**CONAN:** Let's get some listeners involved. Our phone number is (800) 989–8255, (800) 989-TALK. Our e-mail address is totn@npr.org.

And our first caller is Michael, who's with us from Baton Rouge, Louisiana.

**MICHAEL (Caller):** Hi, Neil and Neal.

**CONAN:** Hello. It is—we were talking before the show about how strange it was to be speaking with somebody named Neil.

**MICHAEL:** Right. OK. Anyway, my question is I am—in addition to Neil's work, I'm a big fan of Joseph Campbell and I see a lot of similarities and ideas, and I was wondering how much of a conscious influence, if any, Joseph Campbell was on *The Sandman.*

**CONAN:** Joseph Campbell, of course, featured in that long series with Bill Moyers on Public Television and obviously writes a lot about some of the same subjects you write about, Neil Gaiman.

**Mr. GAIMAN:** Yes. The series—he did *The Masks of God* with something that I was reading right at the beginning when *Sandman*—when I was first putting it all together, and it was just this wonderful sweeping lunatic look at mythology all around the world. And I loved it and it was definitely part of what I was doing. *The Hero with a Thousand Faces*, which is the thing that many people point to, I actually started and I realized I didn't want to read it because I didn't like seeing the nuts and bolts of my craft exposed so obviously. What I like about writing—if you're writing a story with a hero in it, what's nice is somebody will come along afterwards and say, "Ah, yes, you have fulfilled the Campbellian imperatives here. Look, you've got the call and the rejection of the call and the old man and the gatekeeper and you've got all this stuff." But I'd much rather they came along afterwards than that. I had this stuff in the back of my head and was trying to hit things along the way. Otherwise. three-quarters of the way through a book I'm going to be going, "Oh, I should have the reconciliation with the father here, shouldn't I?"

**CONAN:** Too calculated in other words.

**Mr. GAIMAN:** Yes, the stuff you don't want to know. But I loved *The Masks of God.* I just thought it was just this wonderful book and I actually stole a—in *Sandman* No. 8, the one that brings Death in for the very, very first time from Campbell he lists an Egyptian poem about a man essentially in love with death, which begins, "Death is before me today like a man returning to his home after years in a strange land." And I took that and put that into the first appearance—*Sandman* 8, which was the first time that Death appeared.

**CONAN:** Michael, thanks very much.

**MICHAEL:** Thank you.

**CONAN:** OK. Death, I mean, we all have—you know, there's that standardized image of Death, you know, the Grim Reaper, you know, the guy in the baggy cloak and all of that. You envision Death a completely different way. Was that your idea or was that the idea of the artist you were working with at the time?

**Mr. GAIMAN:** It was—actually, it was a very interesting combination of the two. When I came up with the idea of the whole Sandman character, I thought, well, he's the incarnation of dreams. That's good. That implies there are others like him. Then I thought—there's the very famous quote from somebody like Byron or Shelley that "Death is the brother of sleep." And I thought, "Ah, OK. I like that."

**CONAN:** But you made her the sister of sleep.

**Mr. GAIMAN:** Well, I loved the way that the sexism of language works for you. I thought, you know, if I just say in the first episode that Death—that Dream is Death's younger brother, everyone will assume that death is the older brother because language works for you that way. So they won't be expecting a sister, so that'll be nice. And I also remembered from my childhood a story about the angel of death and how when you meet the angel of death you fall in love so hard and so strongly that your soul is sucked out through your eyes and leaves your body, and that's how you die. And I think it's an old Jewish folk story or something. And I just thought, "That's wonderful. I want a Death you could fall in love with."

**CONAN:** Death—your character Death, mischievous, beautiful, absolutely loveable. Her brother, though, Dream, you say he's a hero, but a hero a little unlike a lot of other heroes, not even likeable at times.

**Mr. GAIMAN:** He's an incredibly gloomy bugger and is occasionally blamed for, you know, the Goth movement and stuff, which I'm not really sure that he'll think he certainly had something to do with it, but probably not as much as people think. I wanted a really, you know, Byronic, screwed-up hero. I wanted somebody who was all-powerful and still cannot get out of his own way. And what was then fun was contrasting him with Death, who you expect to be like that, only more so.

**CONAN:** Mm-hmm.

**Mr. GAIMAN:** And she's very good at what she does and she likes it and she gets out and she meets people, you know, because you do if you're Death. And actually what was interesting in *Endless Nights* was doing a story from a very, very, very long time ago, right back at the dawn of time, and you get to meet them, and she was a lot gloomier and she's a lot posier and more melodramatic, and he's actually a lot more cheerful and human. But you get to see why things went the way they did much later.

**CONAN:** Let's go to Leila, who's with us in Tallahassee, Florida.

**LEILA:** (Caller): Hello?

**CONAN:** Hello. You're on the air.

**LEILA:** Hi. I actually just wanted to tell you that the *Sandman* comics are really amazing and the stories are beautiful and I really like the episode that has the serial killers. I was kind of wondering, why did you get so dark there and where did you come up with all that?

**Mr. GAIMAN:** Good question, Leila. The serial killers convention story is probably one of the darkest places I ever went in *Sandman*. In 1988, I was at the British Fantasy—no, the World Fantasy Convention, where fantasy writers from all over the world came together. At that point it was in London and they all came together in London. And I'd just read—I think *Silence of the Lambs* had just come out and it was a book. And I could see the romance of the serial killer just over the horizon and it bothered me. You could see that we were just about to get a wave of romantic serial killers as heroes and anti-heroes all over the place.

**CONAN:** And so you have them all gather in one convention . . .

**Mr. GAIMAN:** Well . . .

**CONAN:** . . . a little like a comic book convention.

**Mr. GAIMAN:** . . . that was the other part of it, which was I—or I'm sitting there late at night brooding over the serial killer thing and in the bar with a bunch of writers, and I looked around and I thought, "I wonder if serial killers have gatherings like this. I wonder if they just get together one weekend a year to be special and have panels on women and serial killing and . . . I"—

**CONAN:** Mm-hmm, and swap trade secrets.

**Mr. GAIMAN:** Swap trade secrets, have an art show, have the awful disco on a Saturday night, like every convention of every kind everywhere. And at that moment, of course, I also knew that having had the idea it was now in the air and I had to get it down before somebody else wrote a serial killer convention story, and it was a very long fourteen months before that story came out.

**CONAN:** Leila, thanks very much for the call.

**LEILA:** Thank you.

**CONAN:** We're talking with author Neil Gaiman. His new book is *The Sandman: Endless Nights.* You can join the conversation: (800) 989-TALK, (800) 989–8255. Or send us e-mail:totn@npr.org. I'm Neal Conan. It's *Talk of the Nation* from NPR News.

[SOUNDBITE OF MUSIC]

**CONAN:** This is *Talk of the Nation.* I'm Neal Conan in Washington.

We're talking with Neil Gaiman, a legend in many subcultures. He's the author of several highly popular comic book series, numerous fantasy stories and novels and recently best-selling children's books. You're invited to join our discussion. Give us a call at (800) 989–8255. Or you can send us e-mail: totn@npr.org.

And for those of you who last opened a comic book back when *Archie* cost a quarter, here's a quick cheat sheet for some of the jargon you may hear here today. Comic books tend to come out monthly. The stories they tell may begin and end in a single issue, in which case it's called a one-shot. Or they may go for several months in what's called a story arc. Gather a bunch of them together in one volume and you have what's often called a graphic novel. There are two main comic publishing houses, Marvel and DC. DC has a smaller mature readers' imprint known as Vertigo. We mentioned that earlier. That's the company with which Neil Gaiman's work is most closely identified. You may also hear talk of the universe in which a series takes place. These are the fictional worlds shared by many of the different titles published by the same company. For example, the DC universe includes Superman's Metropolis and Batman's Gotham. It's also where Neil Gaiman's *Sandman* lives. The Marvel universe is home to the X-Men, the Hulk, and Spider-Man, all of whom who have visited Hollywood recently. It's also the setting of Neil Gaiman's newest series, *1602.*

Neil Gaiman is with us here in Studio 3A. And *1602*, this is going back gunpowder plot and all sorts of things. And what's the idea of this series?

**Mr. GAIMAN:** The idea of this was I'd agreed to do something for Marvel, I wasn't quite sure what, and then September the 11th happened and I thought, "Well, I'm not sure what I want to do, but I know what I don't want to do. I don't want anything with skyscrapers in it. I don't want anything with planes. I don't want anything with guns. I don't want anything that goes boom in a big way." And seeing that most of the Marvel heroes are famed for swinging from and exploding through skyscrapers, that sort of changed the way that—with that set of perimeters. I thought, "Wouldn't it be interesting to do a story set with all of these old characters and to do the Stan Lee, Jack Kirby, Steve Ditko characters that I remembered from when I was a kid and take them again, but as if they were happening four hundred years early."

**CONAN:** Obviously people can tell from your accent that where you grew up was, well, somewhere well east of here, an island called Britain generally. Were comic books as influential amongst kids of your generation there as they were here?
**Mr. GAIMAN:** Well, they were to me. I think so. I think they probably were. There was a wave, which I was a part of, right in the middle of, of English writers coming to America. And Grant Morrison—Alan Moore, of course, was the first and the finest of us.

**CONAN:** Mm-hmm.
**Mr. GAIMAN:** Pete Milligan. There's a whole slew of us Goth. And I think that part of that comes from the fact that we were reading American comics and we were reading them as these strange things. They were like postcards from another dimension. In my case, of course, I was also very lucky because I got to read the Marvel comics from the very beginning. They were being reprinted when I was about seven or eight from the very first *Spider-Mans* and *Hulks* and *Fantastic Fours* in these English reprint editions with names like "Wham!" "Smash!" "Pow!" "Fantastic!" and "Terrific!" all with exclamation marks.

**CONAN:** Let's get another caller involved and this is Tom, who's with us from Redford, Michigan. Tom, are you there?
**TOM (Caller):** Yes. Yes, I'm here.
**CONAN:** You're on the air.
**TOM:** Hi. Well, first I'd like to say just what an honor it is to talk to both Neals. I enjoy your radio program and I've been following Sandman since almost the very beginning. The first storyline I read was the *Season of Mists* storyline and it'll forever be remembered as one of the greatest story lines in comic book history as far as I'm concerned.

The question I have is, I know especially in the world of comic books when you start something as different as *Sandman,* you're not always guaranteed seventy-five issues. When in the course of writing did you realize that you were going to be able to get to an ending point?
**Mr. GAIMAN:** Well, when I started *Sandman,* critical success and commercial failure were more or less synonymous in the world of comics.

People would talk fondly about comics they'd liked which had rarely lasted more than a year. They just tended not to sell anything and get canceled and be remembered fondly.

**CONAN:** The usual thing is to get a call after your eighth issue saying, "Best wrap it up after number 12."

**Mr. GAIMAN:** Well, that was why *Sandman*, the first story line, was eight issues long, because I actually figured that what would happen was I'd tell my eight-issue story line, it would end in number eight, I would get the phone call there and I'd do four short stories to number twelve, and that would be that, and people would remember *Sandman* very fondly as one of these minor, critical successes. No. 8 came out and we looked around and *Sandman* was selling more than anything comparable had sold for twenty years. And suddenly I realized that I really did have this—you know, I could keep driving this. It was about a year before I mentioned casually in conversation to the powers that be at DC Comics that I did envision an end and would like to end when I was done. And they very politely explained back that that was never how things were done and it simply wouldn't happen, but it was nice of me to have asked. And then time went by, and a few years later it was sort of a *fait accompli.*

I think they'd realized that *Sandman* was, for whatever reasons, something unique and that putting another writer on and continuing *Sandman* at No. 76 after I left would just devalue that. And also, on the sheer bland, boring, bottom-line commercial side of things, one reason why a good run-on comics and a writer leaving always meant that somebody else would carry on the comic was that the comic company who owned the characters and so forth would be making some money out of it. With *Sandman*, when it was done, they had ten graphic novels, they had these ten books, and these ten books were selling as well or better than the comic had ever sold. So I think they realized at that point that if they just let it stop and stayed on good terms with me, I would come back and do things like *Endless Nights.*

**CONAN:** Tom, thanks very much.

**TOM:** All right. Thank you.

**CONAN:** Bye-bye.

As we mentioned, *Endless Nights* is illustrated by seven different artists. The volume starts off in the hands of one of Neil Gaiman's frequent collaborators, artist P. Craig Russell. He joins us now from the studios of member station WKSU in Kent, Ohio.

And thanks very much for being with us today.

**Mr. P. CRAIG RUSSELL (Artist):** Oh, thank you. Hello, Neal. And hello, Neil.

**Mr. GAIMAN:** Hey, Craig.

**CONAN:** You guys first worked together on what became one of the most popular *Sandman* stories, an issue called "Ramadan." Craig Russell, tell us how that came about.

**Mr. RUSSELL:** Well, Neil has a way of picking artists almost like casting actors on the basis of what they've been known to do and do well and might do well in the future. So Neil had seen an illustrated book I did, *The Thief of Baghdad*, that had come out a couple years before that. And knowing he was doing an Arabian Knights fairy-tale-style story with a sort of modern twist to the end of it, thought of me as the artist to write the story for. He said, "Do it like you're a thief of Baghdad, only more so."

**CONAN:** Now when you get a script from Neil Gaiman, what does it look like and what's your first reaction when you look at it? Do you say, "Oh, God, he's basically telling me the story," or do you look at it and say, "How does he expect me to do that?"

[SOUNDBITE OF LAUGHTER]

**Mr. RUSSELL:** Well, with Neil's scripts, the usual response is delight, especially reading the ones that are written for comics. We have two ways— we've done four projects together. Two, I've done adaptations of his short stories, and two have been scripts like *Endless Nights* and *Sandman* 50 that were written for comics. So those are the easiest to do. The ones that are written for comics. Everything is there, you know? Every word that's going to be spoken is there. With the short stories, you have to be more of an editor, crossing out lines—"We don't need this, because we're using this picture"—which always makes you nervous when you're crossing out lines of a living author.

**CONAN:** Now . . .

**Mr. RUSSELL:** You feel like, you know . . .

**CONAN:** Yeah.

**Mr. RUSSELL:** . . . he's there behind you.

**CONAN:** Yeah. When you get the script from a writer, say Neil Gaiman, do you ever call him up and say, "No, no, no, no, you know, on Page six we really want to do this instead"?

**Mr. RUSSELL:** No, not exactly that, no. We'll talk before I start working on the adaptation or illustrating the script. Like on the story we did, *Murder Mysteries*, a couple years ago, which was one of his short stories, we talked beforehand and he let me know—sort of underlined something that was implicit in the story, which even though this was Los Angeles and it was in sweltering heat, it was Christmastime. "So be sure to put some sort of sad, tacky little reminders around that this is the season we're in."

**CONAN:** And, Neil Gaiman, similarly, if you get, you know, a look at the artwork, do you ever say, "No, no, no, there's not enough tacky Santa Clauses in there. You need to add some more"?

**Mr. GAIMAN:** Not with Craig. No, I mean it's a lot like, I don't know, ballet or acrobatics or . . . you know, those people in circuses who swing and have to be sure there's somebody there to catch you. I normally will completely trust my artists, and they'll always come through. Because you're trying to give them something to do. With Craig, actually. the strangest way we've ever worked was probably "Ramadan," because I phoned Craig up and I said, "Right, I've written half of this story already and I just wanted to read you what I've done because I need to figure out how I'm going to break it down into panels for you and what kind of pacing you're going to want." And I read it to him, and he said, "Oh, don't touch it." He said, "Just finish it. Send it to me like that, and I'm going to break it down into panels."

**CONAN:** So the pacing, the speed at which the story advances and whether it's close-ups or long shots, essentially—we're talking cinematic terms—that, you think, is the artist's . . .

**Mr. GAIMAN:** No. A lot of the time—I mean. Craig is a lovely example of somebody who I will say to at the beginning, "I will suggest ways that you can do this that should work. If you can see a better way of doing it, you're the artist and I trust you. Go for it." And with our story in *Endless Nights*, which is called "Death in Venice," there's a couple of places where Craig just sort of expanded things. At one point he added a panel that I hadn't written that makes everything somehow deeper and odder and more beautiful.

**Mr. RUSSELL:** I think if you're living with a script—with a writer's script—when you're doing layouts and your thumbnail drawings and working up to the full pages, you just live with it so long and reading it over and over, it almost feels like a three-dimensional object in your mind that you're look-ing at. And once you get that intimate with it, all of a sudden. Other pictures just sort of pop up that aren't changing the story; they're sort of underlining it and expanding it in certain directions, but always in the service of the story that's already there. So if you live with it long enough, it just sort of takes a life on of its own.

**CONAN:** Let me ask you both a quick question, and that's simply a mat-ter of logistics. When you say, "live with it for so long," Craig—how long does this take to do?

**Mr. RUSSELL:** Well, it depends on your page count. I mean, *Murder Mysteries* was a sixty-four-page story. *The Sandman* 50 was about thirty-two. So once you really get going, I might do a half a page a day, so it can be several months . . .

**CONAN:** And . . .

**Mr. RUSSELL:** . . . from start to finish.

**CONAN:** Same to you, Neil Gaiman. How long does it take you to write a comic book that comes out once a month?

**Mr. GAIMAN:** Well, when I started writing *Sandman,* I was young, excited, and every single panel I was writing I'd never written before, and every panel transition I'd never done before, and I could have written about two issues a month. I could write one issue in two weeks. By the time I finished that . . .

**CONAN:** So that's about a page a day, roughly.

**Mr. GAIMAN:** Yeah, or a little bit more than that. By the time I finished *Sandman,* there was sort of roughing-out time. I mean, there's figuring stuff out and drawing little thumbnails and figuring out what you're doing, and then—but I could do two comics a month. By the time I finished *Sandman,* I was up to about sort of—it took me about six weeks every month to write it, and it was just gradually getting later and later.

**CONAN:** Deadlines affect everybody in a lot of businesses. Neil Gaiman is with us, also one of his collaborators, P. Craig Russell. We're discussing *Sandman: Endless Nights,* which is newly published. You're listening to *Talk of the Nation* from NPR News.

And let's get another caller in. Matthew's with us from Arden Hills in Minnesota, excuse me.

**MATTHEW (Caller):** Hello to both Neils.

**CONAN:** Hi.

**MATTHEW:** Yes. I have a question for Neil Gaiman. I'm sorry, it's not really about the artwork, but I was just browsing your website, and I came across a question that you answered in which you said that you would not be surprised if the gods, demigods, and etc. that you wrote about turned out to be true, but you did not expect it. Now one of your constantly reoccurring themes has been the idea that humans have a need to see past the physical world. We have a need to know about story and we have a need to believe in gods, How do you explain that need if we are living in a completely physical world and if, obviously, there's no evolutionary advantage to it?

**CONAN:** And if you could answer that in ten seconds, if you would—no—go ahead.

**Mr. GAIMAN:** Thank you, Matthew. Well, speaking as an author who makes things up, I love making things up. I like the idea of a world in which everything exists, and the joy for me of *Sandman* was creating a fictional universe in which everything could possibly exist. Everything anybody had ever believed was absolutely true. I remember during the *Season of Mists* storyline where I had Lucifer resign as the person who runs hell, close the place down. Throw everybody out and give the Lord of Dreams the key. And bringing characters on from all three stories . . .

**CONAN:** And much hilarity ensues. Yes.

**Mr. GAIMAN:** Yes, with hilarious results as I brought on Greek gods and Egyptian gods, and then I thought, "Well, what about fairies? Can I bring them on? Will everything collapse?" And I brought them on, and no, the structure of belief still held. And then I brought on angels, and it still held. I love the idea that death is an awfully big adventure. I love the idea that all the things that I make up are true. Do I expect it? I have no idea. The joy for me of being a writer is you can be the kind of ultimate agnostic who gets to believe whatever you need for the story. And if ever I write a story in which there are absolutely no ghosts, no gods and nothing but this world, then that's what I believe while I'm writing that story.

**CONAN:** Matthew, thanks very much.

**MATTHEW:** Well, thank you very much.

**CONAN:** OK. Bye-bye.

**MATTHEW:** Bye.

**CONAN:** Here's a quick e-mail question from Joan Lowe in Cleveland: "I have a question about Mr. Gaiman's new comic book series *1602*. We read the first two issues." She's one ahead of me. "I would like to know how many are planned? I especially like the cover art. And can he tell us something about the artist?"

**Mr. GAIMAN:** Yes. Scott, who does the covers, is absolutely wonderful. He's never done any comics work before. He's mainly done playbills. And he's . . .

**CONAN:** For what we call the legitimate theater.

**Mr. GAIMAN:** For the legitimate theater. And he'd sent his portfolio in to Marvel, and Joe Quesada, who's the editor in chief there, saw it and had wanted something that he could use Scott on, and he showed me his stuff and said. "How would he work for *1602*?" And I said, "I think he'll work very well." And I love his approach. And they're absolutely gorgeous covers. It's planned for eight issues. I'm currently halfway through issue seven and have a terrifying feeling that will get halfway through issue eight and look around and grit my teeth and start planning issue nine.

**CONAN:** You could just look outside and say, you know, "And then a big hurricane arrived and everybody died."

**Mr. GAIMAN:** Yes. I must have already written—I've already written at least one hurricane; in fact, I once wrote a hurricane in a *Sandman* story called *A Game of You* which hits New York, so I'm hoping that that doesn't come true tonight.

**CONAN:** P. Craig Russell, thanks very much for being with us.

**Mr. RUSSELL:** Oh, my pleasure.

**CONAN:** He's a comic book artist. He's illustrated many titles, including a story in the new *Sandman* book, *Endless Nights.* He was with us from the studios of member station WKSU in Kent. Ohio. We'll be back with a question or two more for Neil Gaiman when we come back from a break, and we'll also go from comic books to the comics page in the newspapers. Welcome back another cult character. A hint: He's got a big nose, herring breath, and will soon wander onto a Sunday funnies page near you. We'll be back in a moment.

I'm Neal Conan. You're listening to *Talk of the Nation* from NPR News.

[ANNOUNCEMENTS]

**CONAN:** This is *Talk of the Nation.* I'm Neal Conan in Washington.

Tomorrow, join Ira Flatow and "Science Friday" for a special broadcast from San Antonio, Texas, and a discussion of preservation efforts that are under way to try to save the city's missions. That's tomorrow on *Talk of the Nation.*

Today we're talking with Neil Gaiman. His new book is *The Sandman: Endless Nights,* which is newly available in a store near you. We're wrapping up our conversation. Let's go to Cal, who joins us on the line from Cheyenne, Wyoming.

**CAL (Caller):** Hi there.

**CONAN:** Hi, Cal. You're on the air.

**CAL:** Yes. I was wanting to provide Neil an opening to speak about the Comic Book Legal Defense Fund if he wished to.

**CONAN:** And do you work with that?

**CAL:** I contribute by buying nearly everything related in comic t-shirts and Neil's videos and so on.

**CONAN:** All right. What is the Comic Book Legal Defense Fund?

**Mr. GAIMAN:** I'm very grateful. Thank you. The Comic Book Legal Defense Fund is the First Amendment organization that defends the First Amendment rights of comic books and comic book creators and comic book publishers and comic book retailers, who actually are out there on the front lines selling comic books and are the people who are most likely to suddenly find themselves arrested for having sold an adult comic to an adult police officer.

**CONAN:** I see. In comic book stores, or at least many of them these days, there are front sections for everybody, and in the back an adult comic book section.

**Mr. GAIMAN:** That's true. And, as a retailer in Texas recently discovered, that doesn't matter if they don't like the comics they can buy there. No, but the Legal Defense Fund, it's an organization that's now about fourteen years old and has been fighting, sometimes successfully, sometimes not. We managed to prevent the state of California tax authorities reclassifying comics from literature over to sign-painting in order to be able to collect tax on them, which was actually a very, very long, hard-fought battle and, you know, occasionally we lose. There was a guy called Mike Diana—still is—in Florida who was arrested for doing a self-published sort of fanzine comic called *Boiled Angel*; found guilty of obscenity in the state of Pensacola, Florida, and sentenced to a three-year suspended jail sentence, $1000 fine, thousand hours of community service; couldn't be within ten feet of anybody under the age of eighteen, and the local police force were ordered to make twenty-four-hour spot checks of his place of residence, randomly, to make sure he wasn't drawing anything in future. So sometimes you lose.

**CONAN:** Cal, thanks very much for the call. Appreciate it.

**CAL:** Thank you.

**CONAN:** And very quickly, Neil Gaiman, another—well, I'm not sure— well, I guess it's in part legal, but comic book writers and artists have for years struggled with ownership with comic book publishing companies over who gets the rights to what. Has that been resolved? Do you have the rights to *The Sandman*?

**Mr. GAIMAN:** No. No, it hasn't—things are getting better, but there's a sort of one-step-forward-two-step-back thing going on. *Sandman* is owned by Time Warner. It's completely owned by that conglomerate. They could do what they want with it. They don't 'cause they want to keep me reasonably happy. But they absolutely could. Some of the work I've done for DC since has been creator-owned. I did a beautiful series called *Stardust,* which was a fairy tale with Charles Vess, which we owned, we kept the rights to.

But on the whole, it would be a good thing if—yeah, it's one reason why I spend more and more time now doing novels. The last novel, *American Gods,* joy of that is I own it. It's all mine, every word of it. *Coraline,* the children's stuff, it's all mine. When people phone up and say they want to make movies, I can say no if I don't want to do it. I wouldn't have that control over *The Sandman.*

**CONAN:** Well, thanks very much for coming in, and thank you very much for this new book. It's a wonderful piece of work. *The Sandman: Endless Nights.* Neil Gaiman with us here in Studio 3A. Thank you very much.
**Mr. GAIMAN:** Thank you, Neal.

# Maddy Gaiman Interviews Her Dad

## Maddy Gaiman / 2004

**Maddy Gaiman:** Hi. I'm Maddy Gaiman, and the stories you just heard were written and read by my dad, Neil Gaiman. Now, I'm gonna ask him some questions.

**MG:** First of all, what was your first story for children?
**Neil Gaiman:** The first story I ever wrote for children almost nobody in the whole world has ever read or heard and I wrote it when I was about twenty and it was called "My Great Aunt Ermintrude." And it was a story about this lady who has to go off to the desert and rescue a princess and there were lots of dogs and dragons and running around in desserts and mysterious disguises and things and it was the first book I ever wrote. And I don't think it was very good. It had a few good bits in it. but it wasn't really very good and these days it sits in a box in the attic. So that was the very first story I wrote for kids, and then I went on and wrote things for adults.

**MG:** Yeah, Okay. Why did you want to write things for kids instead of just adults?
**NG:** Couple of reasons. And the biggest one is that when you're a writer, and you have kids, your kids don't actually think you do anything really. If they can't actually read what you write. So, I would write and your brother and sister particularly would just sorta assume that I didn't have a real job and that I didn't write anything that anyone would want to read. So that was one reason I wrote my first book for children that got published which was, *The Day I Swapped My Dad For Two Goldfish*, which was sort of to show them that I did something for real. And it was when I started *Coraline*.

**MG:** Okay. Well, which is more fun: writing for children or writing for grown-ups?

**NG:** Probably writing for children, but I think writing for children is actually much harder than for writing for grown-ups as well. So, it's more fun, but you really don't want to waste any words. When I'm writing for children, I'm very, very aware that if somebody likes this book they're going to be reading it over and over and over hundreds of times and I'm aware that some adult is probably going to have to read this to children and that they'll be listening. And I don't want to waste words; I don't want to do the boring bits. When you're writing for kids, you tend to leave out the boring bits.

**MG:** Okay. When you were young did you know that you wanted to become a writer?

**NG:** Yes, I did. I knew I wanted to become a writer pretty much as far back as I can remember. When I was about three, I remember inventing a poem and running to my mum and making her write it down and dictating my poem to her. And I loved the idea of being a writer. I liked the idea of being the things other kids wanted to be as well: I wanted to explore distant planets and ride dragons and things like that. But mostly, I wanted to be a writer, and I think that's probably another reason why I write children's books is because when I started wanting to be a writer those were the books I loved, and they're books that stay with you for always. And they're stories that stay with you for always.

**MG:** Once you realized you wanted to be a writer, what did you do?

**NG:** I wrote! [both laugh warmly] Actually is really what I did when I knew I wanted to be a writer. I wasn't terribly good when I started. I mean writing really is something you get better at as you go. I was, you know, I was probably very good at writing like other people. Which kind of helped . . . but I didn't know what I sounded like, and I couldn't write like me. And it took lots and lots of writing and lots and lots of words before one day I realized that I now sounded like me.

**MG:** What book that you've written have (sic.) made you laugh the most?

**NG:** Well, there was a book I did called *Good Omens* with Terry Pratchett that made me laugh very much because I was writing it with Terry, and I got to laugh at his bits. So, it's harder to write and laugh at your own jokes if you're writing them. Of the books I've done for kids, *Crazy Hair* makes me laugh. I just remember sitting in a Japanese restaurant somewhere in

Florida writing it all down in pencil and just thinking that this was the silliest thing I'd ever written and how funny it was.

**MG:** M'hmm. What book would you recommend I read?
**NG:** Of the things I've written or anything?

**MG:** The things you've written.
**NG:** Well, I've read you *Coraline*, and I've read you all the picture books. I think you're almost probably ready for *Good Omens*. Which you'd probably like because it's like one of the *William* books. Only with various other strange and exciting things happening.

**MG:** Okay. Where do you like to write?
**NG:** I like to write in different places. Um, and I don't like writing if I've been writing somewhere for long enough that it feels like the same place. So, I tend to write somewhere for about a year and then notice that I've been writing there for about a year and move to somewhere else. Um, one of my favorite places to write which I haven't written there for about four years and it's now getting to the point where I'm starting to think: 'Wouldn't it be nice to write there again?' is in the gazebo at the bottom of my garden in the woods. And I get to sit and write and watch the squirrels.

**MG:** [giggles] Okay. What comes first—the pictures or the story?
**NG:** For me, so far—the story. But, on the other hand, the wonderful thing about writing the stories for me is knowing that I have Dave McKean doing the pictures, so I know that I can draw—I can write anything—no matter how silly or strange or impossible, and he'll be able to draw it and make it look good.

**MG:** How do they come together?
**NG:** If I'm doing my job: I write something, I give it to Dave McKean, and then, one day, Dave starts sending me computer files or sending me photocopies, and—all of the sudden—magically, it just works! Uh, *The Day I Swapped My Dad For Two Goldfish* is a lovely example of that. And so actually is *The Wolves in the Walls*. Both of which are done by Dave McKean in completely different styles.

**MG:** Yah. Why do you like audiobooks?
**NG:** I *love* audiobooks. Partly cause the experience of having somebody read something to you is very different from the experience of reading it to

yourself. Sometimes better, sometimes worse, but it's always different. And I love audiobooks that are read by the author because then you hear where the stress goes. You can hear what it's meant to sound like. So, for me, I can think of nothing more fun than getting to read things like *Goldfish* or *Crazy Hair* or *Wolves,* and they all have very different voices. I love the voice of the boy who's talking in *The Day I Swapped My Dad for Two Goldfish.* And I love the way the narrator in *The Wolves in the Walls* uses words and talks about creaking, and cracking, and crumpling noises and sneaking creeping things—and it's great fun—and so I think that's part of the fun of audiobooks is you actually get to—you get to relish that. Plus, everybody likes being told a story. Sometimes you forget that you like being told a story, but it's always nice when somebody just settles down and tells you a story for the night.

**MG:** M'hmm. What made you write *The Wolves in the Walls?*
**NG:** You did. In some ways. You were about four years old, so this was about six years ago, and you woke up from a nightmare. And you were really, really, upset. And I said, "What's wrong?" And you said, "There are wolves in the walls. And they came out." And you showed me the place in the wallpaper where the wolves came out. And you were really quite upset about this. And I just thought, "What a wonderfully cool, strange idea for a story." And for several days after that, I would tell you stories about wolves coming out of walls, and about how, you know, they'd take people prisoner, and they were much, much scarier, much nastier wolves, than the ones in the book. And then I thought, "I'll make this a children's book!" So, I settled down to try and write it, and it didn't really work. And it wasn't very good. So, it took about another couple of years before I actually had the idea for the line, "When the wolves come out of the walls, it's all over." And, as soon as I knew that, I had the whole story. And I sat down and I wrote it, and then I remember actually—to find out if it worked or not—I actually went into your kindergarten class and read it to them and embarrassed you to no end—

**MG:** [giggling] M'hmm. I remember that. Why did you write *Crazy Hair?*
**NG:** *Crazy Hair. Crazy Hair,* again, was your fault actually. Uhm, *Goldfish* wasn't your fault; *Crazy Hair*—I was in Florida, and my hair had gone very strange; I'd gone down for a conference, and the humidity had made my hair all curly and very peculiar, and I wrote you an email about it. And I got back this email addressed to "Dear Mr. Crazy Hair . . ." and I thought, "Huh. I'll write her a poem." So, over several evenings, in a Japanese restaurant in I think it was Ft. Lauderdale, I wrote "Crazy Hair." And I didn't think it

actually was going to be for anybody except you, and then at the academic conference I was at, I had to do a reading, and I read some very respectable academic things I had written, and I read a bit of *American Gods,* and then I read "Crazy Hair." And, afterwards, all of these professors came up to me in lines, and said 'Where can we get "Crazy Hair," we want to send it to our children.' So, I thought, "It's not just me; other people like it too."

**MG:** M'hmm. Okay, what inspired you to write *The Day I Swapped My Dad for Two Goldfish*?
**NG:** Ahh, okay—that had nothing to do with you. That was written many years before you were born actually. Your brother, Mike, when he was about four, five years old, I'd said one of those terrible things to him that parents sometimes say to their children and I asked him something quite horrible and impossible. I think I'd asked him something like, "Isn't it your bedtime?" And he was so offended by this, and he clenched his fists and he looked up at me and he turned red and he said, "I, I wish, I wish I didn't have a dad!" He said, "I wish I had—" and then you could see him trying to figure out what else you could have and he said, "I wish I had goldfish!" And I thought: "What a great, cool, wonderful line! What a wonderful idea." And I wrote the first paragraph of *The Day I Swapped My Dad for Two Goldfish.* And then, a couple of years later, I was writing something, and I was stuck. And just to sort of give myself an idea and to waste a little time, I started looking at the files on the computer to see what else was sitting there and there was something called *The Day I Swapped My Dad for Two Goldfish* with a first paragraph. And I thought: "Oh, I know what the next paragraph is." So I wrote it. And then I knew what the one after that was, so I wrote it. And I looked up two or three hours later and I had written the complete book. So, that was how I wrote that.

**MG:** Wow! Alright, do you tell your children stories?
**NG:** [laughs] What do you think?

**MG:** Yes.
**NG:** [laughs robustly] Yes, I do. I love telling you guys stories. I love reading to you as well. I mean, reading, ya know doing, Diana Wynne Jones or Terry Pratchett or E. Nesbit or Richard Crumpton or P. L. Travers or any of those cool authors aloud is enormously fun. The only time it gets a bit wonky sometimes is when I get a bit carried away. I remember Mike once telling

me off for making things up and I had to explain to him that really was what I did and that's what I do for a living.

**MG:** My favorite book is *The Day I Swapped My Dad for Two Goldfish.* Which one of your books is your favorite?
**NG:** Of the books for kids, I'm really fond of *Coraline.* It is the longest, and it took me ten years to write, and I started it for Holly and I finished it for you. I love *Crazy Hair* because I love reading *Crazy Hair* to live audiences and just watching them start laughing, and I love that. Probably my favorite of all of my children's book is the next one I am going to write. So right now it's a big spooky book called *The Graveyard Book* which I haven't even started, and *that's* my favorite of all my children's books and it can stay my favorite until it's written. And then it will be the one after that.

**MG:** Okay. Well, thanks for answering those questions, Dad. And I'll see you next time.
**NG:** [laughs] Does that mean I'll see you next time?
**MG:** I don't know. I couldn't think of anything else to say.
**NG:** That was great. Thank you, Maddy.
**MG:** Thank you, Dad.

# An Interview With Neil Gaiman

## Jessa Crispin / 2006

From *Bookslut*. Reprinted by permission.

Like many fifteen-year-old girls, my entry into comics was Neil Gaiman's *Sandman*. It offered something I hadn't been aware existed in comic book form: intelligent, funny, beautifully drawn tales of myth woven into real life. Since then, Gaiman has been playing around with form and genre, writing screenplays, short stories, novels, childrens' books, radio plays, and other comic books.

His sense of adventure has paid off in legions of devoted fans. His signing events have hundreds of fans curling around the venue, out the door, and into the street. And dutifully and respectfully, he signs for each person, even until the wee hours of the morning if need be. I sat down with Neil over tea in New York City the day of an event with John Hodgman left him signing until after midnight.

**Jessa Crispin:** You sign for everybody.

**Neil Gaiman:** I do, I sign for everybody. It's stupid. I recently got disabused of something that I had believed for years. I met Stephen King in '92 and I met him at a signing of mine. He came along with his family and he invited me to dinner with them afterwards and the signing went so late that when I finally met him it was eating room service hamburgers on the floor of the hotel room at 10:30 or 11 at night. At the time he was saying, "If I'm booked for an hour and a half, I just leave after an hour and a half." I've always taken that as truth. As a peculiar coincidence I was talking to one of his sons last week and I mentioned that. He told me, "He may say that, but he stays until the end, too."

**JC:** Have you ever shut down an event, where there was a curfew?

**NG:** Yes. Every variant possible happened. The worst ones are the signings where you have an hour there and then you will be replaced by another body in that space and it's not negotiable. You realize you're leaving with several hundred people upset, but there's nothing really you can do.

The worst one ever was in Sao Paulo in Brazil in 2001. Brazilians are lovely people. But they don't hold back on how they feel. And 1,200 showed up and at 7:00 the shop decided to cap the line, thinking that was enough. The five hundred people left behind apparently explained to them in a very enthusiastic and cheerful and Brazilian sort of way that they could of course shut down the line if they wanted to but those five hundred people would destroy their store if they did. And they thought about it for a minute, reopened the line, and I signed for all 1,200. But I only discovered this happened until the end of the day. I stayed until two o'clock in the morning, and I lost my voice.

**JC:** But you have a very open relationship with your fans.
**NG:** (Smirks) Yes. We have an open relationship. Obviously they can see other authors if they want, and I can see other readers.

**JC:** Yes, but with other authors, I don't know their cats' names.
**NG:** That's true. That bit can get weird at times. I can be at a signing and someone will say, "So, how did Fred's operation go?" There have been occasional cat tragedies that I have not blogged. Fred-the-Unlucky-Black-Cat recently went in for an incredibly expensive operation to remove part of his bowel so that he can hopefully eat cat food and actually eliminate it without being sent off for an enema once every two weeks. I decided not to blog that at all because I thought I really don't want to clog the FAQ box with two hundred people writing in with get well wishes for Fred and cat advice. Any time you mention cats, people will write in, "Well, when my cat had this, the only thing he would eat was liquidized sardines. If you liquidize sardines and add acidophilus." I always want to try these things.

**JC:** Did any of them work?
**NG:** Never! Not one. Nothing ever been suggested included by vets who have written in has ever worked. But I will try them every time. Very nobly. Actually, I think I may have learned about this Happy Cat pheromone from somebody writing in. It's this scent that gets released in a month-long slow spray thing and stops them from weeing in places they shouldn't. It did actually work. Happy Cat pheromones.

**JC:** I always wanted to ask you how you were introduced to Kathy Acker.
**NG:** I had read *Blood and Guts in High School* and loved it, which was *Blood*

*and Guts in High School Plus Two, Great Expectations* was in there, and I think *My Death, My Life* by Pier Paolo Pasolini, was that it?

**JC:** I don't have her collected novels, I'm not sure.

**NG:** I loved it. I think I had even seen a TV documentary about her, and I had gotten the impression from the documentary that she was incredibly tall. I was at a party for somebody, it was one of those small literary parties at the Groucho club for a visiting author, who I think might have been Spalding Gray. If it wasn't Spalding Gray, it would have been Tama Janowitz. There's this small, blonde, amazingly cute American lady and we get chatting and suddenly the penny drops that this is Kathy. By that time we were already enjoying talking too much for me to be intimidated. I think we were talking about Alan Moore's *Swamp Thing*, which was at that point her favorite thing in the world, and my favorite thing in the world, and I was already friends with Alan at that point. It was the kind of conversation you don't want to end, so you end up going from there to another bar and to another bar until you finally stop talking. We were friends. It wasn't the sort of friendship where you get to be better friends as time goes on, it was the kind of friendship where you meet, you click, and many, many years later when we were chatting and she said, "Oh darling, I'm so proud of you, you're doing so well." I said, "Well, I was always a writer." She said, "I thought when I met you, you were some sort of groupie."

I introduced her to loads of comic book people, introduced her to Alan Moore. And then our friendship was profoundly rocky and enormous fun for the next decade. I'm not somebody who has very good fallings out with people, but Kathy was somebody who would have enormous and dreadful fallings out with people. At one point she fled England. She moved to New York, and I saw her whenever I'd come to New York, and then she moved back and bought a house in Brighton, sight unseen. This was immediately followed by the falling apart of the British housing market and Kathy moving to San Francisco never having seen her house in Brighton. I got a phone call from her one day saying, "Darling, you can sell my house in Brighton for me, can't you?"

She moved to San Francisco and I ended up with the peculiar task apparently of trying to sell her house and it wasn't something I hadn't quite agreed to do but something I found myself semi-lumbered with. I made a few phone calls and talked to people and established it was much weirder and complicated than that. I think at some point in there Kathy sent the keys to the house in Brighton back and decided that she was mad at me because I hadn't sold it or something. Then I didn't see her or hear from her for a year or two. I think she then turned up at a signing I did, quite unexpectedly, in San Francisco and we had a wonderful time. She rescued me from one of the weirdest signings I had ever been at . . .

**JC:** What made it so weird?

**NG:** As far as I can establish, the owner of the shop who was quite mad, decided there would be a forty-five minute break in the middle of the signing, during which she seemed to have decided that the fifteen-year-old stockgirl who obviously had a huge crush on my books and I should probably go off to the warehouse space in the back and get to know each other as well as possible. Something that seemed to me the most unlikely thing anyone had ever proposed during a signing, at which point Kathy turned up on a motorbike with leopard-spotted hair and rescued me. She was like, "Oh darling!" We disappear into the back and chat and after a while she was saying how delightful it was to see me again and why had I stopped speaking to her. And I thought about explaining to her that I hadn't and that as far as I could tell she had but it was now obviously water under the bridge that I apologized for not speaking to her.

After that we just stayed in touch. I remember once in '94 I got a phone call from her inviting me to spend ten days with her on William Burroughs's farm in Kansas and thought about that for, ooh, a good fraction of a millisecond before saying no, thank you, Kathy, what a lovely offer, I don't think so. I got these great late night phone calls from her ranting about whatever she was interested in. Then she began a relationship with an old friend of mine. A writer named Charles, an English writer. She moved back to England, and I saw her when I was over there and she was so happy to be with Charlie. And then the cancer thing started.

I got a call from her after she came out from having her breasts removed in a San Francisco hospital, so completely horrified by the entire experience. Basically, they gave her a double mastectomy as an out-patient procedure.

**JC:** Jesus.

**NG:** As far as I can tell, a fairly appalling and horrible one. She had nothing further to do with the American medical system. She moved back to England, decided that she'd beaten it, explained to anybody who would listen that any sickness she had in her system was a result of dropping a bottle of water into a grotty canal and lifting it out and still drinking it. It was obviously still icky canal stuff in her system. And then she went back to America and broke up with Charlie and I got an e-mail from somebody one day saying, "I understand you're a friend of Kathy Acker's. She's currently dying in a hospital in Mexico."

I immediately emailed the UK and said, "She's dying in a hospital in Mexico," and a mutual friend of mine and Charlie's, a guy named Igor, said, "She's not dying, she's just got flu, I checked around. She's in San Francisco with flu, she's just being a drama queen." So I wrote back to the guy who said she's dying and said I'm told she has the flu in San Francisco, and they wrote back, "She's really dying."

I phoned her in the hospital in Mexico. We chatted a while. She was very weak. It was good. This week has been a particularly rough one on me because my friend John M. Ford, the writer, died completely unexpectedly. And it's everybody who knew him and loved him is completely devastated, and one reason we're devastated is he was sending us emails the day before and his heart went or his kidneys went in the night and he was gone. With Kathy I never had that. I've always missed her, but I got to phone up and say goodbye. That was good. That sort of somehow made it copable. Then she was gone, and she died in room 101, as Alan Moore said, "There's nothing that woman can't turn into a literary reference."

**JC:** You're not touring much for *Fragile Things,* and usually you're Neil Gaiman: Road Warrior.

**NG:** Mostly I'm not touring much because the *Anansi Boys* tour came very, very close to if not killing me . . . I came off of that tour promising never to tour again. I've mellowed a bit. That one was hell. You saw me in Chicago. I got into Chicago around twelve-ish, dropped my stuff off at the hotel, came out, and did a couple signings of just signing stocks and then straight out to that place, we were there by about five or six, signed stock and stuff in the back for about forty-five minutes, ate some sushi, went on, did half an hour, forty minutes of reading and Q&A, and then signed until 1:30. And then I got into a car and went back to a hotel in the middle of Chicago, got in at about 2:30, I think. I just remember the nice man who brought me something to eat because I was actually painfully hungry by the time I got back to the hotel because I hadn't eaten for eight hours, was the same man who three and a half hours later brought me my cup of coffee, knocked on the door and told me it was time to get up and get in the car and go to the next one.

It just kept on going like that. It was ten days before I had my first day off and I did America and then I did Canada and then I went to England and did it all again. It was a very hard month. For this tour, I would rather have done a reading tour, but really at the end of the day it was just a matter of me turning around and saying, "I will give you a week. You have a week, and however you want to arrange it. And I'd like a day off there somewhere." Then I thought this was going to be so easy and pleasant, and then I realized that actually it butted between two conventions I had already agreed to do, so I went to FantasyCon, and I did two days of events in London for *Fragile Things*, and then I came over here and tomorrow at seven o'clock I'm on my way to Washington DC, and lots of people wanted to know why I wasn't doing the big Washington Book Fair this year, which I kept explaining it would be really boring if I kept turning up every year.

That was one of those where they were disassembling the festival around me at six o'clock as the last few people got to the front. I signed for about four hours there, and the *Washington Post* said I did it because I was a savvy businessman.

JC: Really?
NG: Yeah, they really did.

JC: Were you charging five dollars per autograph?
NG: I just thought that was so weird, the idea that I was still signing because I'm a savvy businessman. I'm signing because it's polite. These people have gotten into line and they came a fair way to be there, and that's how I would like to be treated if I were in line for a book signing, which thank god I never am.

JC: I'm wondering how that would improve your business life. It seems it would be maybe a bad business decision to stay that long.
NG: I don't know. I've never been described as a savvy businessman any-where else in any other context. I suppose I could cut it out and send it to my dad who would be pleased. See? I'm a savvy businessman. Mostly what I am is a really, really crap businessman who did the Douglas Adams thing where what you do is get an awful lot of money so it doesn't really matter that you're a crap businessman.

JC: Especially now that you're doing movies.
NG: That's nice. I now have three completely distinct income sources. The fact that *The Sandman* books sell forever is really nice, and then there's me as a novelist, which is a completely different thing, and then there's movies

where people come along and say, "Here's a million dollars," and you say, "Thank you very much, that's very nice." You kick yourself and you look at the numbers on the check and you say, "I just got a check for a million dollars."

I've realized one of the ways I know I'm not a savvy businessman is I get just as excited by getting a three hundred dollar check for a short story as I did to get for a million. I would get just as grumpy if I didn't get the three hundred dollar check as I would for the million dollar check.

**JC:** But that's why you have an assistant, to straighten all of that out.

**NG:** It's true. My agent thinks I'm hilarious because she's long since learned that the only time I'll call her up thrilled about getting a royalty statement is when it's some obscure country that I barely heard of, and I made back my advance and I'm getting royalties. I phone and say, "Did you see? Did you see? We got ninety dollars from Croatia!" She'll say, "Neil, why are you telling me this?"

**JC:** Your agents must love you, because you seem to be up for any medium, any experiment.

**NG:** I am. I'm not very good at genre snobbery. If it's anything I'm interested in, I'd obviously love to do it. And I keep bumping into people who'd much rather I did one thing or another. My movie agent would much rather I did movies forever and didn't, for example, do TV. Whereas TV is fun, lots of people see it. It's interesting to do TV. I like doing novels, but I'm astonishingly puzzled and grateful that I live in a universe that I have a short story collection published as a major novel. We live in a universe in which the odds of being able to turn to a publisher and say, "Would you like to publish a collection of my short stories?" is right up there with me saying, "Would you like to invest in a zeppelin business?" Doesn't happen very often.

When eight years ago they published *Smoke and Mirrors*, it was with no fuss or fanfare. I said, "Shall I do an author tour for it?" and they said, "No." It was like, why would you tour for a short story collection? Then they were incredibly puzzled when they looked around and it was still selling. I picked up a copy in the offices at HarperCollins this morning and noticed it's now in its seventeenth printing in trade paperback. And maybe later than that, but the one I picked up had a little 17 on it. *Smoke and Mirrors* just came out and just took over. Suddenly I'm in a universe where I have a publisher who is publishing short stories of mine as a major book with quite disturbingly high numbers. If it were me, I would have done a print run of about half that and then gone back to press. With a really cool cover.

**JC:** It is a cool cover, although I was a bit worried about it surviving the airplane trip to New York.

**NG:** Apparently this is tougher than a normal paper cover. The old version used to be much, much weaker. I got to design my cover, which was a first. Me and my editor Jennifer, we actually put together the design. The heart on the back was hand-colored by my doctor. We had colored hearts that were all wrong and we had black and white hearts that were great, so I handed it to my local doctor and asked, "Would you mind coloring this in for me?" and he said, "Not at all." So he colored that heart in, showing us what was red and what was blue, and I sent it back to HarperCollins.

It does look a little more sweet and reassuring than I would have hoped.

**JC:** Really? Because the butterfly is all in pieces, although I guess you can't see that until you take off the translucent cover.

**NG:** I think the translucence works against us. I wanted the damaged butterfly. The fact that it was very dead and damaged . . . I thought that would be the signifier that there were scary, icky bits. Oh well, now it'll take them by surprise and they'll be traumatized by it.

**JC:** I'm sure that they'll be okay. Although you did get a romance audience with *Stardust,* so they might be a little scared.

**NG:** That's the weird thing about not doing the same stuff every time. With every book, you piss off a bunch of people who like a specific thing and are hoping for that specific thing again.

**JC:** Do you actually get emails from your fans complaining about that?

**NG:** No, but what I do get is people coming up at readings and saying, "I like X, I really don't like Y." The ones who read more than one book figure it out. The ones who read only one book tend to extrapolate and go, "Oh, they're all like this." The ones who've done two, go, "Oh, I get it. Some of this may be similar, but mostly they're completely different."

**JC:** I'm sure there are people out there who still wish you were doing *Sandman.*

**NG:** Oh sure. And there are people who wish I'd done nothing but *Neverwhere* novels. And then there are the ones who wish that I'd done nothing but *American Gods.* I sort of worried a bit when *Anansi Boys* was being sold as if it was the *American Gods* sequel. And I kept walking around going (cough, grumble) it's, uh, not. The publisher said, "Yeah, but *American Gods* was a *New York Times* bestseller, and we have to push that." Yeah, but it's a different book. I didn't want people with expectations for more of the same. If you want more of the same with *American Gods,* there's a Shadow story in *Fragile Things.*

**JC:** How did your interest in mythology start?

**NG:** I wish I had an origin story for you. When I was four, I was bitten by a radioactive myth.

I remember the first time I encountered Thor was definitely in comics, which left me interested and excited enough in Roger Lancelyn Green's *Tales of the Norsemen* that I read it until it fell apart. Then I went out with my own money and bought Roger Lancelyn Green's *Tales of Egypt.* Which I read a lot. I was a seven-year-old kid reading ancient Egyptian mythology for pleasure.

**JC:** I ask because it seems so few writers in contemporary literature use myth in their storytelling. Or at least not as many as I would like to read.

**NG:** Mythology tends to be what religion decays into. A sort of second stage religion. Or it's the bits of religion that won't get you shot or harmed if you don't take them seriously enough. There's Jewish mythology, there's Christian mythology, there's Islamic mythology. All of these things sort of accreted around the edge. Nobody is going to call for you to be killed if you don't take the Gospel of the Infancy of Christ seriously.

Which is an awful lot of fun, and I haven't read the new Anne Rice book [*Christ the Lord: Out of Egypt*] but I think she did actually use the Gospel of the Infancy of Christ. At one point a kid gets pushed off the roof and Jesus gets blamed. So he brings the kid back to life so that he can say, "It wasn't Jesus, it was that other kid over there," and then he lets him die again. And then there's a long sequence where Jesus just kills people a lot. They piss him off, so Jesus smites them and they die. To the point where Mary turns to Joseph and says, "If he's going to keep killing people like this, we're going to have to stop him from going out of the house." It's such a great line to find in an apocryphal Bible. How could anyone get from that Jesus to the guy in the New Testament? But obviously, that was the mythological Jesus. They loved the idea of the guy who was forever smiting—a schoolteacher starts to swipe him around the ear because he doesn't learn his lesson and aahhhhh!

Given that we're living in a universe in which religions and mythologies and semi-imaginary things, depending on where you're standing, the level of imaginariness. . . . There are definitely people who look at the entirety of what's going on in the world today as a couple of people fighting over whose imaginary friend likes them better. And then you've got people who say,

"No, no, this isn't an imaginary friend, he's actually the real thing. But that guy over there, he's an imaginary friend." And it's huge and it's responsible for an enormous amount of worry and difficulty and it's why I'm not allowed to travel with eight ounces of shampoo. I'm allowed four ounces. I'm going to have to pour away half of my shampoo before I can put it in my quart bag and put it in my carryon. Which is really bizarre.

And that's because of people arguing over things that many people regard as imaginary. Chiefly, gods, religions, and national boundaries, which are absolutely imaginary. They're completely notional. They don't tend to exist. As soon as you pull back half a mile and look down at the Earth there are no national boundaries. There aren't even any national boundaries when you get down and walk around. They're just imaginary lines we draw on maps.

I don't know where I got to from that. It was more sort of a rant. I just get fascinated by people who assume that things that are imaginary have no relevance to their lives. Things like mythology have no real relationship to what happens to them day by day. There. End rant. Sorry.

**JC:** What's up next? You have *Stardust* and *Beowulf.*

**NG:** They're editing *Stardust* currently. Editing is where I tend to hold my breath a lot. While something is being shot, you tend not to hold your breath. Everyone's just making a film, what will be will be. In the editing phase, there is so much that can wrong. Everyone is so close to it. They showed me a scene when I was in London the other day, and it was the opening scene of the movie. We got to the end, and I said, okay, you have to put back a lot of the stuff you cut down. They said, "Well, we're really concerned about pace." "That's fine, but what you shot was the absolute minimum needed to tell the world that Dunstan and this girl at the faerie market really like each other, really fancy each other. He's besotted with her, she's really taken with him, and she's given him this flower, and now they're sneaking into a caravan in order to get up close and personal. And that information was what you had. You actually trimmed that down for the purposes of pace and speed and now what it looks like is she must be the market slag because they meet and nip off for a quick one." And they actually had the incredibly had the good grace to hang their heads and say, "Oh my god, we hadn't thought of it that way, but you're right." I very much hope that in the next edit, they expand it again.

Having said that, I also know that they spent an interesting few weeks doing things like, they had a version of the film where the opening of the film is a flashback halfway through. They decided they should start with Tristran, stuff like that. Right now the film has at least three endings. From the point of view of those people who have endured *Lord of the Rings*, that's at least one ending too many. Which is in some ways my fault because in a book I can do lots of different endings. I do them fairly fast in an epilogue.

**JC:** Do you have enough distance so that if it's bad you can just walk away?
**NG:** Ish.

**JC:** Ish?
**NG:** No. No, not at all. I will lose sleep if it's bad. Obviously what I'm really hoping for is a film that is absolutely brilliant in every way, beautifully shot, wonderfully made, funny, lovely film I can be absolutely proud of every detail, and then comes out and is a huge and surprising box office hit of absolutely enormous proportions all around, but after seeing it I want people to still sidle over to me and say, "That *Stardust* movie was amazing, but the book was better." That's what I want.

**JC:** I'm sure all of your hopes will be fulfilled without question.
**NG:** That's much more honesty than you'll normally get from somebody getting interviewed about . . . probably, that's what all authors want. You want the most amazing movie in the world, but people coming up and saying, "But the book was better."

There's stuff they've done that is incredibly faithful, and there's stuff where they've gone on their own tack. Some of those things I liked, and some of those things I don't particularly like, and some of those things leads to moments like the amazing Ricky Gervais-Robert De Niro scene which is improvised and absolutely one of the funniest things I've ever seen and wouldn't have given up for the world.

**JC:** Any time you get Ricky Gervais in fancy dress . . .
**NG:** Ricky Gervais in a funny hat, yes. And his delivery is amazing.

**JC:** What about *Beowulf* and *Coraline?*
**NG:** *Coraline* I don't know much about, and that's not me trying to distance myself from a flop. Given the process, it's a stop-animation thing. I've seen some scripts. The ones that I've seen they've gone in and recorded. You've got Ian McShane and Dakota Fanning and Teri Hatcher, which is, um, okay. Songs by They Might Be Giants. It's also that knowledge that this is all going to take . . . once they've got all the voices done, probably right now they're

making sets. It's not like you can go in and watch a day's shooting. In a day's shooting, someone's going to go like (points).

*Beowulf* is really interesting. November 22, 2007 there will probably not be a human being alive in the western world alive who will not know *Beowulf* is out. I know what I've seen so far is a film that looks like Sony Playstation characters. In about a month or a bit less, I go out to Southern California to spend a few days with Roger Avery where we'll get to see a complete cut of the film. I know that *Polar Express* was like version 1.0 version of the technology and *Beowulf* started when it was version 3.0 of the technology and it keeps leaping forward while they're working on it. They're up to version 3.8 or 3.9, and it might hit 4.0 before it gets released. I don't think it's going to look like anything else. I'm enormously proud of the fact that I seem to have written the first animated film to be widely released in America aimed at adults. *Beowulf* is not a kid's film. I think we're only going to make PG-13 because Grendel's blood is green and the dragon's blood is golden. That actually allows us just to get PG-13 rather than the R.

It may be terrible. If *Beowulf* is a disaster, it's going to be a really interesting cool. Which oddly enough, I have to say I'd be perfectly happy with.

**JC:** Why do you have more distance to *Beowulf* than with *Stardust?* Because *Stardust* was yours first?

**NG:** I guess because in the case with *Beowulf,* I'm the one doing the damage to the original thing. I'm the one saying, this is how you turn it into this other thing. Let's turn it into a movie while being faithful, but without hesitating to do damage to the poem if it makes a better film.

With *Stardust,* I'm the one who made the equivalent of the original poem, and Matthew Vaughan is the one not hesitating to do damage to the book if it makes a better film, but I'm the one prepared to nervously start whimpering in the corner if too much damage is done. Yet really loving so much of what I've seen and feeling we're really in there with a chance of something magical happening.

# *Fragile Things*: An Interview with Neil Gaiman

## Eric Lorberer / 2006–07

From *Rain Taxi*. Reprinted by permission.

When last we sat down with the prolific Neil Gaiman, he had just published *American Gods*, a novel that introduced his already acclaimed storytelling skills to the realms of bestsellerdom. Since then he's released an astonishing array of work, including the young adult novel *Coraline*, the graphic novels *1602* and *The Sandman: Endless Nights*, the radio drama *Two Plays for Voices*, the short film *A Short Film About John Bolton*, the novel *Anansi Boys*, and, with longtime collaborator Dave McKean, the children's book *The Wolves in the Walls* and the feature length film *Mirrormask*.

Never one to rest, Gaiman has written the script for the eagerly anticipated film *Beowulf*, is currently writing *The Eternals* for Marvel Comics, and had two new releases this fall, giving us plenty to talk about. *Fragile Things: Short Fictions and Wonders* (William Morrow, $26.95) is a collection of thirty-one (or thirty-two, if you find the "hidden track") stories and poems, a delightful showcase for Gaiman's ability to range widely along the fantasy-postmodernity continuum; the book contains everything from genre pastiches to a strange conversation between the months of the year. *The Absolute Sandman Volume 1* (DC/Vertigo, $99) is a lavish hardcover omnibus of the first twenty issues of Gaiman's groundbreaking comic book series *The Sandman*; with a bevy of "extras" (including Gaiman's astonishingly in-depth proposal for the series) and with dramatic recoloring for this edition, the book is a fitting celebration of a title that thunderously displayed the vast literary potential of the comics medium.

An excerpt of this interview was published in the Winter 2006/2007 print edition of *Rain Taxi Review of Books*.

**Eric Lorberer:** I love the theme of fragility in the new book . . .
**Neil Gaiman:** Thank you! I love the fact that I have a publisher who would actually let me take a theme all the way from the design of the dust jacket into the heart of the book for a short story collection.

**EL:** Did you participate in the jacket design?
**NG:** Oh yes. I said I wanted the transparent paper that's been cursed by librarians and booksellers all over America. My editor Jennifer Brail and I sort of free-associated on fragile things we wanted on the cover. The only thing that I think didn't work as well as it could have done is the butterfly; we hadn't realized until we actually saw the whole thing finished that you sort of lose the brokenness—you fail to see that it's a dead butterfly on broken wings.

**EL:** Yes, it pretties up from the transparency. Of course, everyone will remove the dust jacket and investigate what's under there.
**NG:** That's true. And I got my *Little Nemo* panel in the frontispiece . . .

**EL:** I noticed! You know, it's partly the result of the time we live in, but the history of comics seems to be informing so much work right now.
**NG:** Part of that is, as you say, the time we live in, in that it's now available—I tell people now that this is the golden age, and they don't believe me. But I remember when if you wanted to read an old comic you had to hunt for it a bit. If you wanted to read *Little Nemo*, you couldn't because it wasn't there, or if you wanted to read some *Krazy Kat*, there was maybe one old *Krazy Kat* collection from the early seventies, and you were going to have to find that thing. These days everything's in print, everything's available.

**EL:** And more coming out by the month: *The Complete Peanuts, Dennis the Menace*, everything . . .
**NG:** Yes! I feel guilty—do you have the *Peanuts* collections? I keep buying them but I haven't read them yet.

**EL:** I love them—they're fun to plow through and see that whole world we know so well develop from scratch . . .
**NG:** I remember what it was like to read *Peanuts* anthologies; I would read them out on the grass during school sports events where it was compulsory to go. You know, a cricket game would be going on and I'm just lying in the

grass reading *Peanuts.* Now I have these giant anthologies and I should be doing the same thing: I should be going and lying out in the grass somewhere and reading these *Peanuts.*

**EL:** Highly recommended. But back to your "anthology" . . . it's a great reminder of how storytelling is really your highest value no matter what shape the work takes, but it made me wonder, especially in the wake of the novels, whether you work different things out in short form versus long.

**NG:** Yes, I think you do. If writing a novel is a year's exile to a foreign country, writing a short story is a weekend spent somewhere exotic. They're much more like vacations, more exciting and different, and you're off. "Look at me, I'm writing something that I will finish by tea time!" Having said that, there are some stories, like "Sun Bird," which took about two and a half years to write. And then there are stories in there, like "How to Talk to Girls at Parties," which basically I went off grumpily down to the bottom of the garden at about 11:00 in the morning and came back at about 5:00 in the afternoon with a finished short story. So both kinds of stories exist. But there's definitely a feeling with a short story that it's pure story telling. You're not really worried about theme. You're not going to stay with these characters long enough to live your life with them. And you have different kinds of relationships with them. There are characters in some short stories who exist as people, and there are other characters in different short stories who exist as purely literary constructs. You know, the young man in "Forbidden Brides of the Faceless Slaves in the Secret House of the Night of Dread Desire"—I probably got that right—is a literary construct, and *enjoys* being a literary construct. He has no life off-stage, whereas the young men in "How to Talk to Girls at Parties" were as near to being real human beings as I could possibly get them.

**EL:** Another interesting thing is that a lot of these stories seem to be penned by invitation: somebody is asking you for something. How does that affect the process?

**NG:** It adds an interesting level of desperation. In about fifteen days' time I have to hand in a nine-hundred-word ghost story to the *New York Times* for their Halloween edition. I have no idea what I want to say in a ghost story; it's not like I have any ghost stories sitting in my head desperately needing to be told. On the other hand, little engines have started clicking in the back of my head. What ghost-story ideas have I had over the years that I've never really explored, and also what concerns me right now? I would never be so crass—well I might be actually, because I can be crass—but I would never really want to be so crass as to say, "Okay, I think the war in Iraq is stupid, I think they went in on unverifiable and mistaken premises and have done nothing but make everything significantly worse, therefore I want to write a story about that"—but I could definitely see that being a concern, somehow feeding into what I write, even if the only person who can see the connection is me. Also, what's a nine-hundred-word story? At most we're looking at four pages of text. Therefore you have the kind of story—there's one in *Fragile Things* called "Other People"—which is almost a joke, a short short. It goes in, it does its job, and it gets out again. But I don't want to do a short short, I don't want to do something that feels insufficient, which means that I have to do something that's really compressed. How do I do something that is compressed but still has emotional weight? I have no idea. I may completely fuck up and fifteen days from now I may not have a story to hand in. But right now all I'm doing in the back of my head is chewing it over as a set of problems—and they're really good problems for a writer to have. If you give a writer a pile of blank paper and say you can write anything you like on any subject you want at any length you want, you will probably never get anything at all, whereas if you have nine hundred words to write, and it's fiction that is somehow op-ed fiction, and it needs to tie in with Halloween . . . okay, those are my constraints, that's where I now need to start building something.

**EL:** Doing something for the *New York Times* gives you a certain picture of an audience. Do you think about audience when you are doing other things or things for yourself?

**NG:** I don't think I do think of audience. I might think of audience just in terms of age. And the *Times* audience presupposes a certain level of literacy. But no, I can't imagine there would be any real change. I don't know. It's this weird implicit. The only big difference is you're writing for somebody who didn't pick it up to read you—this is somebody on the subway, this is somebody in a taxi, this is somebody sitting at their desk, this is somebody on a plane, and they're just reading the *Times* because they're reading the *Times*. They didn't buy it to read me. They also probably didn't buy it in the expectation that they were going to be forced to re-read something—so I probably would try and write something that would deliver most of what it had on a first reading. In *Fragile Things* I have at least one short story, "Bitter Grounds," which really doesn't give up very much on a first reading. If you go back to the beginning and start again, figures of speech or whatever will start assuming significance and the whole shape of the story and who the hero is and what's going on will change.

**EL:** You talked earlier about going down to the garden to write, and I know you write a lot while you travel. Can you write anywhere?

**NG:** Yes. But it's easier to write somewhere where there isn't much of an Internet.

**EL:** Fewer places like that these days.

**NG:** I know. Anywhere that I can't check my email is a good place to write!

**EL:** There were a few stories in *Fragile Things* I found particularly intriguing. I really loved the ones for the Tori Amos albums . . .

**NG:** Oh, good! They've been getting odd reviews; one review said, "It was a great short story collection apart from the poems and the Tori Amos-related nonsense." I thought, well, at least one of those Tori Amos-related nonsense pieces was picked up for a Best of the Year Anthology, so it can't be total nonsense.

**EL:** No, no! In fact, I bet this wasn't the one that was picked up, but the one for *Strange Little Girls* is very hermetic, very dense, very complicated, and yet utterly fascinating if you know the album, since it's a covers album that tries to reinterpret these very male songs from different kinds of female points of view. And then your fictions add another level of interpretation. I wondered how that worked—how involved were you with Tori's process?

**NG:** I was involved with *Strange Little Girls* more than any other Tori Amos album, in that I was one of the people who suggested songs, and I was actually the person who went off to the toilet while we were picking songs and came back with a Cindy Sherman anthology saying we could do this . . . and then I think it was Tori who said I should write a short story for each of them. So I did. And I loved, again, the weird and wonderful constraints of writing short stories, some of which were *really* short: you're looking at one-hundred-word pen portraits of fictional women. I think my favorite of them is "Raining Blood," where you're given two contrasting lives and you can pick. Really I just loved the idea of just creating something where each short story is a person and it's just a little fragile moment. Again, these fragile things.

**EL:** So were these different personas coming from both of you or . . .

**NG:** No, they were her. After I came up with the Cindy Sherman idea, she went off with her makeup artist and then sent me photographs of these women—she had an idea of who was singing each song. So the photos would come in and I would sit there and go, I know your story and I know your story . . . you I want to talk to and find out what's going on with you! Sometimes I had a different point of view to hers, and that's fine. I'd write my story anyway.

**EL:** You also have stories set in the world of *The Matrix*, Sherlock Holmes . . . do you like playing in other people's—
**NG:** Sandboxes? Actually that's what it feels like. Playing in other people's backyards. *The Matrix* was sort of an invitation before there ever was a Matrix; the film had been made but it hadn't been shown. It was one of those odd, funny, weird moments where somebody phones you up and says they've done a movie and will you write a short story about it for their web-site. And I thought I was being really clever because I didn't really want to write a story about somebody's movie for a website, so I told my agent that I would happily do it for a ridiculous amount of money—and I thought I named an amount of money so ridiculous that they would say, "Oops, sorry, that's our entire budget." Instead, they said great—you've got three weeks! I thought, "Oh, damn!" Then I thought we should have asked them for twice the amount of money. But then I had my idea for the story, and I loved my idea. And I even got to write—I had read the script for *The Matrix* and there were a couple of things that hadn't quite made sense for me, so I sort of tried to change them a bit: instead of human beings being used as batteries, for example, I had them used for information processing, brains hung out in parallel which seemed, somehow, to make a little more sense.

**EL:** Possibly my favorite piece in the book is "The Problem of Susan," a beautiful, beautiful story. I'm fascinated on a couple of levels. I love how you take Lewis to task in it, but I also think it's a kind of dissertation about how we process children's literature.
**NG:** Right—I think people who read that story as Neil telling off C. S. Lewis are kind of missing the point; people who talk about it being about how we process children's literature are closer to it. The actual problem of Susan in the C. S. Lewis books is a moment that I find deeply problematic . . . you have this weird moment that just seems wrong. And if you're a kid and you run into that you're going, "No, no, that's not right." She was a queen of Narnia. Once a queen of Narnia always a queen of Narnia, she must know that. Yet, just by dint of liking invitations to parties and lipstick and nylons, she's being forbidden paradise. And then there's this point where you grow up and you go, so hang on, let me get this right: everybody else is killed in a train crash,

the entire family is killed except for her, and what does *that* mean? I was shown some reply by C. S. Lewis to some kid saying, that wasn't fair what you did to Susan. And he said, "Ah, she still has time. She's back on earth. She's not dead yet." So that gave me the idea of creating a professor who had been inspired by Susan's character and basing it around her, and talking about how we relate to children's literature and what children's literature means. What sexuality means in terms of children's literature. What being an adult means. What it would mean to have to go and identify these bodies. All of that stuff.

Plus it was enormously fun for me. One of the moments in the Narnia books that I've always found oddest is Pauline Baynes's illustration of Aslan in conversation with the White Witch in the very first book, because he's standing up on his hind legs with his forepaws behind his back, and they're off talking. That's a very strange thing for a lion to be doing. It seems to me that one of the most interesting things about God as a concept, if you decide to believe in God, is that God's ways are unknowable. And God obviously, look at the world around you, does or is responsible for some terrible, terrible, awful things. A young girl kidnapped and kept in the darkness and sexually abused. The deaths of six million Jews. A mudslide that buries a village. All of these things. If God is doing the good stuff, he's got to be doing that stuff too. If people are standing up there saying, my football team just won with help from God, then obviously God just pissed over the other team. So I'm thinking about that and this analogy running through the Narnia books, the idea that Aslan is the incarnation of God and he's not a tame lion, everyone keeps saying he's not a tame lion . . . except that he is a tame lion! He's really nice! He doesn't kill anybody, except possibly some really evil witches who kind of deserve it. Lions, generally, especially not tame lions, are not people you want to go off with, because they could eat you. They can turn on you and they can make life really, really bad for you.

**EL:** They won't keep their paws behind their backs.
**NG:** They're not people—they're lions and they're dangerous! It's worth remembering that Gods, whether they exist or not, are not tame either. And that's one of the other things I wanted the story to be about, the idea that there is an untamed thing. Somehow I thought I could get that all into a short story, and I'm glad it worked for you. I wanted it to be problematic; I wanted you to reach the end of that story and for it to itch. I like the fact that you can find essays online that are replies to that story; I like that academics have started using that story as a basis for papers, because that story, if it's successful, should irritate. It should get under your skin and be something that needs scratching.

**EL:** Another recent book that problematizes our relationship to children's literature is Alan Moore's *Lost Girls* (reviewed in our Fall 2006 Online Edition). I'm about to make us feel old because it's probably a couple decades ago, but I remember an interview in which you praised a book that I also liked quite a lot, an academic study by Linda Williams called *Hard Core.* I wondered if that paraliterary genre, the pornographic, was something that you ever—

**NG:**—wanted to explore? I'd love to write some porn, but I don't know if I have the right engines. When I was a young man and I was tempted to write porn, imaginary parents would appear over my shoulder and read what I was writing; just about the point that I managed to banish the imaginary parents, real children would lean over my shoulder and read what I was writing. Being English, the one pornographic story I that have written— called "Tastings" in *Smoke and Mirrors,* the story collection before this— was deeply embarrassing. It took about four years to write: I would write a page, stop, exit that document with my ears burning and my face red, and then it would be six or eight months before I'd go back and write another page. There's also a little bit of sex in a story called, "How Do You Think It Feels Up There?" But I love the idea of writing sex, and I think Alan found a really good model in Victorian porn. There was a period when I was reviewing porn as a book reviewer—I was reviewing everything, but porn was one of the things I was reviewing—and Victorian porn was far and away my favorite. You knew that if a book was written by Anonymous and had a title like "The Oyster" it was going to be fun, because Victorian pornography was just cooler. There was so much societal repression and yet the porn was fun and kinky in all sorts of really odd and interesting ways. The last time I was actually in a hotel and flicked up a porn movie, there was this horrible feeling that these people were really just going through the motions. They had their list of twelve things that had to happen, and they were just ticking them off, and it was joyless.

**EL:** Well, hotel porn is the lowest common denominator, in that it strives to be pleasing for everybody.

**NG:** I know. But joyless hotel porn! I think for me, it would be more fun to try and write a really good porn movie than it would be to do a porn comic or even a novel—although the joy of doing porn in prose, in truth, is that people do so much more of the work in their heads than they think they do. There are people who have taken me to task for writing an explicitly sexual scene in *Stardust*—which doesn't exist, but they bring enough of themselves to that scene that they read it as hardcore porn. There are a couple of scenes in *American Gods* that I've been told off for as well. One of the most interesting is a supposedly hardcore gay sex scene between a taxi driving Ifrit and an Arabic salesman in New York. And again, I look at it and I think that's really not hardcore sex—you're bringing yourself to it to make it hardcore. Which is one of those things people can do much more with prose than they can with anything illustrative or in film.

I found my biggest problem with *Lost Girls* simply to be, at the end of the day, the Robin Williams paradox: he pointed out that human males have enough blood to run either an erection or a brain, but not both. And I kept finding myself loving *Lost Girls* because it was Alan Moore, because it was so dense, because it was so brilliant . . . I was running the brain the entire time. It was not a one-handed read; it was much more like, "Whoa, there's ten eight-page chapters, and this one is reflective of that, which thematically has this going on, and now it's becoming a meta-fictional construct in which fictional characters are discussing pornographic fictional characters doing things that are obscene and illegal, and yet do not actually exist. Oh my god, this is so cool!"

**EL:** Two people who have pulled it off in recent years, I think, are Chip Delany of course, and also Nicholson Baker in *The Fermata.* Have you read that?

**NG:** Oh, I'm intimately familiar with that book—I wrote a film script for *The Fermata* for Robert Zemeckis! That is a fascinating book, taking a thirteen-year-old's masturbatory fantasy and then creating it into an adult sexual experience. Chip Delany, I have to say from a pornographic point of view, I read it as science fiction. I loved *The Mad Man*, for example, but you read it as if he's turned on by flowers—it's not only gay sex, but it's really dirty gay sex, dirty in the sense of unwashed and grimy. Okay, I can understand that for the person writing this, this is erotica, but for me . . .

**EL:** Well, that book is more about transgression than arousal. But they really work as pieces of writing.

**NG:** They're magnificent pieces of writing! I think that if I really were going to try and do pornography, what would fascinate me about that would be walking that fine line between . . . I remember once—I wish I knew what it was called because I don't—but about sixteen years ago, on a book tour, there was some porno movie on—this was back when they used to have little TV top units to flip through the channels, and you would get five minutes of the movie free before the scramble. I didn't even know it was a porno movie; it was just the most interesting looking thing on. So I pressed the pay button and carried on watching it and kept getting really irritated when these characters would stop the plot to fuck, because I was actually interested in the plot—the fucking was getting in the way. I think the challenge is creating something, as Baker did in *The Fermata* very brilliantly, where the sex is intrinsic—where you never feel that you're stopping something because of the sex. Everything has to be intrinsic plot-wise in the same way, to use the Linda Williams analogy but to move it on a bit, as musicals—in old musicals, like in an old Cole Porter musical, you get the action, then they do a song, which reflects a moment—everything stops while that is being sung—and then you restart. These days in most musicals, the plot keeps moving through the song. I think it would be nice if someone constructed some pornography where the sex continues to propel you through the story.

**EL:** Maybe a pornographic musical?
**NG:** Who knows?

**EL:** Let's talk about your comics for a bit. I know you still have your hand in the game . . .
**NG:** Yes, I'm doing a comic right now called *The Eternals.*

**EL:** Are you intentionally keeping active in the field despite the lure of writing prose, or . . .?
**NG:** I was very uncomfortable with the way that some people, particularly journalists who like very, very simple stories, were starting to view my move from comics to films to best-selling novels . . . it was resembling those little evolutionary maps too much, where you see the fish, and then it can walk, and then it's an ape and then it gets up on its hind legs and finally it is a man. I didn't like that. I didn't like the fact that there was something rather amphibious about me—at least in their heads—back when I was writing comics. So I like continuing to write comics, if only because it points out that I haven't just started to walk upright or left the water. Actually I don't think it's any kind of progression. It's just a different kind of story told in a different kind of way.

**EL:** Are you still looking to find challenges there?
**NG:** I'm very accepting now of the fact that I'm not trying nor do I particularly want to do something on the scale of *Sandman.* I already did *Sandman.*

*1602* was fun, because I got to go, okay, as a kid I loved what Stan and Jack did. I wanted to give some of that amount of fun to people and give me some of that fun back. With *The Eternals* it's much more—okay, I love Jack Kirby, I love even the barking mad Kirby, and I've always wanted to do something with Kirby characters. A really cool thing about *The Eternals* is that Jack never really got to finish it, and then it got badly incorporated into the Marvel universe. The guys at Marvel came to me to ask if I could fix it, could I at least try to take what Jack did and incorporate it slightly better into the Marvel universe so these characters had value. I thought, "That's a fun challenge, sure!"

**EL:** People sometimes say, when they see our graphic novel coverage—
**NG:** I love your graphic novel coverage by the way.

**EL:** Thank you! It gladdens me because I think a lot of non-graphic novel readers are interested in the medium and want to learn more about it, but they feel a bit daunted by it . . . our feeling is that these are just interesting books, as worth reading as any others.
**NG:** That's so funny because the reason I went into comics was much the other way around: I looked at the world of books and just went, "Oh my gosh, if I'm writing novels, I'm on the same shelves as Jane Austen and Charles Dickens and Petronius—whereas with comics, they've only been doing them for a hundred years, and there's stuff that nobody's done before. I think I'll go off and do some of the stuff no one's ever done before."

**EL:** One of those things was obviously *Sandman*—newly celebrated in *The Absolute Sandman Volume 1*. One of the neat "extras" contained therein are some of your original sketches . . . do you often draw out your ideas when writing comics?
**NG:** Yes, but normally no one gets to see them but me—they're not actually done for other people to see!

**EL:** Well, it's fun they were included here. The book also presents your detailed script for the award-winning issue "A Midsummer Night's Dream"—an amazing piece of writing. In the middle of the script, you suddenly have this moment of self-reflection, saying, "This is a fascinating comic to write . . . either it'll work really well, or it'll be a major disaster." What was your sense of the risks you were taking at the time?

**NG:** I have to say that I am somebody who quite likes major disasters! That was my feeling yesterday—I got to see a raw version of *Beowulf*, which won't be out for a year. I said either this was going to be the biggest movie of next year or it's going to be one of those things people compare to *Ishtar*. Either way, I'm very, very happy.

**EL:** And luckily Elaine May's other films are pretty great.
**NG:** They are! In fact I almost saw *Ishtar* the other day, because I've never actually seen it. I know it's supposed to be a heinous disaster.

**EL:** I'm in the same boat. But back to the book: besides all the fun extras, the issues have been recolored and the result is really dazzling—was this done simply for technical reasons, or to suit some vision that hadn't made it into the original series?
**NG:** It was done mostly because we were never happy with the early coloring, but there was no way to fix things back then. It was also done because stuff that looked okay printed on absorbent paper with the technology we had in 1988 looked progressively worse as time went on—you know, the books have now been in print for twenty years, and we are now printing on these amazing presses on glossy white paper.

**EL:** It looks fantastic. One last question for you, Neil: at the start of the interview I mentioned how *Fragile Things* made me realize what an important theme fragility was in your earliest work—which *Absolute Sandman* absolutely confirms. Has revisiting these early issues caused you to have any new thoughts or realizations about the work?
**NG:** It's very, very strange. Reading *The Sandman* opus again, it really felt . . . like it was done by somebody else. In many ways, for the first time ever, I wasn't reading it thinking what was in my head when I wrote this, I was just reading what was on the paper—which you don't get to do often. The main thing I wound up feeling was that it was very much . . . how do I put this? . . . That *Sandman* was very much part of the oeuvre. Occasionally I run into people who've just read my novels, and they'll talk as if that's the only thing I do, and I'll think, "Well, actually, *Sandman* isn't that at all, and it's the biggest thing I've ever done"—it was two thousand pages long, there's a million words of writing there—"so if you really want to understand what I write, you need to read it." So part of the joy of doing *Absolute Sandman* now is getting it into a shape I feel comfortable putting in front of people. And I'm

really pleased about the reaction to Sam Keith's art. People are saying, "Oh, I hadn't realized the level of cartooning, the level of what he was actually doing" . . . and I'm thinking, "Well of course you didn't realize it, because there was a big wad of flat purple across it!"

# Lunching in the Graveyard

## Pádraig ó Méalóid / 2008

From *Forbidden Planet*. Reprinted by permission.

*Here's a very special early Christmas present for our readers: Pádraig Ó Méalóid (who is rapidly becoming our Roving Interviewer At Large, following his excellent chats with Todd Klein and Alan Moore) met one of my very favorite writers Neil Gaiman during Neil's recent busy tour (does Neil do any other kind of tour?) for his new* Graveyard Book. *While poor Neil had to try and combine actually getting to eat some lunch with an interview, Pádraig talked to him about his career,* Miracleman, *the importance of his blog, conventions,* Doctor Who, Stardust, Neverwhere *and whether one should have Wasabi or mushy peas with chips. Over to Pádraig and Neil:*

This interview took place in the Clarence Hotel in Dublin City at lunchtime on Thursday the 30th of October 2008. This was literally Neil's lunch, and I got to ask him questions while he had a spare half hour between other engagements. Neil looked very tired, no doubt due in large part to his partying until the wee small hours the previous night in Manchester with Leah Moore and John Reppion, amongst others. I was suffering from a very heavy cold, so between us there are bits of the interview that, even after repeated listening, I'm still not sure what we were trying to say. Still, here it is, in all its glory . . .

**Neil Gaiman [entering the room]:** Leah and John send their love. They told me that Mel [Melinda Gebbie] is coming to stay with you.
**Pádraig Ó Méalóid:** Mel is coming over for a week. She's coming over next Monday, and she's doing a talk, so I get to do the interview with her as well.
 [Gestures to recording device on table] I mean, I've already got Alan [Moore] and I've got you on this, and my friend Catie [CE] Murphy—I was going to mention her later, she's doing a comic, she's done a lot of

fantasy writing, fantasy novels, and now she has a comic coming out from the Dabel Brothers soon called *Take a Chance*.

**NG:** Did I get given a comic by her?
**PÓM:** I don't think you did.
**NG:** I'm trying to think if I . . . It may have been your friend in Kinsale?
**PÓM:** Kate, Kate Sheehy. I'm meeting Kate in about an hour, off the train, so . . . She was kinda cursing herself 'cause she was going to be here as my lovely assistant, or something like that, you know. I presume your day is entirely filled from here right to the end, so there's no fear of squeezing in a cup of tea with myself and Kate at any stage?
**NG:** No, Cormac [from Repforce Ireland, who was looking after Neil's diary for the day] has built this thing—you are my lunch . . .

**PÓM:** Yeah, I know, I feel bad about that.
**NG:** That's alright, I can talk to you while eating chips.

**PÓM:** Yeah, that's cool. Anyway, I'm now officially going to start.
**NG:** OK, start your official interview! And this is for the FPI blog, the one that I've linked to in the past?

**PÓM:** Yes, for Joe Gordon's thing, and Joe says thank you very much. The Todd Klein interview I did that you put a link to, I sent a mail to the two of them saying, "We got Gaimaned!"
**NG:** I think they can normally tell when they've got Gaimaned.

**PÓM:** Yeah, 'cause it goes Boink! Todd said he noticed an immediate spike in the sales, the orders for the prints.
**NG:** Todd is so nice. Every time I mention it he gets . . .

**PÓM:** Yes, I imagine so.
**NG:** It's the strange thing about a blog, though. You kind of imagine that you're writing to an audience of people who are reading you day by day, and the truth is that you're not. You're writing for an audience of people who are coming in and going out, and some of them are reading you day by day, but some of them are going to catch up every Friday, on what you've done the previous week, and one of the things that I've noticed is, if I mention something I should probably, if it's something important that I want to mention, and I want people to know about, I will try and

remember to mention it three times over a period of about three weeks, because at that point I can catch a lot of people . . .

**PÓM:** I used to just drop in and out myself, and then somebody would say, "There's this on Neil's blog . . ."
**NG:** And they you get caught up for a few weeks, and then you drift out because it's the way that it goes.

**PÓM:** Well eventually what I did was I just put it in as a LiveJournal feed, which is what I should have done all along. It's much easier, 'cause I don't have to do it, LiveJournal does it for me, and it's the one thing I religiously look at every day. I don't necessarily read everything . . .
**NG:** I had to explain to the people at HarperCollins that we used to have one point four million unique visitors a month to the blog, and then over the last few years that's dropped to about four hundred thousand, and they were going, "We've lost a million readers," and I said, "No, no, no, we really haven't. Here's LiveJournal, where you now have seventeen thousand, you know, there's seventeen thousand nine hundred on LiveJournal subscribed to it. You've got this RSS feed here, you've got this RSS feed there, and they're showing up as one hit, but then they're feeding it to another fifty thousand people here, and a hundred thousand people there."

**PÓM:** So you really have to go and search all the bits and pieces to see where it's all going?
**NG:** You kind of do, and then you don't worry, you try not to think about it!

**PÓM:** Well, somebody somewhere presumably gets to do it. Actually, this is something I was going to ask you about later on. You are very successful, you get a lot of hits on your blog, people tend to know what you're doing, and what you're on about, and I think you said something about when you were at Eastercon, that you felt you were . . .
**NG:** [As his lunch arrives] Thank you.

**PÓM:** That is the poshest fish and chips I've ever seen!
**NG:** It's like a work of art.

**PÓM:** Isn't it?
**NG:** [Pointing to a container with a green substance in it] You're going, "That could be mushy peas, it could be Wasabi, it could be . . . How will we ever know?"

**PÓM:** [Carrying on with the question] I think you said you felt that there was a really nice, a really great con going on in the next room that you couldn't go to, or something like that. You weren't being let loose in the wild, kinda.

**NG:** Well, there's definitely . . . I think, I mean the con in the next room, I think I was talking more about the fact that, honestly, more about the con experience than anything else. It's the point where you look around and you realize you are Jumbo the Mighty Elephant that everybody's coming to the zoo to see, and everyone's getting a wonderful day out at the zoo but you.

And as a zoo attraction, it's not a bad thing, it's just a thing. I miss...I miss conventions, I really do. I would love to be able to go to a convention and people say, when I say that, people say, "Why don't you come to our convention? It's a lovely little convention, and there's only a hundred people there," and stuff like that, and I used to believe that. Every time people used to say, "Come to our convention. We've never had more than a hundred people there, and it's lovely, and it's just like little conventions, and we'll all treat you like family," and I'd say, "Great." And I would come to them, and then nine hundred people would show up, and they'd be going, "We've never had this many people here before," and I'd start feeling like a bowling ball on a rubber sheet.

**PÓM:** I know exactly what you mean, yeah. It's the black hole thing.
**NG:** Yeah.

**PÓM:** It just completely distorts the space-time continuum of the con. At the beginning of this month we were at NewCon in Northampton, and because we were there, and because of one or two other things, Alan Moore and Melinda [Gebbie] came along, and they made an appearance here and there, which I think had people's necks craning all weekend, but everyone was very nice, and actually didn't go near him at all, but obviously he could not have set foot near the place if anyone knew he was going to be there, and even at that I think he was quite nervous.

**NG:** You would have had thousands of people, just coming in.

**PÓM:** I got to introduce him to Paul Cornell. I was very pleased to introduce the two *Captain Britain* writers . . .

It's unusual in a way for a writer to be the victim of their own success, because they're generally invisible. You're not. I mean, you do a lot of touring, you're doing a big tour for this, you're going to spend the day doing interviews . . .

**NG:** True, but only up to a point, because if you talk to Cormac about how many authors he has come through who tour, he will tell you how many authors he's had in this month, and it's not like authors don't tour, it's that authors don't—you know, I was in Manchester last night, and they sell out a six-hundred-and-fifty seat university hall, there's this giant monstrous signing afterwards, it's all bizarre, and at some point the head of the program who was there comes down completely baffled, he says, "We didn't get a turnout like this for Martin Amis," and it's not that Martin Amis doesn't tour and doesn't do the media . . .

**PÓM:** I suppose it's that we're all aware that you're touring, where we're not always aware of others. Sometimes someone says, "Did you know such-and-such was in town signing last week?" and no, I didn't, obviously because we're not all reading their blog or wherever it's being mentioned.
**NG:** That's why I love the blog, though, because I'm not the victim—if victim is the right word—of whether or not a shop knows how to promote my appearance any more. I'm not, I don't actually have to worry as much as other authors do about whether a publisher is taking out the advertising and promoting the book.

**PÓM:** You're kinda looking after that one yourself.
**NG:** I'm certainly... I have an amount of control over my destiny from the blog.

**PÓM:** I see exactly what you're saying.
**NG:** Last night I wound up being the first author at Manchester University ever to have a backing band, well, a support band, and, for the end of my signing, they'd more or less been vamping it for as long as they were allowed to, and I went down and made a guest appearance at the Jonathan Coulton gig.

**PÓM:** With a tambourine, I believe?
**NG:** With a tambourine. I did the second verse of "Creepy Doll" . . .

**PÓM:** Which is what? It's a song they do?
**NG:** It's a Jonathan Coulton song. It's lovely, it's like a little horror . . . it's a Stephen King story about somebody with a creepy doll that always follows you. You buy an old house and it's haunted by this thing and you throw it on the fire and it's back the next morning. So. . . And of course you know that because you've read the blog already.

And in the evening I was talking to Jonathan after this was all over, and we were talking about the fact that . . . Johnathan was saying, "If I was a medium successful person, when my contract with the record label is up in music, I cannot understand any reason why anybody would ever sign another contract. Why give that percentage of control and that percentage of your income to a record company who needed to exist as a gateway, but why if you don't need a gateway?" There is no reason to have an intermediary between you and your readers, or you and your listeners. And while I like not being bothered with so many details, and letting people do their jobs, there are places where I feel like I'm now a safety net. Would *The Graveyard Book* have spent two weeks at number one on the children's list if I had been, when it came out? Probably not, not with the blog, because everybody who wanted it knew that it was coming out.

**PÓM:** And another thing I noticed on the blog is that you were getting an awful lot of feedback from people about its availability, its unavailability, and you seemed to be able to chase that up in real time, as it was happening.
**NG:** As it was happening.

**PÓM:** There are some misunderstandings that I see that people at Borders are having, but I suppose that's par for the course.
**NG:** The trouble with the internet is people don't read the actual thing, they read what they think they've been told.

**PÓM:** I'm going to run along, because I see we're already fifteen minutes in and I've a couple of things . . .
**NG:** Go for it.

**PÓM:** How was China? What were you doing in China?
**NG:** Researching a book. I decided it was time to, I really decided it was time to step outside my comfort zone, and it's been twenty years since I did a nonfiction book, and the last nonfiction book I did was, um . . .

**PÓM:** Was that *Ghastly Beyond Belief*?
**NG:** *Don't Panic, The Hitchhiker's Guide to the Galaxy* book.
Then I thought, I want to do a nonfiction book, so I'm doing a nonfiction book about me going to China, and about Monkey, and about Buddhism, and about seventh-century history and sixteenth-century literature, and just, mostly it was that thing where nobody is waiting for it,

and nobody particularly wants a book by me about China, and it seemed like a really good reason to write one.

**PÓM:** Mind you I see that you are—having started off as far as I can see as a comics' writer and then becoming a novelist you've kind of gone back to being a comics' writer. You're doing a Batman story for DC, and are you meant to be writing the prequel, *The Sandman* prequel story? I know you said something about doing that before.

**NG:** I don't know if that will ever happen. Maybe. It's weird, because I talk to people who will tell me with a straight face that I stopped writing comics in 1996, and I say, "OK, let's go to this century. Since 2001, I'd written two adult novels, or had published, two adult novels—*Anansi Boys* and *American Gods*; two children's novels—*Coraline* and *The Graveyard Book;* two major children's picture books . . ."

**PÓM:** That'd be, what? *Wolves in the Walls* and . . .
**NG:** *Wolves in the Walls* and . . .

**PÓM:** *The Day I Swapped My Dad for Two Goldfish*?
**NG:** No, actually that was 1998, so, let's say the *MirrorMask* book. I've done two and a half movies—*Beowulf* and *MirrorMask,* and *Stardust* is my half. And I've done three graphic novel-length works—*The Eternals, 1602,* and *Sandman: Endless Nights.*

**PÓM:** That's a fair body of work just for the past eight years, mind you.
**NG:** But it doesn't seem to me that it's substantially weighted against comics. In terms of page-count that's three books, each of which was more or less novel-length, and about the same amount of work it would have taken me to write a novel, and, you know, hearing people describe my career to me as if it was one of those weird little charts where you start off coming out of the ocean and then you become a monkey, and then, you know . . .

**PÓM:** I think people can only see you as what they see as the primary part of your output. You were a comics writer and maybe other things, and now you're a novelist and maybe other things, and possibly that's it, you know.
I was going to ask you, what did you make of *Stardust* the movie?
**NG:** I enjoyed it. It wasn't the film that I would have made if I'd set out to make a *Stardust* movie, but I thought it was a lovely *Stardust* movie. I could quite happily watch a completely different *Stardust* movie, if that makes

sense. It was very much a "this is a lovely *Stardust* movie." I guess I felt about it, it's weird, because I suppose—with *Coraline* in May, over here, you'll get the Henry Sellick *Coraline* movie which, from what I've seen of it so far, I've very much enjoyed. In May on Broadway you'll see the first performances of the Stephin Merritt *Coraline* which in terms of plot hews, as far as I can tell, exactly to the book, but he's doing some weird and wonderful things, including casting a fifty-year-old lady as Coraline, and casting a man as the other mother, and stuff, and I don't see either of those as being, "This is now *Coraline* legitimized, this is what this is," I see them both as versions, with every bit as much legitimacy as the Irish Puppet Theatre version.

**PÓM:** I know you weren't happy with *Neverwhere*, the TV series . . .?
**NG:** I wasn't.

**PÓM:** Are they remaking *Neverwhere*?
**NG:** There's a film that's meant to be made. I mean, as far as I'm concerned, I remade *Neverwhere* when I wrote the novel. The whole point of the novel was, "No, this is what I meant."

**PÓM:** Certainly the novel was far more satisfactory. The TV series wasn't bad, but it was of its time . . .
**NG:** It wasn't just of its time. Honestly, they could have, its time, it was of its time in the world in which it was up against *X-Files*. It was of its time in a world in which I am saying, "We need to be forty-five minutes long, it needs to be shot on film or it'll look like crap," and they're going [adopts posh BBC accent], "My dear boy, we're the BBC, we've been doing things like this for years. It's like *Doctor Who*, and that's twenty-eight minutes long and shot on video. That's what people love. And by the way, in order to accommodate that we've thrown out half your script . . ." You know it was, I wasn't happy with it, I felt like it had the wrong director, and it needed somebody who was going to say, "It needs to be forty-five minutes long . . ." I loved the fact that when *Doctor Who* came back it was forty five minutes long and shot on film, or looked like it.

**PÓM:** Are you . . . there are persistent rumors that you are going to write a *Doctor Who* story?
**NG:** There definitely are.

**PÓM:** And is there any truth to those?
**NG:** Well, there's truth in the fact that there are rumors.

**PÓM:** Well, that would be a good thing. You know that David Tennant has just announced he's stepping down at the end of next year?

**NG:** So I heard. I was rather sad, 'cause I'd emailed, we were trying to figure out who was going to host my Halloween event for tomorrow, and about a week ago I had this brilliant idea, and I emailed Paterson Joseph and said, "Why don't you host my event, 'cause that will drive people mad, 'cause there's *Doctor Who* rumors about you and there's *Doctor Who* rumors about me, and if you host the event, nobody in the world, and then we don't have to mention anything, but nobody in the world will think, they will feel there has to be something . . ." and I got a thing back from Pat saying he would love to but he's actually right now in Africa filming for the BBC on something.

I mean, he is thrilled by the *Doctor Who* rumors, but I think mostly thrilled because it's suddenly taken him from an actor who nobody really quite knew who he was, you'd have to say, "Well, he was the guy in the Numberwang sketch, or he was the guy from *Peepshow*, or he was . . ." to people going, "Yes, Paterson Joseph, he could be the next *Doctor Who*," and so it's done amazing things for him.

**PÓM:** *Doctor Who* does seem to turn people into just enormous superstars.

I have to ask you the obligatory *Miracleman* question. At what stage is *Miracleman* at?

**NG:** Currently Todd McFarlane is suing me, claiming he owns all of *Miracleman,* and I am going, "You are mad, because as far as I can tell right now, neither of us owns anything of *Miracleman*; it is actually still owned completely by Mick Anglo, who is still alive, and who has asserted his copyright on it, and everything that Dez Skinn said back in *Warrior* days was apparently a lie, and this thing is Mick's, so I don't really see why, why are you suing me now, Todd?"

**PÓM:** I can't help thinking that Todd should just do the right thing and say, throw his hands up and say, no matter what happens, he will never come out the good guy on this one, and just walk away.

**NG:** Yes. I don't know why, it's like, it's all mad.

**PÓM:** The thing is, I think I'm doing a panel at Eastercon next year called "Who Owns *Miracleman*?" which is obviously what all this stuff is [pointing to a file folder on the table marked *Miracleman*] and I'm going to write an accompanying article that I've been promising to write for at least five years, and every time I look into it, it gets a little more complex.

**NG:** Well . . .

**PÓM:** It's very complex unless you go all the way back and say, "Mick Anglo owned it, and kept the rights to it."

**NG:** Yeah, and what was interesting is, there was a trail of lies spread chiefly, as far as I can tell—whether intentionally or unintentionally—by Dez Skinn.

**PÓM:** Thank you for that, for saying, "intentionally or unintentionally"!

**NG:** No, I think Dez made some assumptions about the law, I think there were things that he definitely told people at the time, and that history has proved to be untrue. The biggest one was simply that he'd obtained, you know, there was a version of events in which he had obtained the rights from the official receiver. Then we discovered that Miller & Son was, it never went bankrupt, it had simply been would up.

**PÓM:** The L. Miller properties had been sold to Alan Class, as far as I know, was one of the things I had heard said.

**NG:** No. There are many things that people have said. No, from everything that I can tell, it simply went into voluntary liquidation. It was wound up, and Mick owned *Miracleman* slash *Marvelman* before, during, and after. He held the copyrights on it. L. Miller and Son never made any claims to owning it or to having sold it.

**PÓM:** OK. I was always wondering that, even given that Mick Anglo created *Marvelman*, *Marvelman* was obviously, and was meant to be, almost an exact copy of Captain Marvel, who was of course a copy of Superman . . .

**NG:** Ah, now there it gets, you know, the trouble is, you have this weird magic world in which it is a can of infinite worms, and every time you reach further in there are more worms come out.

**PÓM:** Undoubtedly, yeah. Anyway, I'd better move on, or we'll never get any further. I have to say, I loved the dragon in, was it in *Anansi Boys* that there was a dragon who speaks just like Leslie Phillips?

**NG:** He does! Thank you for noticing.

**PÓM:** I just loved that, and I felt that he should have a book all to himself because that was absolutely super.

**NG:** [Laughs]

**PÓM:** And there's a big man looming over us . . .

**NG:** [To Cormac, who is running his diary for the day] You need me? I haven't even finished my tea, and you need me. What's next?

**Cormac:** The filming.
**NG:** OK.

**PÓM:** Two things: one question, and a photograph.
**NG:** And something to scribble on, or . . .

**PÓM:** I have a few things to scribble on, if that's OK.
[Pádraig produces a camera and two books for Neil to sign, which Neil then signs, while Cormac takes photographs of the two of them.]
  Why red balloons? Red balloons come up in your stories all the time.
**NG:** Well, I was probably bitten by . . .

**PÓM:** A radioactive red balloon in your youth?
**NG:** No! I was going to say P. L. Travers, in my youth, that amazing story in *Mary Poppins* where everybody floats in the park on balloons. It's definitely iconic, in its way, and that would be, if I had to point at anything, that would probably be where the balloons come from.

**PÓM:** Thank you very much, that's great. And your public awaits.
**NG:** They do.

**PÓM:** Is there any possibility, in the next umpteen years, that we could do a long email interview, or is that just taking too much of your time?
**NG:** I was saying earlier, every interview seems to end with somebody saying, "Can I send you a few more questions in email?" Several times they started sending me things that are basically new interviews in email, and I hate doing email interviews, only because there's this point where I've sat there and typed for two hours, producing replies, and I think, at least if I was being interviewed, I'd be having a conversation.

**PÓM:** OK. Let me turn this thing off . . .

I turned off the recorder, and Neil was led away to his next appointment, cup of tea still unfinished. Exactly thirty minutes and thirty-six seconds was what I got, from beginning to end, and I couldn't help feeling that I could easily have spoken to him for another thirty minutes. He did promise we'd get to do something the next time he was in Dublin, hopefully a longer interview, which I look forward to. Looking at my list of question topics, I saw I hadn't got to talk to him about the Comic Book Legal Defense Fund, which I know is close to his heart, and which I'd meant to get to, partly because we'd touched on it before the interview proper started, in relation to CE Murphy's *Take a Chance,* the first issue's profits of which are going to the CBLDF, and which he'd seen preview pages of.

I did get to ask Neil one more question that day, however. After his reading at Eason's bookshop in Dublin he asked for questions, and I stuck my hand in the air and asked, "What's next?" He told us about *Blueberry Girl,* a poem he wrote for Tori Amos's daughter Tash in 2000, which is being drawn by Charles Vess, and which is due out in March 2009, and he held forth at great and comic length about the China book, which is due out god known when. I've always felt that Neil would have a good chance at an alternate career as a stand-up comedian. He's certainly got the comic timing.

*FPI would like to thank Neil Gaiman very much for sacrificing his lunch break and risking indigestion to take part in this interview and thanks to Pádraig for conducting it and writing it all up for us to share with you. The Graveyard Book is out now from Bloomsbury and the fourth and final (and rather beautiful looking) volume of the Absolute Sandman has also been published recently; you can keep up with Neil, his writing, appearances and occasional semi-demonic Salsa making by visiting his very fine online journal.*

# Neil Gaiman Turns His Grad Speed into "Good Art"

## Neal Conan / 2013

**Neal Conan:** A year ago, writer Neil Gaiman told the graduating class at Philadelphia's University of the Arts that life is sometimes hard. Things go wrong in life, in love, and in business and in friendship and in health and in all the other ways that life can go wrong. And when things get tough, Gaiman said, this is what you should do: Make good art. Neil Gaiman's speech became a hit on the Web, and now it's been adapted into a small book. We want to hear from artists today: Is he right? When things go wrong, is work the answer? Tell us your story: 800–989–8255. Email us: talk@npr.org. You can also join the conversation on our website. That's at npr.org. Click on *Talk of the Nation.*

Neil Gaiman joins us now from member station WHYY in Philadelphia. His many books include *American Gods*, the comic book series *The Sandman*, and with graphic artist Chip Kidd, his latest: *Make Good Art*. And, Neil, nice to have you on the program again.

**Neil Gaiman:** It's wonderful to be back, Neal.

**CONAN:** And you don't tell us a story in your speech that illustrates your point about when things go bad, make good art. Do you have one?

**GAIMAN:** I didn't tell any stories, mostly because it was a graduating speech—you know, a commencement speech, and I had twenty minutes to try and squeeze everything that I'd learned or figured out, normally by bitter experience, in thirty years of being a professional writer into nineteen minutes of talking to a graduating class.

But for me, it's been true, pretty much solidly through that thirty years. Things go wrong. If you're a human being in the world, bad things happen. You will bump into things. You will get your heart broken. Things that you thought were going to work aren't going to work. Things you thought people were going to love aren't going to be loved. And when that happens, if you are a creator, if you are an artist—and that was a graduating class of artists—what you have to do is go out and make good art. I think you're absolutely allowed several minutes, possibly even half a day to feel very, very sorry for yourself indeed, and then just start making art.

**CONAN:** When was there such a moment in your life?

**GAIMAN:** Oh, I think the—let's pick a nice moment: 1996, 1997—I'd spent several years working on a TV series in the U.K. called *Neverwhere*, and it came out. And as it was getting made, I started feeling more and more that it was just something that wasn't going to work, that the things that I wanted to happen weren't happening. It wasn't the thing that I'd wanted, and still hoped that when it came out, people would love it. And it came out to deafening silence. People didn't really like it very much. The viewing figures tumbled. And what I did was write a novel. And I wrote *Neverwhere* as the novel. I said, this what I meant. This is the thing.

**CONAN:** (Chuckling)

**GAIMAN:** And I took all of the upset and the frustration with the television series, and I put it into a book and brought the book out. And what's lovely is, over the years since then, the book has gone on to become this much-loved thing. And, actually, a couple of months ago, the BBC did a fantastic adaptation of the novel on the radio starring Benedict Cumberbatch and Sir Christopher Lee and James McAvoy, these fantastic actors. And I thought, OK. Fifteen years later, the thing fixed itself. The wheel turned.

**CONAN:** I'm reminded of Susan Stamberg's memorable phrase: The pictures are better on the radio.

**GAIMAN:** Oh, the pictures are always better on the radio. Somebody at the BBC asked why I'd said yes to the radio, and I said because you have an unlimited special effects budget.

**CONAN:** Like many commencement speeches, yours includes an interesting small confession.

**GAIMAN:** My confession, which was definitely one of those things, I thought, do I tell these kids this or not? And I also tried to preface it with the information that it's not something that you could do in today's era of Google and easily accessible information. But when I started out as a very young journalist, phoning editors and just pitching stories, they would often say, "Well, who else have you written for?" And I didn't want to say, "Well, I haven't actually written for anybody yet." So I would list likely sounding magazines, places that somebody like me might have worked for, and I got the jobs.

And over the next six years, it became this mad point of honor for me to have worked for everybody on the list that I'd said in those first couple of months to people that I'd written for. So I wrote for the *Sunday Times* magazine. I wrote for *The Mail* on Sunday. I wrote for *Time Out* and *City Limits* and all of these magazines in London, just so that later, I could claim that I hadn't actually been lying, I'd just been slightly chronologically mixed-up.

**CONAN:** (Laughing) As you say, that's a little more difficult to get away with these days.
**GAIMAN:** And honestly, I don't recommend it. I don't recommend lying. What I was trying to say to people is that you get work in the beginning as a freelance artist, and you can define artist very, very loosely here in terms of, you know, writing, making art, whatever. You get work however you get work, and you're always faced with this, these weird impossibilities of people will always want to hire you if you have experience, and the only way you're going to get experience is if they hire you, and you do it however you do it.

But what I tried to make clear is something I actually learned from the world of comics that, talking to people seems to apply outside of the world of comics as well, which is how you keep work as a freelancer. What I was saying to people is there are three things you can be. You can get the work in on time; you can be good, really good; and you can be easy to get along with. And as long you get two out of three of these right, you will continue to work.

**CONAN:** Oh, so people will put up with your unbearable personality if you get your work in on time and you're very good.
**GAIMAN:** Absolutely. And by the same token, if you're really nice and you're really good, they'll probably forgive you for being late.

**CONAN:** (Laughter)
**GAIMAN:** But, you know, the problem is when you drop down to one out of three, that's the point when they're going, yes, his work is good,

but he's not very nice; he's always late—why should I bother. So it's that two out of three thing.

**CONAN:** We're asking the artists in our audience if work is their salvation—when things go wrong, is the right answer to make good art? Neil Gaiman is our guest. Our phone number is 800–989–8255, email: talk@npr.org. Let's go to Debbie. Debbie is on the line with us from St. Louis.

**DEBBIE (Caller):** Hi. Thank you for taking my call. Absolutely—I write poetry, and I find that I feel transformed—that my experience is transformed within the poetry. And that once I've completed a poem that I'm very satisfied with, it changes my outlook. I feel a bit released at that moment. Right now, I'm struggling with great poverty, and I have some very dark days. But I find that when I've really put all that into my poetry, not a sob story poem, nothing like that, but just the transformation that I go through internally with that. I find that A, I've completed a piece of work that I'm proud of and that I want to be out there in the world, but also it helped me at that moment, it helped me today. It might not have made me any money today, but it helped me. It'll help me continue to go forward in my life in general.

**CONAN:** So these are not necessarily poems that are about rending of garments and screams of tragic pain?

**DEBBIE:** No. Absolutely not. I don't write that way. I don't wallow in self-pity. I don't want my poems to be that way. They're not tearjerkers. They're not hand-wringers. They're metaphysical, in a sense. They're spiritual, but they're also abstracted from the particulars of my struggle. They're not about that the water was shut off or I don't have electricity. It's not like that. It's what my spirit is journeying through. And one line that I wrote recently was that hope is not a butterfly, it's seeds in amber.

**CONAN:** Hmm. Nice. Well, you should . . .

**GAIMAN:** That's really beautiful.

**CONAN:** Yeah. That's nice and that should be rewarded.

**GAIMAN:** And that feeling of just having created something, it's a very, very real thing, that being able to look around and go, I've just improved the world by something that wasn't there before, even if everything else is going to hell.

**DEBBIE:** Yes, yes.

**GAIMAN:** You made something.

**DEBBIE:** Yes, yes, and that's great. I love that "if the whole world's going to hell," because it sometimes feels that way, but that suddenly I feel like something has been added to especially even to my own life, but just in the universe.

**CONAN:** Well, Debbie, keep adding.

(Laughter)

**DEBBIE:** Thank you, Neal.

**CONAN:** Thanks very much for the phone call. She also said something interesting; she says that they're not making me any money right now. You write in your book—or in your speech, your commencement speech—that the lesson you learned early on was don't write anything for money.

**GAIMAN:** Well, I didn't necessarily learn that. What I learned was whenever I did something where the only reason for doing it was money—and this was a lesson that I learned beginning with being a twenty-three-year-old author hired to write a book about Duran Duran—that whenever I did something and the only reason for doing it was the money, normally something would go terribly wrong. And I normally wouldn't get the money and then I wouldn't have anything. Whereas, whenever I did anything where what prompted my doing it was being interested, being excited, caring, thinking this is going to be fun, even if things went wrong and I didn't get the money, I had something I was proud of. And very often in the long term—and the long term now, you know, could be fifteen years, could be twelve years—I'd look back on it and go, actually that thing worked out. It's looked after me. It came back from the dead. It did something good.

And it's something that, you know, I forget. Sometimes somebody waves a paycheck and I go, "I don't really have any reason for doing it, I'm not interested. But, yes, what amazing money, how can I say no?" And then I do it, and then I regret it. And you can almost feel the universe itself sighing, like why doesn't he learn, this one?

(Laughter)

**CONAN:** We're talking with Neil Gaiman about his new book, *Make Good Art.* It's a graphic representation of a speech he gave—a commencement speech he gave a year ago in Philadelphia. You're listening to *Talk of the Nation* from NPR News.

Todd's on the line with us from Alpine, Texas.

**TODD** (Caller): Yes, sir.

**CONAN:** Go ahead, please.

**TODD:** Oh, I was just calling to say, thanks for taking my call, and whenever I do get down, I love making good art. I run a blacksmith shop, and running a forge and having fire and being able to produce something from nothing always gives me good pleasure.

**CONAN:** And that must be very satisfying, that sort of physical work there?
**TODD:** Oh, it's very satisfying. Not only does it give you something to work towards and taking something from nothing and molding it into something else, but you're knowing you're going to have something that's going to last for generations, that'll be passed on.
**CONAN:** And if you're frustrated, you can take it out whacking a big piece of iron.
**TODD:** Yes, sir. That's one of the good things about it.
(Laughter)
**TODD:** Some things they say about blacksmiths. They're usually very happy people and they like music, not very stressed out.
**CONAN:** Oh, that sounds . . .
**TODD:** You can take it all out with a hammer.
**CONAN:** Sounds like a good profession.
(Laughter)
**GAIMAN:** That's wonderful. It reminds me of—particularly horror writers of my acquaintance. And knowing a lot of horror writers and knowing a lot of comedians, and the way comedians tend to be very harried, worried, troubled people. And people who write horror tend to be incredibly happy and mellow and easygoing. And talking to them, you realize it's because they take all these horrible things and they just put it all on the paper. They're just happy, whereas the comedians trying to make their jokes tend to be much, much, much more worried.
**CONAN:** Thanks for . . .
**GAIMAN:** Blacksmith sounds best of all.
**CONAN:** Todd, thanks . . .
**TODD:** Thank y'all.

**CONAN:** Thanks very much. Appreciate it. One of the things you—the best of advice you say you got from a well-known horror writer, and the fact is it's part of a section of your speech on the difficulties, not of failure, but of success.
**GAIMAN:** Absolutely. I mean, you know, when you're getting to talk to a bunch of graduating kids about to go out in the world, they know to be wary of failure. And you're going to have to tell them a bit about failure, but what nobody warns you about when you set out are the difficulties of success.

The way that you actually have to learn how to say no to projects because you're going to have to spend your first few years, if you're smart, saying yes to anything that comes your way, because you don't know what's going to pay off. I use the analogy in the book of somebody just putting messages in bottles and throwing them out to sea.

And suddenly there comes a day when you go down to the shore and the shore is covered with bottles and all of your messages have come back and everybody's said yes. And now, you're going to have to learn to say no.

But what I said in the speech, and what I say in the book, is the most important piece of advice I was ever given that I didn't pay attention to and I wished that I had, came in 1992 from Stephen King at a signing I did in Boston for a *Sandman* book called *Season of Mists.* And he came down. He saw the lines stretching around the block. He wanted to take me out for dinner, but the signing wasn't done until 10:30 at night. And I wound up in his hotel room with Steve and his family, and he said, "You know, this is really wonderful, this is special. You should enjoy this. Just make a point of enjoying it."

And I didn't. I worried about it. I worried it was going to go away. I worried about the next story. I worried about getting things done. And there was a point, a good fifteen years after that, where I finally started to relax. And I look back and I think, you know, I could have enjoyed it. It all went just fine; my worrying about anything didn't change anything. It didn't get better because I was worried about my next deadline or whatever. I didn't do anything differently; really, I should have enjoyed it.

**CONAN:** Neil Gaiman, you will have a similar problem when your next book comes out, *The Ocean at the End of the Lane*, and I've read a galley, it's a beautiful book. You're going to be pestered with all kinds of demands to do the same thing again. So learn from your success, enjoy it.

**GAIMAN:** Thank you so much, Neal.

**CONAN:** Neil Gaiman joined us today from WHYY, our member station in Philadelphia. He's the author of many novels, children's books, screenplays and comic books, including *American Gods* and, of course, the great comic book *The Sandman.* His latest, *Make Good Art.*

Tomorrow, Chris Hedges will join us for the next in our series of looking-ahead conversations. Join us for that. It's the *Talk of the Nation* from NPR News. I'm Neal Conan in Washington.

# *Trigger Warning*: An Interview with Neil Gaiman

## Diane Rehm / 2015

From *The Diane Rehm Show*, WAMU 88.5 American University Radio. Reprinted by permission.

**Ms. Diane Rehm:** Thanks for joining us. I'm Diane Rehm. Fiction writer Neil Gaiman is the author of more than twenty books for children and adults. He's won dozens of awards, including a Newbery Medal for his bestselling-fantasy novel *The Graveyard Book.* One of this best known works is his eerie children's novel, *Coraline*, that was made into an Academy Award–nominated film. The title of his latest anthology of short stories and poems is *Trigger Warning*, and he joins me in the studio. I invite you to be part of the program. Give us a call, 800–433–8850. Send us an email to drshow@wamu.org. Follow us on Facebook or send us a tweet. Neil Gaiman, it's good to meet you.
**Mr. Neil Gaiman:** It's such an honor to be here, Diane.

**REHM:** Well, thank you very much. You know, I'm looking at the subtitle of your book, *Short Fictions and Disturbances.* What do you mean to convey by that?
**GAIMAN:** I liked the idea. Well, partly it's because when I did my very first book of short stories about twenty years ago, it was called *Smoke and Mirrors*, and I thought I needed a subtitle so I called it *Short Stories and Illusions.* And that was good. So now, I'd set something in motion and when I came to do this, I thought, well, it has to be "short fictions" and something. And I looked at the stories, trying to figure what they had in common. And I thought, well, "disturbances" feels about right. They're the best of the stories, I think, even when they're funny, even when some of them are heartwarming are unsettling. They contain disturbances in our lives. They contain moments that things get turned upside down and some of them do that thing that I tend to do where they don't really settle down in any one

genre so they may trip over the border into horror and then trip back or something. And I thought "disturbances," that's a good word and as with the title, it lets you know that things may not be safe within this book.

**REHM:** Talk about that title, *Trigger Warning.*

**GAIMAN:** Well, "trigger warning" is something that I first ran into online on things like Tumblr or Twitter where if you were linking to something that could contain disturbing content that could potentially upset someone, trigger some kind of PTSD-style flashback, you would let them know that this post or whatever, this image could be very disturbing. And I saw that and thought, "That's such a good idea. That keeps people safe." And then, I noticed that they were now heading out into universities and last year, there was a certain amount of fuss being made about whether great works of literature, for example, should contain trigger warnings and I looked at the screen, no, they definitely shouldn't. You should not put a warning on the beginning of *Romeo and Juliet* saying you may not want to read this because it contains underage sex and suicide and murder. You don't want to warn people. What you want to do is say, if you are a grownup, if you are in a university, if you are studying this thing, it may disturb you and it may challenge you, whatever it is, and you're going to have make the choice. Do you go there, or do you not go there? And for me, I started reading the argument, started seeing university professors explaining why they didn't want trigger warnings on things in their classes and felt that the whole idea of putting a warning on literature is one that just fascinated me. And I thought it's absolutely a topic for discussion. It's absolutely something that's interesting and out there. I know that several of these stories would upset people. I put something in the introduction, which many people have read as a joke and it actually really wasn't, when I mentioned that I have a friend who cannot cope with tentacles and there is a giant tentacle in one of these stories. And people have said, "Well, you can see Gaiman, you know, joking about this thing, making light of it." I'm going, "No, no, this is my friend Rocky. I have seen her in a sushi restaurant when somebody walked past with something tentacular on a plate and watched her sweat, fall, faint."

**REHM:** Wow.

**GAIMAN:** This is somebody who cannot cope with tentacles. But the point for me is that we all have, well, most of us have, those places which—and I'm not just talking about things that upset us. That's one thing. But those places where it's like the earth is kicked out from under your feet.

**REHM:** But it's fascinating to me, and you've just mentioned your introduction, it's fascinating to me that you did write this long introduction to your collection of short stories. That's fairly unusual.

**GAIMAN:** When I was a boy and first discovering collections of short stories, I loved any single author short story collections in which the author would tell you something about the process, something about the way in which these were written, the situation they were in, who the story was written for, maybe what inspired it because as a kid who wanted to be an author more than anything else in the world, this was like being taken backstage.

**REHM:** From what age did you want to be an author?

**GAIMAN:** I don't ever remember not wanting to be an author. I do remember times when I thought it would be a complete pipedream. I mean, when I was—put it this way. When I was about ten years old, eleven years old, at the age when most kids are fantasizing about being sport stars or athletes, I was working on a grandiose fantasy in which I was the author of *Lord of the Rings.* Now, and because I was ten and had a very strange kind of mind, in my fantasy, I needed to have a copy of *Lord of the Rings* with me and then I needed to accidently slip into a parallel universe exactly the same as the one we were in, except Tolkien had not written *Lord of the Rings.* And then, it got a little bit problematic because I was going to have to find an adult to type the entirety of this copy of *Lord of the Rings* that I had because I thought, I can't just send my book into a publisher. They will figure out there's something dodgy. It's going to have to be a giant typed script and I'm ten and I can't type. I don't even own a typewriter. So I'll have to get an adult to do it. And then, my fantasy would always get into trouble because I'd go what do I do with this adult? This adult will know that they typed out this thing. How am I going to pay the adult? Maybe I'm going to have to murder the adult because they can't know. But that was the kind of strange mad fantasy that I would have.

**REHM:** And what were your parents' reactions?

**GAIMAN:** I think on the whole, because I don't think I ever explained my fantasies about being a writer to my parents, they just loved me reading. They were very happy with me reading, except, obviously, before family events, weddings, bar mitzvahs, things like that, at which point they would frisk me because I would always have a book on me somewhere and they would lock in it the—they would find the book and lock it in the car.

REHM: Because otherwise you'd go off and find a place to read.
GAIMAN: They would find me sitting quietly under a table with my book.

REHM: So you went through school where?
GAIMAN: I was educated in England in a handful of schools in the south of England.

REHM: What was your father doing at the time?
GAIMAN: My father was doing a whole bunch of things, primarily owning a vitamin company and doing property, buying and selling property.

REHM: And your mother?
GAIMAN: My mother was a pharmacist.

REHM: A pharmacist.
GAIMAN: And both of them were—it's very strange. A few years ago, I was doing a signing in Barnes and Noble, Union Square and my father, who was in New York for the week—he's dead now. He's been dead for about six years, but he was there and he slipped in just to watch me at this mega signing. There were fifteen hundred odd people there and I was just signing away. And my agent, Merrilee who is very wonderful, my literary agent, walked over to him and she said, "You know, isn't this amazing? Isn't this wonderful?" And he said, "Yes." And she said, "You must have always known, though, that it would be like this." And my father looked at her and said, "I had a son who wanted to be a writer. I thought I'd be supporting him for the rest of his life." And . . .

REHM: Isn't that something?
GAIMAN: That—and what was great about that is they'd never let me know that. He'd never—I'd never got that from him.

REHM: Are you an only child?
GAIMAN: No. I had two sisters, neither of whom wanted to write, but both of whom—it's pretty strange, that thing when you get to be a—I have three kids and now, you know, adults. The youngest is in college. But it wasn't

until I'd been a father, you know, three times and watched this thing happen that I realized that I must have been a strange kid.

**REHM:** Neil Gaiman, his new *Short Fictions and Disturbances* is titled *Trigger Warning*. You can join us, if you like, 800–433–8850. Send us an email to drshow@wamu.org.

**REHM:** And welcome back. Author Neil Gaiman is with me. He's written more than twenty books of fiction for children, young adults, and adults, including his bestsellers, *The Graveyard Book*, *The Ocean at the End of the Lane*, and *Coraline*. His newest is what he calls a collection of short fictions and disturbances. It's titled *Trigger Warning*. At the same time, Neil, you've just come out with an illustrated version of one of the stories, *The Truth is a Cave in the Black Mountains*. And this is an illustrated version, which I've had such fun reading. You've read this story in concert halls, accompanied by a string quartet. Let's hear a little of it and then hear how it came about.

> You ask me if I can forgive myself. I can forgive myself for many things, for where I left him, for what I did. But I will not forgive myself for the year that I hated my daughter, when I believed her to have run away, perhaps to the city. During that year, I forbade her name to be mentioned. And if her name entered my prayers when I prayed, it was to ask that she would one day learn the meaning of what she had done, of the dishonor that she had brought to our family, of the red that ringed her mother's eyes. I hate myself for that. For nothing will ease the hatred, not even what happened that final night on the side of the mountain.

**REHM:** Talk about eerie.
**GAIMAN:** You know, there's something about having a string quartet that makes an author feel invulnerable. I think all authors should have string quartets behind them. It's a wonderful thing.

**REHM:** How did that come about?
**GAIMAN:** Completely accidentally. Like all the best things in life, it just turned up. I was invited to do something on the stage of the Sydney Opera House. And they said, "We would love you to do an appearance at Sydney Opera House." And I'd just finished. The story had not even been published yet, *The Truth Is a Cave in the Black Mountains*. And I thought, well, that's about seventy minutes long. That would be perfect for what they're asking me, because they said, you know, no more than ninety minutes on the stage.

I wrote back and I sent them the story and they'd asked if I would do something that in some way would have some musical theme . . .

**REHM:** Ah.

**GAIMAN:** . . . and perhaps some visual theme. And I suggested Eddie Campbell, the artist whose illustrations are in that book, could do some paintings that would be projected behind me as I spoke. And they suggested FourPlay String Quartet, who are—they're like a rock band of string quartets. They're these four Australian, classically-trained musicians, who still do things like *The Simpsons'* Theme or the *Doctor Who* Theme as part of their repertoire. And they sent me some of their records and I just thought, "These guys are amazing." I sent them the book. They put the music together. I went out there. We fine-tuned it a little bit in rehearsal, did it on the stage of Sidney Opera House, got a standing ovation, and thought, "We have to do this again. That was so much fun." And wound up, last year, doing a micro-tour: The Warfield in San Francisco, Carnegie Hall, which was amazing, the Barbican in England, Edinburgh. I'm just . . .

**REHM:** Wow.

**GAIMAN:** . . . It was so wonderful. I felt like I was getting to make movies inside people's heads. And adults don't get read to. They don't, you know, it is the tragedy of adults. People read to us when we are children and we love that and we can make stories up in our heads. But all too often, once you're a grownup, you've lost that thing. People will not read you stories. And suddenly, you can watch people shifting in their seats at the beginning, going, he's going to be telling me the story for seventy minutes. And then, at the end, they're on their, you know, and there are moments in the middle where you can literally hear a pin drop. People aren't breathing. They're just being really still because you're in a quiet bit that's exciting and they don't want to miss a second of it. So wonderful.

**REHM:** I think that might happen now, actually. If you would read for us a story from *Trigger Warning*. And it's part of a group of stories, and this is titled, "July Tale."

**GAIMAN:** Yes. It's part of the calendar of tales, twelve stories I wrote, each inspired by something somebody had said to me on Twitter. And this was July.

> The day that my wife walked out on me, saying she needed to be alone and to have some time to think things over. On the first of July, when the sun beat down on

the lake in the center of the town, when the corn in the meadows that surrounded my house was knee high, when the first few rockets and firecrackers were let off by over-enthusiastic children, to startle us and to speckle the summer sky, I built an igloo out of books in my backyard.

I used paperbacks to build it, scared of the weight of falling hardbacks or encyclopedias if I didn't build it soundly.

But it held. It was twelve feet high and had a tunnel through which I could crawl to enter, to keep out the bitter Arctic winds.

I took more books into the igloo I had made out of books and I read in there. I marveled at how warm and comfortable I was inside. As I read the books, I would put them down, make a floor out of them. And then I got more books and I sat on them, eliminating the last of the green July grass from my world.

My friends came by the next day. They crawled on their hands and knees into my igloo. They told me I was acting crazy. I told them that the only thing that stood between me and the winter's cold was my father's collection of 1950s paperbacks, many of them with racy titled and lurid covers and disappointingly staid stories.

My friends left.

I sat in my igloo imagining the Arctic night outside, wondering whether the Northern Lights would be filling the sky above me. I looked out but saw only a night filled with pinprick stars.

I slept in my igloo made of books. I was getting hungry. I made a hole in the floor, lowered a fishing line and waited until something bit. I pulled it up. A fish made of books: green-covered, vintage Penguin detective stories. I ate it raw, fearing a fire in my igloo.

When I went outside, I observed that someone had covered the whole world with books, pale-covered books, all shades of white and blue and purple. I wandered the ice floes of books.

I saw someone who looked like my wife out there on the ice. She was making a glacier of autobiographies.

"I thought you left me," I said to her. "I thought you left me alone."

She said nothing. And I realized she was only a shadow of a shadow.

It was July, when the sun never sets in the Arctic. But I was getting tired and I started back towards the igloo.

I saw the shadows of the bears before I saw the bears themselves. Huge they were and pale, made of the pages of fierce books, poems ancient and modern, prowled the ice floes in bear shape, filled with words that could wound with their beauty. I could see the paper and the words winding across them and I was frightened that the bears could see me.

I crept back to my igloo, avoiding the bears. I may have slept in the darkness. And then I crawled out and I lay on my back on the ice and stared up at the unexpected colors of the shimmering Northern Lights and listened to the cracks and snaps of the distant ice, as an iceberg of fairy tales carved from a glacier of books on mythology.

I do not know when I became aware that there was someone else lying on the ground near to me. I could hear her breathing.

"They're very beautiful, aren't they?" she said.

"It is *Aurora Borealis*, the Northern Lights," I told her.

"It's the town's Fourth of July fireworks, baby," said my wife.

She held my hand and we watched the fireworks together.

When the last of the fireworks had vanished in a cloud of golden stars, she said, "I came home."

I didn't say anything. But I held her hand very tightly and I left my igloo made of books and I went with her back into the house we lived in, basking like a cat in the July heat.

I heard distant thunder. And in the night, while we slept, it began to rain, tumbling my igloo of books, washing away the words from the world.

**REHM:** Neil Gaiman, reading "July," a story in his new collection titled, *Trigger Warning*. You know, I marvel at your imagination. Can you tell me how it works?

**GAIMAN:** Mostly, it begins with daydreaming. Which was something that I only really realized when I was talking some years ago to one of my daughter's classes at school. I went in and there's a bunch of seven-, eight-year-olds, and the first question they asked was, "Where do you get your ideas?"

**REHM:** Hmm.

**GAIMAN:** And authors always get asked where we get our ideas. And we get asked it and we don't really know and we get scared. So we tend to come up with flip, funny answers that aren't even funny. But when you've got seven-year-olds asking you, you owe them a real answer. So I tried to explain that most ideas begin with the same process as daydreaming. Your mind is just wandering a little and you're sitting there and you start thinking things like, what if, or if only, or what would happen when? And I was giving them the kind of examples that you give school kids. I was saying, "Okay, what if you discovered that your school teacher was going to kill and eat one of you at the end of term? But you didn't know which one it was?"

**REHM:** Oh, my heavens.

**GAIMAN:** And suddenly that's a story. It's a story beginning.

**REHM:** Yeah. Yeah.

**GAIMAN:** What would happen if you shrank tiny? What would happen if you were invisible? They're lovely, just starting places. And for me, so many of these stories began in that kind of way, just with following a weird chain of thought. When I was about fourteen years old, I didn't have a girlfriend. But some of my friends did. And I thought, "Well, how do I cope with this?" You know, I'm in an all-boys school. So I write a girl's name on my exercise books. And when asked about her, I said, "No, she's nothing, we're just friends," so that people would think I had a girlfriend. And as an adult, I was asked to write a story for a book of love stories. And I started thinking, wouldn't it be strange if that girl—if I was an adult and she turned up in your life? What would happen if you had made up a girlfriend when you were fifteen, but now you're in your thirties and she's emailing you and you bump into her? And how does that work? And it's just that—the what if? Wouldn't that be interesting? What could I use that story to do? What could I tell people with that story? And, of course, normally, for me, the first draft, I'm finding out what I'm saying.

**REHM:** Hmm.

**GAIMAN:** The second draft, I've figured out what I'm saying and now I'm trying to make the theme consistent. I'm trying to make sure that it is about the thing that I discovered that it was about while writing it.

**REHM:** And you're listening to *The Diane Rehm Show.* And, indeed, that does turn into a story.

**GAIMAN:** It does. It's called "The Thing About Cassandra." And it was a story that I got to write that was basically about the gulfs between us, about the imagination, and about loneliness and how we cope with it.

**REHM:** All right. We've got lots of callers. I'm going to open the phones, 800–433–8850. First, to Jordan in New Milford, Conn. You're on the air.

**JOURDAN:** Oh, good morning. Now, I'm an author. I wrote the book *Me Squared.* And I'm currently working with an indie filmmaker because I wrote a little short story spinoff called "Josephine's Job." It's a sci-fi story about cloning. And I had some questions about creative control. Because Mr. Gaiman, I really enjoyed the film adaptation of *Stardust.* And I wondered, how much creative control did you have over that? And how much creative control do you think an author should have when there's an adaptation of somebody's work being done?

**GAIMAN:** When I was a very young author, my first graphic novel, a book called *Violent Cases* was adapted to the stage. And they did it in what I thought, as an author, was the best possible way, in that they just took the text of the graphic novel and did it on the stage. And I was amazed when I saw things that were huge and important in the book became trivial on stage. And things that were almost trivial in the book suddenly became important on stage. And I realized that you cannot necessarily simply move something from one medium to another. It needs to be translated. It needs to work in its new medium. Which is one reason why I tend—rather than hoping for creative control—what I tend to try and do with things like *Coraline*, with things like *Stardust,* with some of the things that are happening in the future, to find filmmakers whose work I love and respect, find collaborators whose work I love and respect—Henry Sellick making *Coraline.* And for me, the way that I did that was I finished writing *Coraline.* I'd seen Henry's work on *The Nightmare Before Christmas*, which he directed, and on *James and the Giant Peach*, I thought, he is perfect for this. Sent it to him. He called up. And just made sure that Henry had the option and Henry got to make it.

**REHM:** So it's trust.

**GAIMAN:** I think it's trust. And I think it's a matter of finding people whose work you like and respect. Because no matter how much control you think you have, unless you're actually making the film—which, in a couple of cases, you know, there have been—a few years ago I was invited to do a short film for a series of silent films and television in the UK. And I figured the only way it work would be if I directed it. Because otherwise I would be writing a one-hundred-page script for a ten-page film. And I knew that nobody was going to get the sense and the sensibility in what I wanted. So I just directed it and I made it. And at that point, you have a sense of, "Because I say so."

**REHM:** Neil Gaiman, his new book is titled, *Trigger Warning*, subtitled, *Short Fictions and Disturbances.* And we'll take a short break here. More of your calls, comments, when we come back.

**REHM:** And we're back. I'll go right to the phones to Rachel in Rockville, Maryland. You're on the air.

**RACHEL:** Hi.

**REHM:** Hi.

**RACHEL:** I wanted to know what Mr. Gaiman's favorite video was, like YouTube video.

**GAIMAN:** What a great question. Okay. I understand you're actually calling from school.

**RACHEL:** Yeah. Actually, school just started so I'm skipping for you.

**GAIMAN:** I will answer quickly then so you can get back. Thank you so much. I think my favorite video and this is—this would sound creepy but it's also true, is my wife. She did a TED Talk, Amanda Palmer, she did a TED Talk called, "The Art of Asking."

**REHM:** "The Art of Asking."

**GAIMAN:** "The Art of Asking." It goes from her time as a human statue to her time doing the world's most successful music Kickstarter and how she learned to trust people and to ask for things. And I am in awe of it. I watched her take it from this idea that she wanted to do to thirteen minutes of pure heart and honesty and soul-baring onstage and I look at that video and I just think that it's so perfect. So it's got to be that.

**REHM:** Rachel, I hope you'll take a look at that. I'm sure you'll enjoy it. And thank you for calling. To another high school or perhaps junior high school person, Garrett in Columbia, Maryland. You're on the air.

**GARRETT:** Hi. I'm Garrett. I'm thirteen years old and I've recently written my first novel. It took me seven months to do.

**GAIMAN:** Well done.

**GARRETT:** So I was wondering how I can progress as an author, you know, and maybe what I do with a novel once I've finished it and think it's pretty decent.

**GAIMAN:** Well, the great thing that you have that I did not have and nobody had until relevantly recently is you have the web. So you have so many ways to get your novel out into the world. You can put it up on Amazon as a thing. You can get it printed these days cheaply and easily and give copies to your friends or possibly, if you have enough chutzpah, sell copies to your friends and family. You can put it up on the web for people to read and just invite readers and get comments. What do you do next? You write your next book 'cause that's how you get good. And you've come so far by spending seven months and actually finishing it. I tell people that the most important thing you can do is finishing things. You learn more from finishing a story that isn't great than you ever will from starting and abandoning a great story.

**REHM:** I think that Garrett is truly on his way. In the email he wrote, he says, "I got up early to spend a couple of hours every day on it." That is a writer.

**GAIMAN:** That's absolutely a writer and that's so smart. My friend, Jean Wolf, who I think is now in his eighties and one of the finest writers that we have still creating in America today, for much of his adult life, would set his alarm for quarter to 5:00 in the morning and before there was anybody in the house, he would get up and he would write from 5:15 to until about 6:30 and that was his writing time. He'd just write a page, a page and a half each day. But if you write a page and a half each day, you've written a novel at the end of the year.

**REHM:** Absolutely. Garrett, good luck to you. We'll be rooting for you. Let's go to Janet in Highland, Illinois. You're on the air.

**JANET:** Yes, thank you. Neil, is there a disturbance that you are trying to heal as you write? I find it perfect that there should be no warning on literature, because it's vicarious healing. And when it comes at the right time, it's what you need to be whole. And I'm still fishing in your igloo and wondering what I'm going to pull up. But is it healing for you to write the story?

**GAIMAN:** It's absolutely. It's always healing. And I found, there was recently a book about my career, for want of a better word, called *The Art of Neil Gaiman.* Which was a lot of—heavy on the visuals, but essentially, it was an account of everything I've done. And the writer of it, Hayley Campbell, I gave her access to my attic and all of the tubs of papers up there. And she included in there, just a small note written in one of my notebooks while I was writing, I think it was probably *Stardust.* Possibly something else, and it just said, "When things are bad, I go to the writing place." And that's so true. It's always been my way of healing myself, my way of creating a world that I can control. When things are out of your control, when you write, you're God. When you write, the world does, you hope, on a good day, what it's meant to do. And you come away from a period of writing, you come away from a story with a certain amount of insight into what you've done. But of course, the strange thing is it's not until you re-read something, for some reason, fifteen, twenty years later, that you suddenly realize what you were writing, what you were saying, and why it was important for you to write that story at that time.

**REHM:** Tell us about the story "Orange." I know you wrote the entire tale while in the airport and on a plane in one trip.

**GAIMAN:** You know, sometimes you get lucky. There are stories in that book that took me literally years to write. Most of them took weeks to write. And then there was "Orange," which I had let an editor down. I had an editor in Australia and I'd had to pull a story that I'd written for him because publication schedules on something else just meant that he couldn't publish it. And he said, "Well, will you write me something?" And I said, "Well yes, but it's not like I have an idea and now we're literally forty-eight hours away from your deadline." And he said, "Well, just anything." And I got to the airport, and I'd been thinking about just some comments that a friend of mine had been making about her little sister who had started using orange tanning cream. An overabundance of orange tanning cream. And was leaving orange smudges on the fridge and on the walls as she passed. And that was sort of sitting there in my head. And I had a vague idea for a short story and then I suddenly realized how the story could be told. And it was that moment of thrilled excitement where I went, if I do the story as a set of answers to a questionnaire, to an interrogation but you don't actually find out what the questions were, you're forcing the reader to use their imagination to fill in the gaps. And the reader is going to have to create a story in a very strange and upside down way. And I just sat down in the waiting room, you know, waiting to board, and just started writing it. And I remember writing some of it in baggage claim while waiting to change airports. And then landed in Australia and the story was done.

**REHM:** Read a little bit of that for us.
**GAIMAN:** "Orange."

Third subject's responses to investigator's written questionnaire.

Eyes only.

1. Jamaima Glorfindal Petula Ramsey.
2. Seventeen on June the ninth.
3. The last five years, before that, we lived in Glasgow (Scotland). Before that, Cardiff (Wales).
4. I don't know. I think he's in magazine publishing now. He doesn't talk to us anymore. The divorce was pretty bad and mum wound up paying him a lot of money, which seemed sort of wrong to me. But maybe it was worth it, just to get shot of him.
5. An inventor, an entrepreneur. She invented the Stuffed Muffin™, and started the Stuffed Muffin chain. I used to like them when I was a kid, but you can get kind of sick of stuffed muffins for every meal, especially because mummy used us a guinea pigs. The Complete Turkey Dinner Christmas stuffed muffin was

the worst. But she sold out her interest in the stuffed muffin chain about five years ago to start work on My Mom's Colored Bubbles. Not actually ""yet.

**REHM:** Fantastic. And that came to you? You just went with it. What it tells me, as I talk with you, and you recount these bits that come into your head from conversations, is how superb a listener you are. And whether that might be a piece of advice you would offer to young Garrett.

**GAIMAN:** I think it's a piece of advice I would offer to anybody who wants to be a writer. Listen to people. Listen to the way they talk. I was incredibly lucky, because as a very young man, I wound up, although I wanted in my heart to write fiction, I became a journalist. And I became the kind of journalist who would do interviews with people and then have to play back the tapes, and I'd realize I had six thousand words worth of interview and I wanted to somehow get it all into two thousand words worth of magazine article. So I would become obsessed with speech patterns and how to reproduce speech patterns while still squeezing what people said into the smallest amount of time. And listening to how people actually talk, as opposed to the way they talk on television, on movies, talk in books, is incredibly useful to you. You watch them start a sentence, and then stop and go back. You watch them hesitate, you watch them change course on the way. And the more you can do that, the more you can listen to people, and the more you can eavesdrop sitting in a Starbucks and just listening to the conversations at nearby tables or being on a Greyhound bus and listening to kids in the seat in front of you is a wonderful, wonderful thing.

**REHM:** Let's go to Kate in Detroit, Michigan. You're on the air.

**KATE:** Hello, good morning.

**REHM:** Hi.

**GAIMAN:** Hello, Kate.

**KATE:** Hi. I'm a schoolteacher of eighteen brilliant, extraordinary kids who are aged eight and nine. And some of them are tilted in their wonderment toward the grotesque and funny and interesting. Science-fiction kinds of thinking. And I was wondering if you had any suggestions for an entree onto the slippery-slope of science fiction for those kinds of kids.

**GAIMAN:** You know, there are—Diane is holding up my books for me.

**REHM:** Yes.

**GAIMAN:** But, you know, let us take my books as a given. Let's recommend some other wonderful writers. Madeleine L'Engle's *A Wrinkle in Time* is a great science-fiction book for kids. There's an author named Diana Wynne

Jones, who wrote magic, fantasy, and weird stuff. And she wanders between fantasy and science fiction, but anything by Diana is absolutely worthwhile. And I think, right now, when they get a little bit older, there are people like Cory Doctorow, whose book, *Little Brother*, is a wonderful sort of Big Brother, *1984*, but for kids. What I think is marvelous, though, is there's so much good stuff for young readers right now. And young readers who like weird genre-type stuff. It's out there and it's on the shelves.

**REHM:** I hope that helps. And I really would, very definitely, recommend Neil Gaiman's illustrated book, *The Truth Is a Cave in the Black Mountains*. And you're listening to *The Diane Rehm Show*. Let's go now to Robert in Birmingham, Alabama. Hi, you're on the air.

**ROBERT:** I'm doing fine, Diane. Thanks. And two quick things, Diane. Because I just absolutely adore you. Number one, thank you so much for being, for making accessible to the masses of people who listen to you, the most complicated of subjects around the world.

**REHM:** Good.

**ROBERT:** Thank you for that. And secondly, your husband must have been an extraordinary man to be able to share you with the world.

**REHM:** Thank you.

**ROBERT:** And that being said, my question is, there was something about provisos on certain literature. I, as a person of African descent, certainly believe that there should be an advisory on certain literatures. In terms of being able to decode it. Because great writings like your author has there, these things are translated into movies and things like that. And then we get an Academy Award situation where it's lily white. And so I'm very, very concerned that I really think some of these things do—if I'm an African person reading this literature, that somehow gets translated as being universal, it's Euroversal. So, I really think that a proviso should be put his literature, because it inferiorizes so many people around the world.

**GAIMAN:** You know, I think, I would agree with you up to a point on that. I think the most important thing is to insist, as we were talking earlier about control of movies as an author, and one of the big things for me is being absolutely clear on race in books translating to race in movies. I wrote a novel called *Anansi Boys* in which all of the lead characters are of African descent. Most of them are Anglo-Caribbean. And I was approached shortly after it came out and hit the bestseller list by a major Hollywood director and producer, saying we want to turn this into a movie. And I said great. And they said, obviously, we're going to make the lead characters white.

And I said no, I'm not selling it to you. And I—you know, and they were going, no, but you don't understand. Black people, it wouldn't work, and maybe white people, and I'm like no.
**REHM:** Wow.
**GAIMAN:** Go away. I'm not selling it to you. And with my novel, *American Gods*, which we're currently adapting for television, the only thing that I absolutely held the line on is to make sure that everybody understands that any people of color in the book are going to be people of color on the screen.

**REHM:** I have one last quick question. And I hope for a quick answer. Is there a line you would not cross for children's literature?
**GAIMAN:** Yes, and I had to discover that when I was writing my last novel, *Ocean at the End of the Lane*, and figure out for myself whether it was for children or for adults. And I decided it was for adults because I was not convinced that it offered hope. And I want all children's literature that I write to have hope in it.

**REHM:** Neil Gaiman. His newest collection of short fictions, poems, and what he calls "disturbances," is titled, *Trigger Warning*. What a great pleasure to talk with you.
**GAIMAN:** Such an honor to be here, Diane.

**REHM:** Thank you. And thanks all, for listening. I'm Diane Rehm.

# It's Neil's World. We Just Live in It:
# An Interview with Neil Gaiman

## Joseph Michael Sommers and Maggie Grace Sommers / 2017

Previously unpublished. Printed by permission of Joseph Michael Sommers and Maggie Grace Sommers.

This collection could have been complete without the addition of a new interview from Neil Gaiman. Likewise, a dinner can be complete without a dessert course, but who doesn't care for a slice of pie with their meal?

More to the point, what kind of madman would I be to not take the opportunity to speak with the author I have studied for decades and read since I was a teenager?

On July 26, 2017, having read through well over a thousand previous interviews with him over the course of the year prior, I chatted with Neil Gaiman about some things more recent that had not yet been attended to by others, some things that would be forthcoming from him, and some things that I greedily needed to know and understand as an academic, parent, and human being, generally-speaking, from a man who grasps the human condition better than most.

There are things we did not get to, both due to the space constraints of this volume and the time constraints of one of the busiest authors writing today. I very much wanted to ask him about who he was reading right now and who he was listening to because music so crucially informs his work. I wanted to ask him about writing for *Doctor Who* and if he regretted not getting to write for Peter Capaldi, a man to my mind who would embody the voice of Gaiman's writing. I also wanted to know if he might write for Jodie Whittaker, the Thirteenth Doctor and the first woman to occupy that role, in the future. Given Gaiman's capacity to write women so well—if nothing else—I wanted to slip that bug in his ear. I very much wanted to know, in as Seinfeldian a way as I could ask, if he had figured out yet what his deal was with angels was as they are some of the most complex repeated motifs and characterizations he crafts across his writing.

I didn't get to ask him about those things, but I did get to ask him about these things.

And, this time, I had some help.

**Neil Gaiman:** Hello.
**Joseph Michael Sommers:** Hello, Neil! How are you doing?
**NG:** Apart from having a cough, I'm great.

**JMS:** [laughter]
**NG:** So, I will try not to cough in your ear, but I am good.

**JMS:** I would have no issue with that [laughter]. Ok, I know that you are incredibly busy, so if you are ready, I will begin.
**NG:** Good.

**JMS:** For this collection, I've been reviewing about forty years' worth of interviews with you and by you, and one of the first things I wonder about Neil Gaiman in 2017 is how you approach, or rather, what is your approach at this point to your writing and how has it evolved as you have grown more comfortable in your authorial voice. I guess I should ask if you think you have grown more comfortable, as it certainly feels like you have.
**NG:** I think I must have. It's interesting because I did something recently that I almost never do—I found four pages I wrote in 1985, maybe earlier, maybe '86 but I think it was '85, and it's the original four pages of a version of *The Graveyard Book* that was written, looked at, and put away, and I hadn't looked at it since.

And it was really interesting looking at that, you know, and I loved it for all the wrong reasons. I loved it for all the wrong reasons. I loved it because it was a really interesting little portrait of my son Mike when he was two, and it had things in there that I had long forgotten, like his first words. But it was interesting watching me still flailing as a writer—flailing in a nice sense—you know, you're twenty-four or twenty-five years old, and you don't quite have a voice yet, but you have lots of other people's voices. And you don't really have a plot yet; you're not sure about the plotting thing, but you're kind of throwing mud at the wall and seeing what sticks.

There was a thing that I thought was a Jerry Garcia quote, but I have googled it now many times and the only person I have found either saying the quote or attributing it to Jerry Garcia is me. (JMS: [laughter]) Your guess is as good as mine, but, it's that, "Style is the stuff you get wrong." The idea being that if you wrote absolutely—if you were writing perfectly style-free, you would be writing perfect prose. It's the stuff that you give up on, it's the stuff that you don't do right that tells people it's you. So, that's also the stuff that only emerges if you've been writing for ten years, fifteen years, twenty years that emerges after the first couple of million words.

I know I sound like me. And I know if I look at the short story collections or even the nonfiction stuff that there are a lot of different me's. And they're all—sorry: I'm being distracted by the most amazing fawn! (JMS: [laughter]) Just walking backwards and forwards in front of my writer's cabin. Normally, I see sort of deer in the distance—this one is just like, "Yaaah. I dunno. I'm lost. I'm here." So, anyway, the point being that, at this point, I've been writing for . . . pushing forty years, and I definitely sound like me now. And I look at things like *The Graveyard Book*, as it is now, and I go, "I love you. You are the authorial voice that I wanted in the book." It has the voice of a classic, English children's book, and that was the feeling I was going for.

And then you look at that next two, *The Ocean at the End of the Lane* and *Fortunately, the Milk*, or whatever else came out after that, or even *Norse Mythology*, and they're obviously all written by me, and they're obviously all different voices.

**JMS:** One of the things that I have noticed going through your work, and at my age I have had the pleasure of growing up with you, or, I should say, growing up with your work, is that one of the things I have noticed, certainly as a boy and certainly as I've grown older, is that you've got one of the most idiosyncratic and playful senses of humor *particularly* when you're somehow doing dark, or even gallows humor, and yet you fill the experience with what I can only describe as being warm, even friendly, to a reader no matter how disturbing the context. I'm thinking about things like that first bit of *The Sandman* with Dr. Destiny or even your shorter works like "Orange," and certainly *Good Omens*—How does your humor operate in your fiction? How does it fit in with the fantastic and the imaginative and certainly with the darker bits? It feels very unique in contemporary fiction.

**NG:** You know, I'm not a horror writer. Even though horror and humor are really close, and I'm not a horror writer because I would never want to spend a year in the horror place writing a novel. When I do go there, I find things tend to get gently funny. And I think a lot of that is also the same phenomenon from a different angle . . . I think, as the thing where people will say to me, "Why are your bad guys so interesting?" And, I go, "Because, with all the characters, I always try to do the thing where if you met them at a party, you'd want to hang around with them."

**JMS:** [laughter]

**NG:** And, you know, there is a level in which—I love appalling people! My wife doesn't. She has a very low appalling-people tolerance. I will get fascinated by them [laughter]. I will talk to appalling people, and go, "Oh! You really are appalling!" As long as they're interesting, and, you know, make little mental notes, and go, "Ahhhh! Ok. My gosh—all of the things people say about you are true . . . And you have no idea. How fascinating."

   I think part of it also is that I like stories where you get light in the bleakest places, and the flipside of that, I guess, is that in most of my stories you get bleakness in the lightest places.

**JMS:** That's fair. You mentioned something earlier that I'd like to pick up on: You mentioned your wife (Amanda Palmer) and, if I'm wrong about this, please correct me, but your son, your youngest son, Anthony is . . . is he two now?

**NG:** He is! He's twenty-two months to this point.

**JMS:** I have been perusing your bibliography in front of me, which is amazingly long of course, and it appears as if you're busier than ever with [the television adaptation of] *American Gods*, with the adaptation of *Good Omens*, with the writing of *The Seven Sisters* [The second *Neverwhere* book], your ubiquitous online presence . . . as a father myself, I have a very practical question: How do you do it? How do you find the time?

**NG:** I fail. I really fail. Normally, my life is juggling eggs. At the point where the baby turned up . . . at the point where Amanda was very pregnant, my life started to turn into the sound of eggs hitting the floor.

   *Seven Sisters*, right now, is a year late. And it will probably be two years late by the time it gets handed in. *Good Omens* is . . . I know how many things I should have done in the last few years that in any normal last few years I would have got done. There's a couple of children's books that are begun that I would have finished. I would have been wrapping up *The Seven Sisters*, and, instead, mostly, it's just been *Good Omens*. Part of that is the madness of television because you never finish. You hand in a draft, and you go, "Ahh! Here we go—here are all six scripts now in their third draft—

we're done." And then, three weeks later, the notes come in after the director and the producer have been on the technical reconnaissance and they say, "Ok. Well, we don't have one of these, and we're not gonna get one of those. Could you lose these? Could we build this? Could we do stuff with this?" Suddenly, you're back writing the thing you thought was over. And the only thing that keeps me going on that is the fact that the script does seem to be getting better and better. And it's gonna be this huge production: the biggest thing the BBC has ever done and the biggest thing I've ever done.

So, from that point of view, it keeps taking priority, but, having said that, Ash (Anthony) also takes priority. Especially, also, I guess, since I'm an old dad. And it's harder to leave him—I know how fast they grow and change at this point. And I'm much more easily persuaded to do something like, you know, "Here, look after the baby for three hours!"

Yah, nobody really has to twist my arm; I'm like, "OK."

So, how do I do it?

I fail. A lot right now.

I am sure that as he gets bigger I will get back on top of stuff. It's weird—having known people who are genuinely prolific—Terry Pratchett springs to mind, or my friend Kim Newman who was twenty-three and I was twenty-two when we did our first book together . . . Those are people who were really prolific. They would do their two thousand words a day. Kim used to do things like write entire novels in a long weekend and stuff. I do not have any of those facilities. On the other hand, I'm also not as nuts as somebody like Douglas Adams who'd have to be locked into a room to write. I do enjoy writing, and not only do I enjoy writing, but it kind of sorts my head out. It makes me a happier person and easier to get on with. If I'm writing, everything's good.

So, you look, if you're me, at the shelves upon shelves of books that I've written, and the fact that when small children ask me how many books I have written I have to say, " I don't know." And a lot of that is just 'cause I keep working relatively slowly and relatively steadily. Year in and year out, and I do stuff. And also I like to have more than one thing on a go for when I get stuck. It's an immense sort of reassurance to me even right now that if I get absolutely stuck on *Neverwhere*, there's a goofy book about frogs in Central Park that I could go and just start writing chapter two of.

**JMS:** I have to tell you, as an academic, when you mention failing, or that sort of feeling you get as you mention these folks that you consider prolific—this last book on your work I did—I just counted up your bibliography, and there were seven single-spaced pages of your work. Books, comics, movies, adaptations, etc. and as you were speaking, I looked at that and thought, "Dear lord, I wish I could fail that well."

**NG:** Awe, thank you. It's really odd. You know, it's odd when you're in that weird kind of zone between your first lifetime achievement award and the grave, and you just sort of look at all the stuff you've made and you don't, if you're me anyway, go, "Oh my gosh—look at all this stuff I made!" You go, "Ahhh! I haven't done this book yet. I haven't done *this* book yet. I haven't done this short story . . ." And there are stories I feel guilty about; I mean genuinely guilty about. There's a big one . . . The story is all there. I just need one of those really nice periods of about ten days when I can write a story for me because nobody is waiting for that one.

**JMS:** As I look at 2017, it strikes me as one of the more exciting years recently—particularly with the release of *Norse Mythology.* I remember paging through it when it first came out, and the first thought that struck me was that it reminded me in some fashion of what Seamus Heaney had done with his verse translation of *Beowulf.* And it got me thinking: What kind of project was that for you? Was it a translation, or a novelization, or an adaptation of the *Prose* and *Poetic Eddas*? What was that work for you?

**NG:** It was sort of all of those things. It's very much not a translation of the entire, ya know, a retelling of the *Prose* and *Poetic Eddas.* It loses a lot of the goofy plots of the *Eddas* where Odin shows up in disguise and there are long questions and answers and people say: "Well, how *was* the world created?" And he says (in a very Odinic voice), "I will tell you how the world was created." So, I decided that I wasn't gonna—what I wanted to do was just tell the story, and then a lot of it was sort of beginning with my favorites and just going into the *Eddas* . . . and it was always simplest if there was only one version: The Marriage of Thor one [for example] only exists in the *Poetic Edda.* So, that's fun—I get to go into the *Poetic Edda,* and I get to take something that's basically a three-page poem, a four-page poem and retell it and try and get all of the detail right. But there's a fiction in my head when I was writing it with the idea that all of this stuff, wherever possible, was being told not written, and it was being told in Viking times, and the idea was there that, very subtly, it was being told in (unintelligible)'s time. So you're in a pre-Christian Iceland. There was one thing that made me smile—describing, I think, a giant's wall as bigger than a cathedral. And I thought, "Yeah, we'll, we'll drop that one in there."

But part of that also is the fact that because the *Prose* and *Poetic Eddas* are collected a couple of hundred years after Iceland has already gone

Christian, we don't know what the pre-Christian version would have been. We don't really know what the versions of the stories would have been that people would have told to each other. So, what I was trying to do was go into that. I tended to have lots and lots and lots of versions of the *Prose* and *Poetic Eddas*—I keep promising myself that for the paperback edition of *Norse Mythology*, I'll actually do some notes. Because, I thought: "Academics will be much happier if I did that!"

**JMS:** [laughter] (*Side note*: Of course, he is correct.)

**NG:** The problem with the way that I did it was that because *Norse Mythology* was—I've described it as "my knitting." I don't know if you have ever had an aunt or a friend who knits, but they always sort of have knitting in their bag, and they take it out when things are dull or when they have a down moment, and with *Norse Mythology*, I agreed to do it at the end of 2008/ beginning of 2009. It took me about three years of thinking to go, "I think I have got the voice in my head. I think I can do this voice which will work for kids, but work for adults too." Just putting this sort of weird voice together, and then I started writing it . . . but I would write it one story at a time. And then I'd go off and do something else. And then, three months later, four months later, I'd look up and go, "Ahh! I have here—I've got a week! Time to do another story." And by that week, I would have lost my last copies of the *Prose* and *Poetic Eddas*. So, I would be much more likely to head off at that point to Project Gutenberg or the web and wind up reading [laughter] four different Victorian translations, and then going, "These are weird." and then go digging in any other version I could find.

It was always sort of what was around at the point where I was ready to write the next one, and I did this for about four years. And, at the end of that four years, the lovely people at Norton were starting to cough politely and said, "You know, you did sign the contract with us in 2009 . . . It's 2015 now. You know, could we have our book please?"

**JMS:** [laughter]

**NG:** So, that was the point where I looked at what I had done. I went, "Ahh! Here are the holes . . ." and I went off, and in a week of madness, I wrote, filled in all the holes, and wrote "Ragnarok." I'd been pushing off writing "Ragnarok" until the very end. I knew that I couldn't—I knew it needed. . . it would be the capstone on the arch that I would need to build everything off.

**JMS:** Well, as we are talking about mythology and adaptation, I have to ask you about *American Gods* on STARZ . . . It's the sort of show that defies description. It's a feast for the eyes and the mind—just incredibly bold television. I suppose my question is, after going through such a long period of getting it on the screen, do you like it, love it, or is it everything one could hope, and what was it like watching it come to life?

**NG:** I like most of it. I love lots of it. And then there are bits of it where I go, "Oh guys . . . no." It was a wonderful mixture of delight and frustration watching it—

**JMS:** Really?!

**NG:** Well, you don't get to see the frustration. And you shouldn't. What's that wonderful line about nobody should see sausages or the law being made?

**JMS:** [laughter]

**NG:** You don't want to know what goes into it. You don't want to know what the backstage grumbles, the casting missteps that might have happened but didn't just because we got lucky. Casting has a weird sort of magic sometimes, and sometimes you really do get lucky.

There are bits of *American Gods* that I completely love, and I'm fascinated by the fact that the bits that I love the best are the bits I had nothing to do with at all. The episode four ("Git Gone") which is the Laura biography where they invented, of course they had to invent a new Laura, the one in the book was a small town travel agent, and there aren't any small town travel agents anymore. They've gone the way of the small town buggy-whip sellers. So, I loved that episode. I loved in the episode after the very weird David Bowie/ Media chewing out the Technical Boy scene, and I'm looking at this going, "This is . . . This is wonderful."

I also look at it and go . . . I don't think, just in a day-to-day thinking kind of thing, that 1999 was that long ago, and then I look at the book and then I look at the TV series and I go, "My gosh, I was writing this book in a world before smart phones. I was writing this book in a world full of modems with things that got you online. A dial-up world." And there's an awful lot of places I just look at it and go, "Actually, probably more by accident than anything else, I got a bunch of stuff right."

**JMS:** Given its success and what will eventually happen with *Good Omens,* I have to ask, I'd be remiss if I didn't: Have the powers that be finally found religion and realized that doing a proper *Sandman* as a serialized television show would be something that . . . it's literally already written, laid out, ready-to-go with seven to eight seasons of television majesty—has there been any movement made on it yet?

**NG:** The trouble is . . . there's a beautiful saying in Sussex, when I was a boy, they'd say, "I've lived too near the woods too long to be frightened by an owl," and, in my case, I have seen them find that religion . . I have seen them lose that religion. [laughter] There was an HBO *Sandman* series that was going to happen in 2009, 2008—it never happened. There was talk of doing a network television show, and then it went back to feature films, and it stayed in features for a while, and then it went from Warners over to New Line . . . which seemed rather baffling. And then, I saw an interview with the writer at New Line saying, "This is crazy. It should be a TV show."

I very, very much hope that one day that HBO or Showtime or whichever Time Warner subsidiary is allowed to do it as TV does it as TV. I very much hope that if it's done that it won't be network TV. I've watched attempts to try and turn *Sandman* into something that would work on network TV and all of the features suddenly become bugs. It's a no-brainer for you just as it's a no-brainer for me because you go, "Well, look: Here's two and a half thousand pages of story," and that's what they want. It's already there and it already exists, and all you have to do, really, is to tell these stories. And you're in business.

But . . . but what? You know, it sort of petered out a bit. I suppose it sort of petered out because it really doesn't have anywhere to go. It's very logical to me just as it's logical to you. Neither of us is running HBO or Time Warner or Warner Brothers movies . . . It would be wonderful to think. Especially, weirdly following even the success of tiny little bits of *Sandman*. I'm fascinated and amused to see that . . . rather like the tip of a starfish that regrows an entire starfish that *Lucifer* is now in its third season and a successful TV show. And I go, "Really?!" And I remember going, "I think I'll put him in a piano bar in LA called 'Lux,' and that will be fun!" And look what that's turned into.

Sandman could be even better than that.

**JMS:** As part of my job to read pretty much everything that you write, I seem to recall reading an idea on your twitter. It was sort of like a proposed idea about *The Graveyard Book* and something yet to come. I think it was entitled *Silas and Co.*, and it was kind of akin to what *The Hobbit* and *The Lord of the Rings* were. And I suppose my question for you would be: When could I buy this and could it be just as soon as possible?

**NG:** [laughter]The problem with something like that is, of all the books out there, it's probably the one that I would like to write the most. I also know that it's going to be *enormous*. It's called *The Honor Guard*. And/ or possibly be Volume One of *The Honor Guard* or whatever. It will probably get written after, of the major works . . . I have to finish the *Neverwhere* book. I need to probably do *American Gods 2*. . . . There's a very big, very weird children's book that I want to write because it's a lovely, peculiar idea that is probably my oldest idea that I haven't used. In the same way that *The Ocean at the End of the Lane* was sort of plot stuff that was in my head since age eight or nine probably, this is stuff from when I was twelve or thirteen. And it feels like it's really good—so that needs to get written. And then I would probably start on [*The Honor Guard*]. But it really . . . I don't mind the fact that, by the time I get to it, Ash may well be seven or eight years old because hopefully he'll be in school at that point, and I will have more writing time.

**JMS:** Alright . . . I'm about to try something rather dangerous if you'll let me.
**NG:** Perfect!

**JMS:** Just talking about *The Graveyard Book* and all these children's books yet to come, it occurs to me as a professor of children's literature that I should probably ask you some question about the children's literature that you've done. And, I certainly could, but the thought had occurred to me . . . one of the interviews I include in this book is the one with you and Maddy when she was young because it's perfect in every way. And when I thought about the questions I wanted to ask you as a children's literature scholar it occurred to me that they were very scholarly and, as such, boring.

So, I thought, if you wouldn't mind, I'd like my co-interviewer, my seven-year-old daughter, Maggie, to do it. She's thought of some questions from the things of yours she has read with me or read alone, and would you mind it if she would ask you a few questions?

**NG:** Absolutely not—that sounds like the most fun possible!

**JMS:** Maggie?
**MGS:** Hi, Mr. Gaiman! I'm Maggie Sommers.
**NG:** Hi, Maggie!
**MGS:** Hi! Would you mind if I asked you a few questions about your books?
**NG:** No, I would love it if you would ask me some questions about my books.
**MGS:** Great! The first question is: Why did you name your book *Blueberry Girl?*

**NG:** I named *Blueberry Girl* "Blueberry Girl" because "Blueberry Girl" didn't even start out as a poem. It started out as book. It started out with a friend of mine, one of my best friends, a lady called Tori Amos, who was having a baby. And she phoned me up and she said, "Will you write something for the baby I haven't had yet?" And I said, "Of course!" I said, "What do you call the baby?" And she said, "Well, we don't have a name for her yet, but we call her 'The Blueberry.'" And I said, "Good!"

So, I wrote a poem called "Blueberry Girl." And this was while I was writing a book called *American Gods*, and I sent "Blueberry Girl" off to Tori, and she loved it, and she read it to her baby, and I had it handwritten, and it was up on her baby's wall. Her baby is called Natasha. I didn't think—I thought that would be the end of it—but every now and again, I would be asked if I would read it to somebody who had heard it or who knew that it existed. So I read it at a few readings, but I would always ask people who were recording what I was doing to turn off their recorders, to stop taping, and they always did. So, for years—I'd say this isn't really mine to read to you, this is Tori's for whom I wrote it. Then, a few years later, the artist Charles Vess, had loved "Blueberry Girl" so much and he heard me read it once and he said, "Could you let me draw it?" And I phoned Tori, and said, "This was always yours—would you like it to go out into the world?"

She said yes.

She supports some really good charities that help people who've been hurt and we made sure that a bunch of the money from *Blueberry Girl* goes to them. And we did it as a book. And that's why—it's called *Blueberry Girl* because the bump that wasn't yet a girl called Natasha was called the blueberry.

**MGS:** Thanks! Why did you make *Instructions* a poem?

**NG:** *Instructions* is a poem because . . . many years ago, I was in Boston. I got caught in the rain, and I went back to my hotel room to dry off, and, at some point, while doing that, I remember just thinking, "Wouldn't it be interesting to try and tell somebody how to get through a fairy story as if it were a set of instructions? As if it were a manual?" And I sat, and I wrote it. And it was published in my short story collection. And it was printed as a poem in a few books.

And then, again, Charles Vess, having done the beautifulness of *Blueberry Girl*, said, "Let's do something else together." I loved Charles' art so much, I said, "Anything you want." And he said—"Let's do 'Instructions.'"

**MGS:** Cooooool. My Daddy says that you have a daughter who dreamt about wolves in the walls. Do you have any idea why she dreamt about them?

**NG:** Uhm, could you say that again love?

**MGS:** Sure! Daddy said that your daughter dreamt about wolves in the walls and that became *The Wolves in the Walls*—Do you know why she dreamt about them?

**NG:** I think it was because the house we were living in back then was very, very old. It was a big old house, and there were definitely things that were in the walls that would make scratchy-scritchy noises. And I always figured that it was mice or rats or bats. But sometimes you'd be falling asleep and you would hears something going *scritchy scritchy scritchy scritchy scratch*, and it would be moving along the wall. And it would be moving on the inside of the wall. And you'd go, "I wonder what you are, little thing that's going *scritch scritch scritch*." But Maddy, my daughter, woke up—I went upstairs, and she was crying and I said, "What's wrong?" And she said, "There were wolves. In the walls of our house. And they came out. And they took over our house!" And I said, "No, you were dreaming." And she said, "No, I wasn't dreaming 'cause I can show you the place in the wallpaper where they came out." And so she pointed to the place in the wallpaper where they came out.

**JMS:** Would you like to ask him about *Coraline*?

**MGS:** OK! [pause]

**JMS:** [laughter] We typed them out after she wrote them up for you, and then she made little emendations to how they were typed up so that they were written just as she wanted to ask them.

**NG:** Maggie, what would you like to know about *Coraline?*

**MGS:** Well . . . Daddy, can you help me with this one part?

**JMS:** Sure. We started reading *Coraline* at bedtime, but when it started to get a little scarier, we moved our readings earlier in the day because it got to a point where she was having nightmares. So, Maggie—What are you thinking about right there?

**MGS:** Well, why does the other mother want Coraline so much?

**NG:** I think that one of the things that I wanted to say with *Coraline* was that sometimes people who don't give you as much attention as you would like still love you. And, sometimes, people who give you lots and lots of attention don't always have your best interests at heart. So, I think, for me, with the other mother, I wanted to create somebody who when you first meet her, you can understand why Coraline would go, "Oh this is actually—this is kinda cool. She's much more interesting than my real mother." But, then she would get creepier and creepier. And I wanted to show Coraline having to learn to be brave, and having to understand that being brave means that when you're scared, you do the right thing anyway. That was important to me.

**MGS:** Thank you for letting me ask you a few questions, Mr. Gaiman.
**NG:** You're welcome, Maggie. You're a fantastic interviewer!
**MGS:** [giggles] Thank you.
**JMS:** Thank you very much, Neil.

# Key Resources

Abbruscato, Joseph. "Being Nobody: Identity in Neil Gaiman's The Graveyard Book."
   *Gothic Fairy Tale In Young Adult Literature.* Eds. Joseph Abbruscato and Tanya Jones.
   McFarland, 2014. 66–82. Print.

Bealer, Tracy L., Rachel Luria, and Wayne Yuen. *Neil Gaiman and Philosophy*: Gods Gone
   Wild!. Open Court, 2012. Print.

Błaszkiewicz, Maria. "Allegorizing the Fantastic: A Spenserian Reading of Neil Gaiman's
   *Neverwhere*." *Basic Categories of Fantastic Literature Revisited.* Eds. Andrzej Wicher, Piotr
   Spyra, and Joanna Matyjaszczyk. Cambridge Scholars, 2014. 127–143. Print.

Bowen, Jared. "Neil Gaiman—Lowell Lecture Series, April 4, 2017." *YouTube.* YouTube, 20 Apr.
   2017. Web. 28 July 2017.

Brisbin, Ally, and Paul Booth. "The Sand/wo/man: The Unstable Worlds of Gender in Neil
   Gaiman's *Sandman* Series." *Journal of Popular Culture* 46.1 (2013): 20–37. Print.

Buchanan, Jenni. "Reading Rainbow Blog." *Reading Rainbow.* N.p., 2 Apr. 2015. Web. 28
   July 2017.

Buffington, Sean. "Q&A with Neil Gaiman." *YouTube.* YouTube, 24 June 2013. Web. 28
   July 2017.

Burstyn, Franziska. "Alice and Mowgli Revisited: Neil Gaiman's *Coraline* and *The Graveyard
   Book*." *Inklings: Jahrbuch für Literatur und Ästhetik* 30 (2012): 72–86. Print.

Campbell, Hayley, and Audry Niffenegger. *The Art of Neil Gaiman.* Harper, 2014. Print.

Camus, Cyril. "Fantasy and Landscape: Mountain as Myth in Neil Gaiman's Stories.
   "*Mountains Figured and Disfigured in the English-Speaking World.* Ed. Françoise Besson.
   Cambridge Scholars, 2010. 379–391. Print.

———. "Neil Gaiman's *Sandman* as a Gateway from Comic Books to Graphic Novels." *Studies
   in the Novel* 47.3 (2015): 308–18. Print.

———. "The 'Outsider': Neil Gaiman and the Old Testament." *Shofar: An Interdisciplinary
   Journal of Jewish Studies* 29.2 (2011): 77–99. Print.

Carroll, Siobhan. "Imagined Nation: Place and National Identity in Neil Gaiman's *American
   Gods*." *Extrapolation: A Journal of Science Fiction and Fantasy* 53.3 (2012): 307–26. Print.

Cates, Isaac. "Memory, Signal, and Noise in the Collaborations of Neil Gaiman and Dave
   McKean." *Drawing From Life.* Ed. Jane Tolmie. UP of Mississippi, 2013. 144–162. Print.

Chabon, Michael. "Neil Gaiman on Terry Pratchett and Writing, in Conversation with Michael Chabon." *YouTube*. YouTube, 13 Mar. 2015. Web. 28 July 2017.

Cheverton, Sarah. "'Hanging Out with the Dream King': An Interview with Neil Gaiman." Star& Crescent. N.p., n.d. Web. 28 July 2017.

Coats, Karen. "Between Horror, Humour, and Hope: Neil Gaiman and the Psychic Work of the Gothic." *The Gothic in Children's Literature*: *Haunting the Borders* Eds. Anna Jackson, Karen Coats, and Roderick McGillis. Routledge, 2008. 77–92. Print.

Collins, Meredith. "Fairy and Faerie: Uses of Victorian in Neil Gaiman's and Charles Vess's *Stardust*." *ImageTexT*: *Interdisciplinary Comics Studies* 4.1 (2008) Web. 8 Sep. 2016.

Croci, Daniele. "Watching (through) the Watchmen: Representation and Deconstruction of the Controlling Gaze in Neil Gaiman's *The Sandman*." *Altre Modernità* 11 (2014): 120–35.Print.

Curry, Alice. "'The Pale Trees Shook, although no Wind Blew, and it Seemed to Tristran that they Shook in Anger': 'Blind Space' and Ecofeminism in a Post-Colonial Reading of Neil Gaiman and Charles Vess's Graphic Novel *Stardust* (1998)." *Barnboken* 33.2 (2010): 19–33. Print.

Czarnowsky, Laura-Marie von. ""Power and all its Secrets": Engendering Magic in Neil Gaiman's *The Ocean at the End of the Lane*." *Fafnir*: *Nordic Journal of Science Fiction and Fantasy Research* 2.4 (2015): 18–28. Print.

Daniels, Keith. "Missy." *Neil Gaiman*. SuicideGirls, n.d. Web. 28 July 2017.

David, Danya. "Extraordinary Navigators: An Examination of Three Heroines in Neil Gaiman and Dave McKean's *Coraline, the Wolves in the Walls, MirrorMask*." *Looking Glass*: *New Perspectives on Children's Literature* 12.1 (2008) Print.

Dean, Tanya. "Piano Guts and Other Mothers: Staging Fantasy in David Greenspan and Stephin Merritt's Musical Adaptation of Neil Gaiman's *Coraline*." *Journal of the Fantastic in the Arts* 24.2 (2013): 264–74. Print.

Evans, Timothy H. "Folklore, Intertextuality, and the Folkloresque in the Works of Neil Gaiman." *The Folkloresque*: *Reframing Folklore in a Popular Culture World*. Eds. Michael Dylan Foster and Jeffrey A. Tolbert. Utah State UP, 2016. 64–80. Print.

Fleming, James R. "Incommensurable Ontologies and the Return of the Witness in Neil Gaiman's *1602*." *ImageTexT*: *Interdisciplinary Comics Studies* 4.1 (2008) Print.

Frostrup, Mariella. "Open Book, Neil Gaiman Special." *BBC Radio 4*. BBC, 27 June 2013. Web. 28 July 2017.

Gaiman, Neil. "Neil Gaiman's Tribute to Terry Pratchett." *BBC Arts*. BBC, 9 Feb. 2017. Web.28 July 2017.

Gamble, Nikki. "Neil Gaiman Interviewed by Nikki Gamble." *Just Imagine*, 1 Aug. 2014. Web.28 July 2017.

Goodyear, Dana. "Kid Goth." The New Yorker. The New Yorker, 19 June 2017. Web. 28 July 2017.

Grossman, Lev. "Interview: Neil Gaiman and Joss Whedon." Time. Time Inc., 25 Sept. 2005. Web. 28 July 2017.

Harris-Fain, Darren. "Putting the Graphic in Graphic Novel: P. Craig Russell's Adaptation of Neil Gaiman's *Coraline*." *Studies in the Novel* 47.3 (2015): 335–45. Print.

Jahlmar, Joakim. "'Give the Devil His due': Freedom, Damnation, and Milton's Paradise Lost in Neil Gaiman's *The Sandman: Season of Mists*." *Partial Answers: Journal of Literature and the History of Ideas* 13.2 (2015): 267–86. Print.

Jenkins, Henry. "Neil Gaiman: The Julius Schwartz Lecture at MIT." *YouTube*. YouTube, 09 Nov. 2015. Web. 28 July 2017.

Jones, Robert William II. "At Home in the World Tree: A Somaesthetic Reading of the Body at Home in Neil Gaiman's *American Gods*." *Open Library of Humanities* 1.1 (2015) Print.

Katsiadas, Nick. "Mytho-Auto-Bio: Neil Gaiman's Sandman, the Romantics and Shakespeare's 'The Tempest.'" *Studies in Comics* 6.1 (2015): 61–84. Print.

Klapcsik, Sá. "Neil Gaiman's Irony, Liminal Fantasies, and Fairy Tale Adaptations." *Hungarian Journal of English and American Studies* 14.2 (2008): 317–34. Print.

Klapcsik, Sandor. "The Double-Edged Nature of Neil Gaiman's Ironical Perspectives and Liminal Fantasies." *Journal of the Fantastic in the Arts* 20.2 (2009): 193–209. Print.

Kosiba, Sara. "'Flyover Country': Neil Gaiman's Extraordinary Perceptions of the Midwest." *Midwestern Miscellany* 38 (2010): 106–19. Print.

Krewson, John. "Neil Gaiman." *The A.V. Club*. The Onion, 03 Feb. 1999. Web. 28 July 2017.

Lancaster, Kurt. "Neil Gaiman's 'A Midsummer Night's Dream': Shakespeare Integrated into Popular Culture." *Journal of American & Comparative Cultures* 23.3 (2000): 69–77.Print.

Llompart Pons, Auba. "Another Turn of the Screw: From Henry James's Gothic Children to Neil Gaiman's Children's Gothic." *Weaving New Perspectives Together: Some Reflections on Literary Studies*. Eds. María Alonso Alonso, et al. Cambridge Scholars, 2012. 171–184. Print.

McCabe, Joel, ed. *Hanging out with the Dream King: Interviews with Neil Gaiman and His Collaborators*. Seattle, WA: Fantagraphics, 2005. Print.

Mellette, Justin. "Serialization and Empire in Neil Gaiman's *The Sandman*." *Studies in the Novel* 47.3 (2015): 319–34. Print.

"Neil Gaiman: By the Book." *The New York Times*. The New York Times, 05 May 2012. Web. 28 July 2017.

Noone, Kristin. "The Monsters and the Heroes: Neil Gaiman's *Beowulf*." *Weird Fiction Review* 1 (2010): 139–53. Print.

Parsons, Elizabeth, Naarah Sawers, and Kate McInally. "The Other Mother: Neil Gaiman's Postfeminist Fairytales." *Children's Literature Association Quarterly* 33.4 (2008): 371–89.Print.

Penny, Laurie. "Neil Gaiman Interview: 'It Was Much, Much More Fun Being Absolutely Unknown.'" *New Statesman,* 13 Nov. 2013. Web. 28 July 2017.

Porter, Adam. "Neil Gaiman's Lucifer: Reconsidering Milton's Satan." *Journal of Religion and Popular Culture* 25.2 (2013): 175–85. Print.

Prescott, Tara. *Neil Gaiman in the 21st Century: Essays on the Novels, Children's Stories, Online Writings, Comics and Other Works*. McFarland, 2015. Print.

Prescott, Tara and Aaron Drucker. *Feminism in the Worlds of Neil Gaiman*. McFarland, 2012. Print.

Reed, S.A. "Through Every Mirror in the World: Lacan's Mirror Stage as Mutual Reference in the Works of Neil Gaiman and Tori Amos." *ImageTexT: Interdisciplinary Comics Studies* 4.1 (2008) Web. 8 Sep. 2016.

Richards, Linda. "January Interview: Neil Gaiman." *January Magazine*, n.d. Web. 28 July 2017.

Robertson, Christine. "'I Want to be Like You': Riffs on Kipling in Neil Gaiman's *The Graveyard Book*." Children's Literature Association Quarterly 36.2 (2011): 164–89. Print.

Romero Jódar, Andrés. "Paradisical Hells: Subversions of the Mythical Canon in Neil Gaiman's *Neverwhere*." *Cuadernos de Investigación Filológica* 31–32 (2005): 163–95.Print.

Round, Julia. "Transforming Shakespeare: Neil Gaiman and *The Sandman*." *Beyond Adaptation*. Eds. Phyllis Frus and Christy Williams. McFarland, 2010. 95–110. Print.

Rudd, David. "An Eye for an I: Neil Gaiman's *Coraline* and Questions of Identity." *Children's Literature in Education: An International Quarterly* 39.3 (2008): 159–68. Print.

Rusnak, Marcin. "Playing with Death: Humorous Treatment of Death-Related Issues in Terry Pratchett's and Neil Gaiman's Young Adult Fiction." *Fastitocalon: Studies in Fantasticism Ancient to Modern* 2.1–2 (2011): 81–95. Print.

Sanders, Joe. "Of Parents and Children and Dreams in Neil Gaiman's *Mr. Punch* and *The Sandman*." *Foundation: The International Review of Science Fiction* 71 (1997): 18–32.

——. *The Sandman Papers* Ed by Joe Sanders. Fantagraphics, 2006, Print.

——. "Tidings of Discomfort and Joy: Neil Gaiman's 'Murder Mysteries.'" *New York Review of Science Fiction* 20.11 (2008): 1–6 . Print.

Slabbert, Mathilda. "Inventions and Transformations: Imagining New Worlds in the Stories of Neil Gaiman." *Fairy Tales Reimagined*. Eds. Susan Redington Bobby and Kate Bernheimer. McFarland, 2009. 68–83. Print.

Smith, Clay. "Get Gaiman? PolyMorpheus Perversity in Works by and about Neil Gaiman." *ImageTexT: Interdisciplinary Comics Studies* 4.1 (2008) Web. 8 September 2016.

Sommers, Joseph Michael. *Critical Insights: Neil Gaiman*. Salem/ Grey House Press, 2016. Print.

Spiegelman, Art. "Neil Gaiman in Conversation with Art Spiegelman." *YouTube*. YouTube, 12 June 2014. Web. 28 July 2017.

Sung, Eunai. "Neil Gaiman's *Stardust* and the Victorian Fantasy." British and American Fiction 20.1 (2013): 81–104. Print.

Sutton, Roger. "It's Good to Be Gaiman: A Revealing Interview with Newbery Winner Neil Gaiman." *School Library Journal*. N.p., 1 Mar. 2009. Web. 28 July 2017.

Tally, Robert T. Jr. "Lost in Grand Central: Dystopia and Transgression in Neil Gaiman's American Gods." Blast, Corrupt, Dismantle, Erase: *Contemporary North American*

*Dystopian Literature.* Eds. Brett Josef Grubisic, Gisèle M. Baxter, and Tara Lee. Wilfrid Laurier UP, 2014. 357–371. Print.

Tiffin, Jessica. "Blood on the Snow: Inverting 'Snow White' in the Vampire Tales of Neil Gaiman and Tanith Lee." *Anti-Tales: The Uses of Disenchantment.* Eds. Catriona McAra and David Calvin. Cambridge Scholars, 2011. 220–230. Print.

Vespe, Eric "Quint." "Quint Has a Long Chat with Neil Gaiman about STARDUST, BEOWULF, CORALINE, SANDMAN, DEATH And . . ." *Aint It Cool News.* N.p., 29 Dec. 2012. Web. 28 July 2017.

Wearring, Andrew. "Changing, Out-of-Work, Dead, and Reborn Gods in the Fiction of Neil Gaiman." *Literature and Aesthetics: The Journal of the Sydney Society of Literature and Aesthetics* 19.2 (2009): 236–46. Print.

Wehler, Melissa. "'be Wise. be Brave. be Tricky': Neil Gaiman's Extraordinarily Ordinary *Coraline.*" *A Quest of Her Own.* Ed. Lori M. Campbell. McFarland, 2014. 111–129.Print.

White, Claire E. "A Conversation With Neil Gaiman." *Writers Write.* N.p., Mar. 1999. Web. 28July 2017.

———. "Interview With Neil Gaiman." *Writers Write.* N.p., July 2001. Web. 28 July 2017.

Wilkie-Stibbs, Christine. "Imaging Fear: Inside the Worlds of Neil Gaiman (an Anti-Oedipal Reading)." *Lion and the Unicorn* 37.1 (2013): 37–53. Print.

# Index

Lightning Source UK Ltd.
Milton Keynes UK
UKHW011832050320
359851UK00001B/82